In Defe

CW00859780

of the R

Evidence and symbolism in support of God

To all the Buckleys
For all your friendship
over the years.

Hamish 20/8/17

H G H Ramsay

ISBN: 978-0-244-91521-6

With updates 2014-2017

Includes cross references and bibliographical references

My grateful thanks to:

My wife and my mother, for their continuing support and edits

Isabel Allum, for prophetically calling my writing into existence

Phil and Heather Warren for their unceasing love and support

My friend, Richard White, for his feedback, encouragement and general editing

Dedication

This book is dedicated to my mother, Sarah, my wife, Louise, and my sister Alexandra, for their ceaseless support.

This book is also dedicated to my Herschel ancestors: William Herschel; his sister Caroline Herschel; John Herschel; and William James Herschel.

Index to chapters

1. In Defence of the Realm

"It is the Glory of God to conceal a thing;
but the honour of Kings is to search out a matter"

(Proverbs 25:2 New King James Version)

<u>Why is this book for you?</u>

This book is for you if you are resisting, or holding back from faith in the God of the Bible because you need some evidence that the Bible makes sense. Science – particularly evolution, seems to suggest to you that the God story you have heard or read about is simply a myth, or worse: a lie.

This book seeks to challenge much of the hopelessness that might dissuade you from placing your faith in God. These pages set out a profound belief that God is as good as His inerrant word. He can be trusted.

You certainly don't have to be a scientist or an academic to read this book – indeed I am just as happy to take a general description from Wikipedia as I am from a particular academic. This book seeks to address some evolutionary and other scientific, evidential, philosophical and associated symbolic issues in a topical and accessible way. It extracts many current pro-Christian authors' scientific and evidential works and adds many further personal insights drawn from my scientific family's legacy. It aims to assist you in your decision to take a leap of faith, with confidence, or to add fresh zest to a flagging faith.

I believe that it is important to consider the evidential with the spiritual and symbolic, as God intended for us to enjoy both. It is clear He uses symbolism in the bible, particularly in the context of spiritual things (and the book of Revelation is pregnant with examples) so it is helpful to understand a little about symbolism. Whilst the spiritual and symbolic do not provide 'proof' as such, and may appear incongruous in the context of a book citing evidence, they still have a place in our thinking, because they provide pictures or analogies by which we can get a better view of God's Kingdom. Science, without a recognition of the creator, who is spirit by nature, only provides a part of that picture. After all, evidence may assist in taking a leap into faith, but at that point its purpose can lessen. Thereafter, faith drives the relationship with God who develops that faith and gives it strength.

The purpose of this book is to help take you to the point of faith. After that, it's about you and God, in your secret place with Him.

<u>Why did I write this book?</u>

I initially wrote this book for me, alone. It started with the legacy my own scientific family left the world.

This journey of discovery expanded to cover not only their works, but the works and contribution of many others. Some of this is well known and some is not, but all of it spoke to me in some way. I brought much of it together, covering a wide spectrum of disciplines, from science to archaeology, from philosophy to prophecy, and so on. By referencing them and distilling my own thoughts in the light of all current thinking, I could determine my own position. This, as it turns out, supports the things God says about Himself and therefore encourages me in my faith.

Then a thought occurred to me: perhaps you, my readers, might also find this interesting, or helpful.

There has been a great deal published in this area in the last decade or so. But this book is different, because nothing comes close to starting the journey from inside a well-known family of original scientific thinkers.

This is not a biography, however.

Whilst the book starts with my dynastic family that have collectively contributed a large scientific legacy, these scientists were people of a certain era, and their voices now need to be heard in the context of more contemporary thinking and science. Those voices are also included here, up to the point of publication.

Future hope?

There are many difficult issues facing the world at present. We don't need to recite them all here. Taken together, they dampen much future hope for us and the next generation. They can skew and obscure the good promises of God who has publicly declared that He has made plans to prosper people and not to harm them[1]. So, with such difficulties facing our planet, is there really any hope? What future, if any, can we leave our children?

No temporal solution has yet satisfied the deep yearning in the human soul for these answers, so can the solution be found elsewhere? And if we suggest that a solution can be found, then how do we build a case for trusting that solution, particularly if it might sound a little 'fanciful'?

The good news is that there is still a solution. It's not a formula, or some rule, but a *person*. A real, living leader, and one who has seen and understands all of the issues in great detail. Because I have come to know Him, I have chosen to pin all of my own hope and trust in that person, that leader.

That person is Jesus Christ. And the story about Him is contained in His biography, the Holy Bible. The Bible contains everything necessary to show us how to live righteous relationships with each other and with Jesus, so it would seem like a sensible place to consider how relationships should be lived.

Some say that as Jesus died some 2,000 years ago, the things written down in the Bible must be outdated. But He didn't give us an end date by when the things He said about Himself would be outdated. He didn't give us that option. He never intended to, because they apply for all time. And to further entrench His legacy, God gave us the Holy spirit, by which an ongoing, real, and tangible relationship can still be found. The Bible shows us how Jesus lived, which was selflessly, showing great love for others. And His life is the most compelling life of anyone who ever lived or will live. People were magnetised to Him. Jesus talks endlessly about a brighter future. So, if He is telling the truth, we should learn from Him.

Yet some also believe that the Bible, including the things that Jesus says about Himself, and the things stated about His creation are fanciful and the stuff of myth. To believe the Biblical account and take it at its word, to *take such a calculated risk*, to be able confidently to stick one's head above a parapet and suggest that all we need to do is to listen to Him, we need some facts and figures, because no one would do such a thing blindly. We need to establish some trust in Him, and we need to have some basis for believing in Him and His own promises about a brighter future. We need to know He can, and does, deliver on His promises and never breaks them, as our own leaders often do.

In my own darkest and most challenging moments, I too needed to *know* that He is true and that I can rely on Him. I do believe that I have come to understand that, uniquely and without possible comparison to anyone before or after Him, Jesus Christ is as good as His word.

If this Jesus can offer the hope we seek; then that is good news and it is certainly worth taking a small risk to read just a few more chapters to find out whether God is a God of myth, or a God of living truth.

<u>A scientific heritage which compelled me to raise questions about faith in Jesus the person of hope</u>

I was born on the last day of 1966 in Reading. The last day of the year, Hogmanay, is an appropriate day for someone with Scottish ancestry to be born.

For me, there is, however, something much more special than a Scottish birth date for a son of Scotland, that I learned about my family as I grew up. We were descendants of one of the world's greatest scientific dynasties. That dynasty was particularly active during the Age of the Enlightenment and the surname of that dynastic family is Herschel.

My name is Hamish Graham Herschel Ramsay, and a lineal ancestor of mine was Sir William Herschel. William discovered the planet Uranus in 1781, and infra-red in 1800.

William's sister Caroline was also a remarkable character, being a woman scientist in an age where women were barely recognised, let alone praised for any work they did. She carried out pioneering work on the cosmos, charting comets and so called 'double stars'. She was honoured by the King for her work.

William had one son – John Frederick William Herschel, the greatest scientist of his age, and a major inspiration to Charles Darwin in his pioneering work on the Origin of Species. His genius began to flower early, being a child prodigy, and John made significant contributions particularly to astronomy, photography and mathematics, for which he was awarded the

Copley Medal. He won a second medal later in life. A polymath, he passed out from Cambridge as senior wrangler, but was also variously a lawyer; Master of the Mint; pioneer photographer; chemist; an artist capable of turning a camera obscura drawing into a thing of beauty; competent poet; and quite a lover too! He had twelve children! Somewhat irritatingly for all lesser mortals, no one really had a bad word to say about him.

John Herschel's distinction shone from his early thirties. It was so recognised in his day, that the young princess Victoria created him a baronet on the occasion of her Coronation, in order that he would be present to see her ascension. One of his daughters even became a lady in waiting. Such honour from such humble beginnings.

He died full of years; and his obituary was almost obsequious in its deference to him. His was a golden life in a golden age as one of England's greatest sons.

On John's death, his eight pallbearers included the Duke of Devonshire, Sir Charles Lyell the geologist, and Sir John Lubbock the banker and vice president of the Royal Society. The Lubbocks were close friends of the Herschels and Sir Neville Lubbock, one of his sons, married Constance Herschel, one of John Herschel's daughters. Paying homage, was none other than Charles Robert Darwin, who saw him interred as the nation required, quite deliberately next to that other great scientific pioneer, Sir Isaac Newton. Interestingly, when Darwin passed away, he too was buried right next to John Herschel in Westminster Abbey: a striking testament to the evolutionary debate that was started between Darwin and Herschel, and whose ghostly presence seems to ring down through the ages, as they continue to speak to us through their respective legacies.

Coincidentally, I found later in life that John Herschel and Isaac Newton may be proximate in more ways than one, for I discovered that my maternal grandfather, Robert Alan Wimberley Bicknell joins me by marriage through his Wimberley relatives to Isaac Newton's family. The Wimberleys and Newtons are related, which makes Isaac 'distant family' of sorts.

This improbable confluence of scientific families – Newton and Herschel, and of their geographic proximity as they lie in state, is something I did not know at the time I became engaged to my wife. Following a conversation with a member of my family regarding a suitable place to propose, I chose the Little Cloister in Westminster Abbey as a mark of honour to my wonderful ancestor. It was pregnant with meaning for me.

Yet years later I was to discover that I could equally have been honouring another, more distant relative: Sir Isaac Newton.

Now John Herschel's eldest son was another pioneer. This was Sir William James Herschel. William James was the discoverer of the permanence of fingerprints, which he introduced to Scotland Yard. Fingerprint identification is still in use to this day, (a recent development being to identify the owner of a cell phone) though it is beginning to give way to DNA 'fingerprinting'. William James was a scholar, and also compiled a standard and exhaustive 'harmony' (chronology of Christ's life) of the four Gospels.

All these men have left legacies that are profound and to which I refer in this book.

William James' eldest son was another Sir John Herschel, who became a vicar and the last baronet, leaving no male heir.

A Christian heritage married with science

Every single one of these men, including Newton[2], were Christians and somehow held on to a faith when the scientific world was constantly breaking new frontiers, some of which did not appear to be favourable to the traditional biblical account. They wisely retained an open mind, preferring to avoid an absolute reconciliation when repeatable evidence was pouring forth month after month from all sorts of different disciplines. It is to William Herschel and his son John (1st), that I owe my greatest debt of gratitude, for the moral influence that they have sent me down through the ages. They remained steadfast in their faith in God, though the precise nature of that faith differed slightly from father to son.

These two men were absolutely central to the Age of the Enlightenment (a.k.a. the Age of Reason) and they had an authority recognised by their peers and by men and women of the day. When they spoke, people listened.

Following William's discovery of Uranus (which he initially called Georgium Sidus ("George's Star") named after his patron, George III), he pronounced, perhaps reflecting the earlier words of Edward Young that:

"The un-devout astronomer *must be mad*"

We will never know whether this was simply stated with a rash excitement, made in the heat of the moment, but it does appear to be an extraordinary statement to make nonetheless. 'Devout' here cannot *really or honestly* be read to apply to an astronomer who is faithful to his work to the extent he obtains breakthrough. 'Devout' is not used like this, and would be an extraordinary statement to make from someone who had no belief, sounding incongruous rather than witty. To me, and I would state that this is a personal opinion, this statement appears to give glory to a God who has created stars as numerous as sand on a beach because, one would argue, *how else* could one explain the complexity and beauty of the heavens? It portrays for me an emotional statement about the numinous, made from a rational man who otherwise did not make emotional or irrational statements. But his son John, who towered over all the specialist scientists in their own chosen fields, made an equally strong statement when talking of scientific discovery generally, and of God:

> "All human discoveries seem to be made only for the sole purpose of confirming more and more strongly the truths that come from on high and are contained in the sacred writings."

Isaac Newton had this to say:

> "He who thinks half-heartedly will not believe in God; but he who really thinks *has to believe* in God" (my emphasis)

So then, taken together, these men believed that scientific discovery should be made for the purpose of understanding God more closely, and of revealing some of the mysteries shrouded in the Bible. Surely there can be no more exciting thing to do than to take a book which makes some outrageous predictions about the future, and then to make a breakthrough discovery, which then attests to the things stated thousands of years earlier?! The Bible actually addresses that very issue too, which is the quotation with which I open this book:

> "It is the glory of God to conceal a matter, but the glory of kings is to search out a matter" (Proverbs 25: 2)

We, human beings, are all 'kings' in this context, so it is to our own glory to search out what God has hidden like treasure about Himself, to surprise us about Him and His nature.

According to Newton, anyone with half an ounce of intelligence would conclude that God exists. Now, God exists. Newton believed it; my grandfathers believed it, and by now you have probably concluded that I do too.

And I particularly like this insightful quote from Newton:

> "Gravity explains the motions of the planets, but it cannot explain *who set the planets in motion*" (my emphasis).

Atheistic evolution attempts to use science to disprove the existence of God (see the chapters on Evolution). But in this quotation from Newton, he hits on a point which I believe can be extrapolated from science generally. Science can explain many things but it cannot prove, or disprove God. It cannot prove who put the planets in motion (though God makes clear from Genesis that it was Him). Whilst Newton is making an assumption that there clearly is a 'who' that was behind creation of planets and planetary motion, science cannot inform a conversation about actual existence, although modern philosophers have reached this point[3].

Either modern atheism, or the most brilliant scientist who ever lived, is correct. Both cannot be right: and I doubt many would take on Newton. Newton on atheism writes:

> "I have a fundamental belief in the Bible as the Word of God, written by men who were inspired. I study the Bible daily. Opposition to godliness is atheism in profession and idolatry in practice. Atheism is so senseless and odious to mankind that it never had many professors."[4]

Science does not prevent us observing what God said about His creation. When we discover something scientifically and can see that it is supported in the Bible, we can all agree that the probability that God exists is higher, because the things he said about His creation and of God Himself appear to be true. As Herschel says, science seems to provide "more strongly the truths that come from on high and are contained in [in the Bible]".

It is a popular modern notion that John Herschel experienced something different that set him apart from many people of his age. Some say that he had undergone a genuine spiritual conversion through the agency of his wife, Margaret. The actual truth of that modern conclusion does not quite come out through the family's collections of letters. However, it is fair to say he was, by upbringing and persuasion, a Christian, and being influenced by this background, would have considered becoming a minister after his graduation. He entertained many theological discussions with friends and relatives during his life, that are documented. His answers to Darwin's theory about evolution show that he was predisposed to think in Christian terms about Darwin's conclusions and this partly, but not wholly, contributed to his rejection of them.

Both Newton and the Herschels contended that what they discovered added to, rather than detracted from their understanding of how God intervened in creation, as set out in God's Holy book. It continues to do so, as this book will show.

A central consideration within the debate about science and God, is evolution. This important scientific theory has done much to damage people's faith in God. Fortunately, there are now very good reasons to revisit Evolution; and to revisit what has been taught as 'scientific fact' about Evolution at school. Atheists are resisting a retraction with all that they have, but in my view, they are losing the rational argument. The universe and earth and all that is in it really does look designed, and everything points to one simple conclusion, namely that it looks designed, because it is. And if it is designed, then it has to have a Designer. We look at Evolution later in this book, as my family had a key part to play in the debate.

I wish to allow you, my reader, to recognise that some brilliant men and women have considered science and evidence and yet this has bolstered, rather than diminished their faith. By showing you what they did, and how science now supports the biblical account, then maybe, just maybe, it will be enough to open your eyes and let God speak to you to enable you to take that precious step of faith; faith for a hope and a bright future.

Now let's look at light.

2. God is light

"God is light; in Him there is no darkness at all"

(1 John 1:5)

<u>Herschel's prism: light became so much broader than we previously thought</u>

In 1800, William Herschel, already famous from his discovery of Uranus almost thirty years earlier, was fiddling with a prism. He had decided to see whether light had different temperatures in different parts of the colour spectrum. This might assist him to understand whether stars of different colours had different temperatures as well, as he had clearly observed many different hues during his night watches.

After focusing a beam of light on his prism, a clear display of light composed of seven colours refracted out of the glass, which every schoolboy knows follows the mnemonic:

> "Richard Of York Gave Battle In Vain – Red, Orange, Yellow, Green, Blue, Indigo and Violet."

Herschel indeed observed different colours had different temperatures. But to Herschel's surprise, as he moved his array of thermometers off the hotter red end of the spectrum into the darkness beside it, the temperature rose and yet the instruments were not bathed in visible light. Herschel was a man of observation. This meant only one thing. Light did not end with the visible. He had found something else out about light.

He called this "dark light". But he still called it 'light'.

Herschel had in fact discovered infra-red, which is beyond the visible spectrum of the human eye.

Darkness and Light

Now the Bible says some interesting things about light and makes room for invisible things like infra-red as well. It says that God is light; but that there is no darkness in Him (from 1 John 1:5). But it also says this:

> "For by Him all things were created, things in heaven and on earth things **visible and invisible**"
> ...Colossians 1:16-17

Therefore, Herschel had called his discovery 'dark light' because he could not observe it with his eye, but perhaps it was not 'dark' at all. Perhaps it was just invisible to us, to the human eye. In fact, when viewed through the right instrument, it is radiant and not dark. You need to use an infrared spectrometer to see it, however.

Just because we cannot see it, doesn't mean it is 'dark'. It still has qualities associated with light such as radiance and wave formation. So, light is light even if it is invisible to us. But *real* darkness is not simply what we cannot see; it is the absence of light.

Light holds everything together

We turn again to that part of Colossians that says that He created:

> "Things **visible and invisible** ...in Him all things are **held together**"[5]

Now, God said about Himself that in Him all things are held

together (see above) and we know that God is also light from our opening quotation to this chapter (1 John 1:5). Therefore, it would be a strong affirmation if we saw that statements made two thousand years ago about God, before the discovery of electromagnetism, were consistent with the nature of light? Does light – electromagnetism, indeed hold all things together? And therefore, if God is light, it follows that God holds everything together.

Once Herschel had discovered that there was light beyond the visible, scientists have gone on to discover that the invisible spectrum is very wide and includes radio waves, microwaves and ultra violet as examples. In fact, the whole spectrum is collectively part of what is known as the electromagnetic spectrum.

Electromagnetism

There is some debate about who really discovered the existence of electromagnetism as a force, but around 1820, Hans Christian Ørsted first connected electricity with magnetism but could not explain his discovery and so it was left to André-Marie Ampère to do so a week later!

The involvement of electromagnetism as a force which holds matter together was explained during the 1900s using increasingly refined models. The first was proposed in 1900 by JJ Thompson who discovered the electron. He proposed a 'plum pudding' model where the electrons were embedded on the edge of the atom. Ernest Rutherford went on to propose that the positive charge was concentrated in the centre of the atom, with remote electrons found at the outer reaches of the structure, leaving open space inside. Later Niels Bohr developed a quantum approach to the explanation of the atom, and thereafter the neutron was discovered, and so on, until a far bigger, better picture of the structure was available. The forces holding atoms together include the electromagnetic forces. These electromagnetic forces hold electrons to the nuclei of atoms, and also hold atoms together to form molecules and also tie molecules together with other molecules to make objects.

So, 'light' seems to hold all mass together. It has relationship with mass. And we know that from Einstein's great formula, $E=MC^2$, where the speed of light is C, M is mass and E is energy. As there is relationship between light, energy and mass, it would not be surprising to learn that light might "create" mass. We will look at that later.

God is light, and light is electromagnetic in nature and holds all matter together. In saying that 'in Him all things are held together', The Bible has attested to the truth, discovered almost 1900 years later.

Transcendent light: over all, through all and in all

As the Bible says light 'holds everything together', it follows that light – God - must permeate through everything and around everything. Light must permeate everything in the known universe (and beyond).

Ephesians 4:6 says:

"There is…one God and Father of all, who is over all and through all and in all."

Now this statement has massive and profound implications for us. Whilst light is over and through everything, this verse says that it behaves in a *fatherly* way. Psalm 139:17-18 also explains that God has intelligence about each of us. This is what is said about the number of thoughts He has for each of us:

"How vast is the sum of them. If I were to count them,

16

they would outnumber the grains of sand."

God is light that pervades all, with intelligence.

<u>Intelligent light: the 'omni' of God</u>

This intelligent light – God – has been described as "omnipresent, omniscient and omnipotent" - literally, "all present, all knowing and all powerful". It is possible to see from the physics how that can be. This trilogy of 'omni' features has always been said about God. If God is light, as the Bible claims Him to be, then it seems that now, some 2000 years later, we can see that the all pervasive nature of light can support 'omni' style features.

We see **omniscience**, for example in:

> Psalm 139, which says: "You have searched me, and you know me."

> 1 Corinthians 2:10. We know that one person of the Trinity is the Spirit, and 1 Corinthians 2:10 says:

> > "The Spirit searches all things."

> Hebrews 4:13:

> > "And no creature is hidden from His sight, but all are naked and exposed to the eyes of Him to whom we must give account"

We also see **omnipotence** in a variety of ways:

> **in power:** Job 37:23: "The Almighty is beyond our reach and exalted in power"

> **in creation:** "By the Word of the Lord the heavens were

17

made, their starry host by the breath of His mouth" (The Jewish Rabbis believe that he created the universe with one word: "heh", which has a breath like quality about it):

> Hebrews 1:3: "The Son is the radiance of God's glory...sustaining all things by His powerful word"

in salvation: Romans 1:16: "For I am not ashamed of the gospel, because it is the power of God that brings salvation to everyone who believes..."

in resurrection: John 10: 17-18: "...I lay down my life, only to take it up again. No one takes it from me, but I lay it down of my own accord. I have authority to lay it down and take it up again. This...I received from my father."

in understanding: Psalm 147:5 "Great is our Lord and mighty in power; His understanding has no limit.

And finally, we see **omnipresence** in a number of places in the Bible:

> Psalm 139:7-10: "Where shall I go from your Spirit? Or where shall I flee from your presence? If I ascend to Heaven you are there! If I make my bed in Sheol, you are there! If I take the wings of the morning and dwell in the uttermost parts of the sea, even there your hand shall lead me, and your right hand shall hold me."

> It can be seen in the lives of every believer: Galatians 2:20: "If I have been crucified with Christ it is no longer I who live, but Christ who lives in me."

He is present even in the darkness, as He reminds Job in Job

38:19: "what is the way to the abode of light? And where does darkness reside? Here he is reminding Job of His acts of creation, when He separated light from darkness and commanded light to shine out of darkness.

Isaac Newton said this about God in Principia Mathematica:

> "The true God is a living, intelligent, and powerful being. His duration reaches from eternity to eternity; His presence from infinity to infinity...He governs all things and knows all things that are or can be done. He is not eternity and infinity, but eternal and infinite; he is not duration or space but he endures and is present. He endures forever, and is everywhere present; and, by existing always and everywhere, he constitutes duration and space. This most beautiful system of the sun, planets, and comets could only proceed from the counsel and dominion of an intelligent and powerful Being...He is omnipresent not virtually only, but also substantially; for virtue cannot subsist without substance. In Him all things are contained and moved."

Isaac Newton understood this aspect of the nature of God profoundly.

How does this Omnipresence and Omniscience function?

We don't know how omniscience and omnipresence function, but it has to do with operating outside the boundaries of the material realm. We gain some clues about this 'extra-material' functioning from the Bible, together with reported personal experience. This is therefore speculative, but still worth noting.

One intriguing article cites a study by Southampton University of 2,000 cardiac arrests. They documented something of 'awareness' that survives clinical death even though the brain has shut down completely[6]. Some people reported time slowing down or speeding up, others of a bright light; still others of a sense of fear and drowning, and in one case the article quotes that:

> "One man even recalled leaving his body entirely and watching his resuscitation from the corner of the room. Despite being unconscious and 'dead' for three minutes, the 57-year-old social worker from Southampton, recounted the actions of the nursing staff in detail and described the sound of the machines.
>
> "We know the brain can't function when the heart has stopped beating," said Dr Sam Parnia, a former research fellow at Southampton University, now at the State University of New York, who led the study.
>
> "But in this case, conscious awareness appears to have continued for up to three minutes into the period when the heart wasn't beating, even though the brain typically shuts down within 20-30 seconds after the heart has stopped.
>
> The man described everything that had happened in the room, but importantly, he heard two bleeps from a machine that makes a noise at three minute intervals. We could time how long the experienced lasted for.
>
> He seemed very credible and everything that he said had happened to him had actually happened."[7]

This also appears to accord with the mystical experience of a number of characters in the Bible: Enoch was taken up into heaven by faith (Hebrews 11:5); Philip on the road to Gaza from Jerusalem is taken away by the Holy Spirit, 'appearing' at Azotus (Acts 8:40); and

Paul attests to a man he knew 14 years previously (and therefore not Enoch) who was 'caught up to the third heaven' (2 Corinthians 12: 1-4)

Today we hear of this happening in certain Christian circles occasionally, to assist with the work of the Holy Spirit around the world.

The Southampton University near death experiences permit an answer to be given to the challenge of being somewhere else 'in spirit' despite the obvious presence in a different place of the material body, and this phenomenon appears to be more widely experienced than simply at death. God is light and that light emanates from His throne, and permeates everything. It lies in, throughout and around everything, and that 'everything' is contained within Him. He issues billions of thoughts every second by His Spirit (light) in all directions[8] and, because of His 'omni' nature, this light, which knows the mind of God[9] and so acts as His emissary, searches out[10] everything and reports back everything He sees[11]. His thoughts alone allow Him to be in all places at once, as He is unbounded by material things that He created, unlike us. But some of us, it appears, are fortunate enough to experience it when we become very close to God.

Being created in the image of God, there is sense in which God stamped His design 'hallmark', as it were, within us, in terms of the way we function as humans. We know that our own 'intelligence' operates using electricity in a similar way to the way He governs the universe. Our mind issues thoughts and instructions, which are sent out via electrochemical impulses through synapses, from our brain to various parts of the 'universe of our bodies'. The pulses often return, to be checked by the central intelligence, our mind itself. Sometimes parts of the body malfunction and pain may be felt and understood from the central 'throne' of our minds. It is a microcosm of the way in

21

which God operates throughout the universe, but in our case, it is limited by the requirement for a material medium through which to operate. The picture is, however, analogous and consistent with God being light.

God is in everything, so this has profound implications for us, as He must know us intimately

It is a very humbling thought for us all then to recognise that we cannot escape God. If God were a powerful, but evil being, it would be a very ominous thing indeed; but this power exists only from a place of pure love, as of course God is love[12].

But this knowledge of God's omnipresence and omniscience still places a great responsibility on us to behave correctly, as we are *known*. Imagine if everyone you despised could see what you thought, and how you acted in those secret places? I would shudder to think that this were possible, and how it might be abused by them. But because God is light and love, and this light permeates the entire universe, it is not only possible, but it is simply a fact that God knows us intimately and better than we know ourselves.

It is also a great relief to know that He is a God of love, for He is the definition of love itself. I do not believe that anyone can honestly make the case that He has abused them in exercising His love, nor do I believe that it is theologically possible to do so. He exercises that absolute power with great care, and with great, great love, for our benefit.

This knowledge also means that there is no point holding anything back from God. He knows it all already. It is in fact a great relief to feel then that in confessing what we may have done wrong, we are doing so to someone who would actually respond: "I know. I just wondered how long you were going to take to tell me that. Now please can we get on and work together for a change?"

His Omniscience therefore means that we are not bringing something new to God when we confess. If we can accept that He already knows what we have done, confessing it is less frightening than it might be otherwise; and is not really about a fear that God might find out; but rather a fear about being true to ourselves and authentic about our own failures. That is where the biggest hurdle and the fear really lies: within us.

We have already seen that God is Omnipotent, so it would be helpful to know a bit more about the scale of power He can wield. As God created all things visible, and invisible, we might be curious to determine just much He has used by measuring the energy stored up in His creation.

The awesome background power in the universe exercised by the Lord in creation

The answer to the extent of power used by the Lord already within creation is beyond our ability to comprehend seriously. We can gain some sense of the scale by looking at something very simple: for instance, the energy stored up within a single cubic centimetre of space. Apparently, if my research is correct, every cubic centimetre of space contains more energy than the total energy contained within all of the matter in the known universe.

There is something called 'residual energy' or 'zero-point energy'. It's what is left when one sucks out all of the air from space and then freezes it to absolute zero. Sucking out the air aims to take much of the energy out of space. Having cooled that space to minus 273.15 degrees Celsius, scientists have discovered that there is still some residual energy contained within it that cannot be removed. This residual energy is quite substantial. One cubic centimetre of this pure space still contains energy which is equivalent to between **100 and 300 million**

suns! That is the 'residual' energy left in a cubic centimetre after scientists have taken out all of the energy that they are able to do, using conventional means. Energy is not of itself God, but represents the awesome and excessive power at His disposal. No wonder that those who have seen Jesus, see Him as burning brighter than the sun, as Paul described in Acts 9:3!

Now that means your average living room is fizzing with power! It is power you cannot see; and although you live in the material world, that world is far less important than the invisible world which God also permeates, and which fizzes with far more power. It takes vast power to hold everything together; power that is beyond our imaginings to conceive. Only a God can do this; only a person who has eternal power can do this. Nothing we can do or explain is capable of this.

This awesome background power also informs us what God has available to Him to create something out of nothing, or as the theologians like to say: "Creatio ex nihilo".

We will look at creation later.

Quantum entanglement and Jesus; 'intelligent' light that knows what each bit is doing

Now light has another strange property. As every schoolboy knows, light has both wave-like properties and particulate properties, but one cannot measure both at the same time. It appears to have a sort of mutually-exclusive double character. Isaac Newton proposed that light was like particles, (and Einstein showed in 1905 that light was indeed made of particles called photons) and James Clerk Maxwell proposed initially that it was like waves.

Until recently no one knew whether light existed as waves or as particles, or both simultaneously.

24

No one seemed able to measure both 'states' at the same time. No one knew whether light was capable of switching between the two either. However, more recently, a strange phenomenon has emerged concerning this particle-wave duality, called 'quantum entanglement'. The movement of one light particle *appears to engage and affect the movement of another particle*, thus giving the simultaneous appearance of waves. In fact, *they seem to 'decide' to be waves or particles and may even delay that choice.*

Whilst clearly this is new and lightly tested and there is much to learn about the nature of light, this particle-wave duality, the ability to be either or both at a given moment, might shed some light on some extraordinary Bible verses.

In Matthew 17:1-3 it says that:

> "After six days Jesus took with Him Peter, James and John the brother of James, and led them up a high mountain by themselves. There He was transfigured before them. His face shone like the sun, and His clothes became as white as the light. Then appeared before them Moses and Elijah, taking with Jesus."

What is going on here? The visible Jesus is becoming more like His resurrected body; more light- like. This is the clearest statement that if God is Light, then Jesus, whose light was so strong that His clothes became whiter than anyone could bleach them (Mark 9:3), must be God. Simultaneously other figures – Moses and Elijah - appeared out of nowhere, from the invisible spectrum, to become visible. We do not know whether their bodies had mass, but they appeared. They were clearly not dead images, but live figures, as they were talking with the still living human being, Jesus. They disappeared equally quickly after the Lord boomed from a cloud that enveloped all three: "this is my son in whom I am well pleased[13]: listen to Him!"

Thus, Jesus is able to flip between His physical human body and His resurrected, light-fuelled and filled body.

In John 20:19, the crucified (dead) Jesus appeared within a locked room. The verse says:

> "On the evening of that first day of the week, when the disciples were together, with the doors locked for fear of the Jews, Jesus came and stood among them and said, "Peace be with you".

Jesus apparently walked through a wall, or appeared out of nowhere before the disciples, and spoke. He then breathed the Holy Spirit (very much light, as we shall see next), onto the disciples (Jn 20:22). Thomas is then told of this (verse 25) and replied that unless he was able to see for himself the nail marks and actually put his finger into the wounds in Jesus' hands and side, he would not believe that Jesus had risen.

A week later, Jesus appeared again behind locked doors, but this time Thomas was present. Thomas did as he had stated, believed, and exclaimed: "My Lord and my God" (verses 27-28).

Here, Jesus walked through walls, or appeared out of nowhere, but has a body that was clearly made of material sufficient for Thomas to feel. It is also clear from Acts 1:4 that Jesus ate with the disciples after He appeared.

So – this man of light could walk through material, or appear from nowhere, to appear in solid form and eat.

Now the Bible says clearly that God is light. We have learned that light can be waves and/or particles. We have also learned that light is the entire electromagnetic spectrum. Light can indeed travel through solid objects. X rays, for example, do just that. It is therefore no barrier to entry for light to travel through objects. Furthermore, if quantum entanglement has any truth to it, we see that this light can switch from waves to particles, 'at its own choosing'. So, although I do not suggest for a minute that "this is how God did it", we do at least have some rationale for suggesting that if God is light and that light is embodied as God, this light can simply materialise at will, through the exercise of God's own intelligence. From science, it appears possible for light to do this. This point of quantum entanglement about light 'knowing' what it is doing is taken up again later when omnipresence is considered.

The Bible has made some extraordinary statements millennia ago that can now be seen to be capable of some sort of rational explanation and are therefore trustworthy, given the nature of light.

The Holy Spirit is brilliant light

It is time to consider the Holy Spirit; or third person of the Trinity.

It is the Holy Spirit that is that part of God that is the light that permeates throughout everything and holds it all together. He gives power to Jesus at Jesus' baptism, when He comes as a dove to descend on Him to provide power for Jesus' ministry. He gives Jesus His *light* at Jesus' transfiguration; He allows Jesus to walk through walls. His light is *blinding.*

We see from Paul's dramatic Damascene conversion experience that God can appear as blinding, white light. In Acts 26:13, Paul says: "I was on the road, and it was noon...when I saw a light from heaven, brighter than the sun, shining around me and my travelling companions"[14].

And again, in Matthew 17:2 Jesus is transfigured before Peter,

James and John and His face: "shone like the sun, and His clothes became as white as light."

In Revelation, it says that John of Patmos saw one 'like a son of man' and that "His face was like the sun shining in all its brilliance."

And this light is transcendent. When Moses met the Lord to converse with Him and take instructions for proper living for his tribe, he would return, with a face that was radiant (Exodus 34: 29-35), so much so, that he would have to cover his face with a veil. The Lord's light had permeated his very being, and he reflected that light, rather like a luminous watch does, when charged by the light of the sun.

Blinding light is just one aspect of Holy Spirit. He is also known as the 'creator spirit' as He embodies creative qualities. He exists as a fine artist, replete with a full palette of colours to paint with.

We know that visible light consists of seven different colours, so if the Holy Spirit is that light, then there ought to be biblical proof that <u>He exists as seven colours</u>. Given what we have been through in this chapter so far, it would be incredible if that were in fact the case.

<u>Holy Spirit exists as a perfect 'seven', including seven colours</u>

If we turn to Revelation 1:4, we learn that there are 'seven spirits' of God. We learn that these seven spirits are in fact represented as seven lamps surrounding the throne of God. We are given a picture of spirits that surround and encircle the throne.

Now if we turn back to Isaiah 11:2, we also learn that the spirit of God is sevenfold. Here, the descendant of Jesse - Jesus - is described as having this sevenfold spirit resting on Him, to assist in the righteousness of Jesus' ministry. These sevenfold spirits each depict a different characteristic of God:

Spirit of The Lord
Spirit of wisdom
Spirit of understanding
Spirit of counsel
Spirit of power
Spirit of knowledge
Spirit of fear of The Lord

Taken as a whole (the Holy Spirit), these characteristics provide everything that is necessary for us as human beings, to rely on, and to turn to, in knowing God.

In more recent times, the missionary H.A. Baker wrote of his time in China ministering to orphaned children in his classic Christian account called: "Visions Beyond the Veil". These young orphans could not read or write, and had scant knowledge of the Bible. Baker would hold services in which he invited the presence of the Holy Spirit to come, and began to see that the Holy Spirit did indeed come, falling heavily on these children. They would fall under, as Smith Wigglesworth calls it, the 'unction' of the Spirit, in which He would transport the children, together, to Heaven and provide them with visions of their eternal destiny. I cannot recommend this book to you highly enough. He wrote down their experiences. This is what they saw.

> "Many times, have older and younger children seen the Holy Spirit as **seven lamps**. At times of special outpouring of the Holy Spirit, these **seven lamps of fire** were seen let down from heaven into the room in our very midst. At other times in the visions of the throne of Christ in heaven, children saw the "seven lamps of fire burning before the throne, **which are the seven Spirits**

of God" (Rev. 4:5). We all knew that **the seven lamps meant the Holy Spirit** was in our midst.

At that time the Lord said, "the Holy Spirit will descend to give you power to preach the gospel, to cast out demons, and to heal the sick; the **Holy Spirit is in seven colours, red, blue**, and other colours."

Here then, is a reasonably contemporary account of visions of the Holy Spirit comprised of seven spirits of God, and <u>seven colours</u>.

<u>When seven light-based (as opposed to painted) colours are combined together</u>, as every schoolboy knows, it forms <u>white light</u>. As Baker notes, "these people have also seen the Holy Spirit **brighter than the noon-day sun**".

So, in order to test this account, we must look to what the Bible says. I had spent much fruitless time searching my Bible for references to seven colours, and could not find anything. But when I did come across the reference, I smiled to myself, and said under my breath: "Of course! It had to be that!"

<u>Light of seven colours</u>

There is a stunning verse in Ezekiel which finalises the point I need to make. This verse says, part-way through Ezekiel's vision of The Lord on His throne:

"Downward from what appears to be His waist, I saw what looked like fire giving brilliant light all around Him. This brilliance around Him looked **like a rainbow in a cloud on a rainy day**."

(Jewish Bible, Ezekiel 1:27)

After the flood The Lord set **His rainbow**: a covenant sign of His

Holy Spirit, that demonstrated that he would not destroy the earth by flood again. A rainbow is of course refracted white light and is composed of seven different colours.

So, there you have direct biblical proof that the **Holy Spirit is a sevenfold, rainbow coloured set of spirits that combines to form the Holy Spirit as light, brighter than the sun**.

And the point of telling you all of this? It is simply astounding that we can learn from the Bible that the Holy Spirit is bright light composed of seven different spirits of seven different colours, and had been recorded faithfully in the Holy Bible almost two and a half thousand years ago.

Isaac Newton discovers that light is composed of seven colours

Who was it that discovered that light was split into a spectrum of seven different colours? It was none other than Sir Isaac Newton and he described his colour experiments in his book "Optiks" in 1665!

Furthermore, he showed that split light could be recombined into white light again, by passing the 'dispersed' rays, as he called them, back through a prism again. But if one ray went in, it would come out the same. In other words, to ensure that light became 'perfect' white light, all parts are combined and have their place. This is an extraordinary correlation with what we have just read about the Holy Spirit! The Holy Spirit is naturally perfect, being God, and being composed of seven different colours, combining to provide white, perfect light, brighter than the noon day sun. I sense divine providence! None of the seven spirits that comprise the Holy Spirit is the final conclusion or fullness of God by itself. However, when combined to form pure, white light, the fullness is revealed. (Interestingly, though, there is a subset of 'fullness' representing a trinity of colours which we will consider later).

Now Newton based his view that light was composed of seven different colours on non-biblical history. Some people consider his views to be cultic, ludicrous or based on Sophistry and, regarding the latter, they would be right. But Newton stumbled upon the right conclusion, even if he did so using the wrong root. Newton stated that there were seven different colours based on his understanding of ancient Greek Sophists, and despite some discussion on the question of colours from Goethe to Isaac Asimov, generally it is held that that the blue part of the spectrum is composed of three different hues, which will be of no surprise to any Bible scholar. If Newton had considered what the Bible said about light, he might have given more credit to his creator God than the Sophists.

3. Colour

"White...is not mere absence of colour;
it is a shining and affirmative thing,
as fierce as red,
as definite as black...God paints in many colours."

GK Chesterton

As we have looked at the *science* of light in comparison with the Bible, it might interest you to know that colour also plays an important *symbolic* role in the Bible. The reason for mentioning colour here is that although symbolic, the Bible is remarkably *consistent* towards the use of colour.

From a study of this symbolism, we see that the primary colours have a direct comparison with the Trinity which is explored further in the next chapter, and given that there are seven colours that represent the seven spirits of the Holy Spirit, it would not be surprising to find that each of these colours have characteristics in keeping with the spirit or colour, to which they are assigned.

Colours of God

In fact, as becomes clear, we can go further and state that these colours are set in the order of redemption of man – which is the gospel of Jesus Christ.

It is hardly surprising that these strange coincidences arise, given the use and mention of the rainbow in the Bible as we began to understand from the last chapter.

The first time that the rainbow is mentioned is following the

Noahic flood in Genesis 9:13:

> "I set my rainbow in the cloud and it shall be for the sign of the covenant between Me and the earth."

Now the important point here is that God does not say in that verse that he set any old rainbow in the cloud, but that he set *His own rainbow* in the cloud, and that 'it shall be a sign of the covenant between Me (God) and the earth'. Therefore, the rainbow is His very own rainbow – which as we learned from Ezekiel 1:28 in the last chapter, is the Holy Spirit, as the Lord was surrounded by the fire of this Holy Spirit, which looked:

> "like a rainbow in a cloud on a rainy day".

The use of similar words within Genesis 9:13 and Ezekiel 1:28 is too much of a coincidence to be overlooked. It is clear that God wishes the reader to take note that He set a colourful aspect of Himself, the Holy Spirit, in the sky as the stated covenant reminder. It is important, therefore, to understand what is being referred to when the use of colour is stated or alluded to in the Bible, as it reflects something important that God wants to tell us about His nature in the context in which the colour is mentioned.

We see from Proverbs and from various references to colour usage throughout the Bible, that an intriguing pattern emerges about man's redemption which I record in the table below. The redemption 'story' follows the order of colours set out in the rainbow.

Thus, starting with **Red**, we learn from biblical language (see below) that Red corresponds with the **atoning Spirit of the Lord**, for which atonement was made by **Christ's red blood**. Continuing thereafter **with the colours in the order in which they appear in the rainbow**, we see a story emerge about man's redemption.

Colour order	Characteristics	Spirit order (from Isaiah 11: 1 -5)	Bible references in Proverbs
1.Red	**The grace of redemption over sin, love** (E.g., blood of Christ (**red**) cleansing us from sin and death; washed clothes white in blood of Christ in Revelation 7:14; and how Christ loved us and washed us from our sins through His **blood** in Revelation 1:5)	...of the Lord	Proverbs 16:6 ("Through love and faithfulness sin is atoned for; through the **fear of the Lord a man avoids evil**")
2. Orange	**Separation of Good and Evil through Christ's intervention, judgement** (E.g. [Christ] will rule the [nations] with a rod of iron (**orange**) in Revelation 19:15; removal of rust (**orange**) from Ezekiel's pot as a judgement over Jerusalem in Ezekiel 24:6, NASB; and breaking nations with an iron (**orange**) sceptre)	...of Wisdom	Proverbs 9:10 ("The fear of the Lord is the beginning of **wisdom**")
3.Yellow	**Purity and holiness, purging through fire** (E.g. Gold (**yellow**) refined in fire in Revelation 3:18; God the refiner	...of Understanding	Proverbs 2:5 ("Then you will **understand** the fear of the Lord...")

	purifying Levites like **gold** in Malachi 3:3; faith greater than **gold** in 1 Peter 1:7)		
4.Green	**Healing, renewal, resurrection, immortality** (E.g. The leaves (**green**) of the trees are for the healing of the nations in Revelation 22:2; and Aaron's almond staff that budded overnight with **green** leaves and a crop of almonds in Numbers 17:8)	...of Counsel	Proverbs 8:14 ("**Counsel and sound judgement** are mine..")
5.Royal Blue	**Eternal presence of the Lord** (E.g. Emanating out before the throne is an eternal sea (**blue**) of glass in Revelation 4:6; lapis lazuli throne (blue) in Ezekiel 1:26; Mordechai wearing royal robes of **blue** and white in Esther 8:15)	...of Might	Proverbs 8:14 ("...I have **strength**")
6.Purple	**Royalty and priesthood** (Clothed Jesus in purple Mark 15:17; **purple** raiment on Kings of Midian (Judges 8:26))	...of Knowledge	Proverbs 2:5 ("Then you will...find the **knowledge** of God")
7.Violet		...of Fear (of the Lord)	Proverbs 1:7 ("The **fear of the Lord** is the beginning of **knowledge**...")

Taking the last entry of Proverbs from the table above, first, which says that:

> "The fear of the Lord is the beginning of knowledge" (Proverbs 1:7),

we learn that a respect and awe for the Lord ('fear') will begin a transformation in a person from ignorance to knowledge, as that respect will foster learning and will be, as that particular proverb continues: "a graceful ornament on your head" (verse 9).

From there, the fear of (i.e. respect for) the Lord will lead to **knowledge of God Himself**:

> Proverbs 2:5: "Then you will understand the fear of the Lord <u>and</u> find the knowledge of God." (NKJV)

But fear of the Lord is also the entry point to many other benefits, which as we see include wisdom (Proverbs 9:10) and redemption (Proverbs 16:6), spiritual might and strength (Proverbs 8:14). The Lord speaks to Job in Job 38: 2, asking who "darkens my counsel by words without knowledge?", before continuing with a lengthy discourse about His mighty deeds. This, in turn, equally implies that counsel can only be given with knowledge from God (as confirmed again by Job in chapter 42:3).

And this fear, or respect of the Lord ultimately leads to the final benefit: the Spirit of the Lord – being total freedom in redemption from sin:

> "Now, the Lord is the Spirit, and where the Spirit of the Lord is, there is freedom" (2 Corinthians 3:17)

This is the final state of the Christian – a redeemed whole person, free from sin and given freedom, which means freedom from death and decay, enjoying immortality.

There is a sense in colour in which man's *journey to faith* travels from the top of the table (red – the need for atonement of sin) downwards towards his final state at the bottom (blue/violet – our princely royalty re-established). So, man travels from redemption through Christ's blood; to judgement of his sin by the presence of the Holy Spirit in us; to the separation of sin from himself as his old self battles with the new presence of the Holy Spirit within him; through to healing from the damage of sin; and then sanctification and purification to become the person the Lord designed him to be: more like Him. He then spends the rest of his life eternally with God, from the time of his saving, onwards.

This is the gospel, described in colour, and we can look at this in more depth next.

Of course, many of those processes in that journey of faith can happen simultaneously, rather than sequentially. For example, faith ensures Christ's redemption for a person, and eternal life with Him instantaneously.

We can see this from the statement Christ gave to the thief on the cross. All the thief said was:

"...remember me when you come into your kingdom"[15],

which, with the preceding statement he made to his fellow felon, as Duncan Smith makes beautifully clear in his book 'Consumed by Love', is a full confession and then acknowledgement of Christ as his saviour. Christ was the one to whom the thief had pinned his last hope, and who was saved by his seemingly meagre acknowledgement of Christ as king of a future kingdom.

The very next thing to occur after this thief's statement is Christ's own statement:

> "Truly I tell you, today you will be with me in Paradise."[16]

So that was it. In an instant, the thief was saved from damnation.

Colour theology

I want to explore the topic of colour theology in a little more depth.

There are many characteristics to colours that are mentioned in the Bible. The Bible is often described as a 'pauper with words', and it takes study to discover its gems and hidden meanings, by revelation with the assistance of the Holy Spirit. The colour allusions to which I have referred are not exhaustive and there are plenty of others as well, which a variety of Christian writers publish from time to time.

However, for my purposes I wanted to show how these colours attest to the gospel, which we have just noted above, and to look into their meaning as aspects of light. Take pure white light. That light, as Isaac Newton's prism experiment showed us all, is obtained by adding all seven colours as light sources. White light represents absolute purity, for God is light. But as we move towards one end of the colour spectrum or the other, we start to move into places where that light is no longer visible, for example, as we progress into the infra-red or ultra violet part of the spectrum.

Is there a place in this spectrum that is actually *dark*?

Darkness is set apart from light

The difference with darkness, and this is crucial, is that darkness **cannot be made using light sources, for as the Lord said in**

Genesis:

> "God said, "let there be light", and there was light. God saw that the light was good, and he separated the light from the darkness."[17]

And it is true that every school child knows that you cannot make darkness from light sources, **but it is only observed from the lack of light <u>reflected back</u> from a created material thing – like paint**. But people don't know the biblical rule for this. Neither did the ancients. Yet it was set out there in the fourth verse of the Bible, as clear as day is from night.

God separated light (which we saw from above that He created) from darkness (which He also created[18]), so it is impossible for anyone to create darkness from light.

Generally, darkness and the symbolism associated with it has to do with the material, created, but now decaying Worldly realm. This material realm is decaying from the effect of sin on it. This created realm, which includes darkness, will pass away, leaving only absolute pure light forever and a day. In Revelation it confirms this, for it says:

> "The city does not need the sun or the moon to shine on it, for the glory of the Lord gives it light, and the Lamb is its lamp. The nations will walk by its light....**there will be no night there**."[19]

And so, whilst pure light contains all the visible colours of the 'light spectrum', there is no other end of the electromagnetic spectrum that is absolute darkness. Sorry: doesn't exist. Now you know why: God has spoken. But we will now look at the non-white and visible part of the light spectrum in a little more detail.

The gospel in primary colours

As these seven rainbow colours have ancient symbolic meaning, some of which have been set out in the table above, and that these meanings taken together describe a redemptive purpose, it implies that 'God the Holy Spirit' has always existed from time immemorial as a redemptive God, even though 'God the Son' (Jesus) appeared physically at more recent date in history.

The redemptive rainbow set over Noah following the flood began with red, and ended with purple, and was divided into seven colours.

There are some colours that are more special than others within the spectrum. They are symbolically 'divine' in nature, and the world calls these 'primary colours'. They have special characteristics and each relates to a specific person of the Trinity. In fact, as the other colours of the spectrum can be made by mixing them, it follows one can obtain pure white light from these divine colours alone. They are, as it were, set apart. Let us now consider each divine colour.

The 'divine' colours

The colour red is one of three primary colours which in the material world cannot be subdivided further and neither can it be created from other colours. It is therefore a colour that cannot be made less complex by man unlike blended colours, because it cannot be made more basic than itself. Because red and the other two primary colours cannot be simplified or 'controlled' as it were, by man, it stands, symbolically, for something absolute, or "divine", in its nature.

Red

Our first primary colour, red, has its Hebrew root in the word

41

"Oudem". Oudem means "red clay"[20]. We know that Adam – man – was made by God from the earth, so in what seems like a biblical pun, we learn that 'Oudem' is also the root of the word 'Adam' which means 'man'. So red earth and man are linked by the same Hebrew word. The creation of man by God is something that man has no ability to undertake, or control. Creation of man is a divine appointment only, and likewise the colour red in its own fundamental nature attests to this.

We therefore have the initial stage of the gospel, being the creation of man by God, from clay.

It is also associated with the colour of blood, both to represent life[21], and also to represent the sacrifice of blood-letting by Jesus Christ, for the redemption of our sin.

Therefore, red is the colour associated with God the Son.

Yellow

Yellow is the second primary 'divine' colour. Yellow, the colour of fire, is associated in the Bible with purging and refining of faith:

> "That the trial of your faith, being much more precious than of gold that perisheth, though it be tried with fire, (yellow) might be found unto praise and honour and glory at the appearing of Jesus Christ. (1 Peter 1:7, KJV)"

So we enter the trials of man, and the difficulty that God explained would be visited on man due to his sin: "In painful toil you will eat [of the grain of the earth amongst the thistles and thorns]..."[22]. But through faith in Jesus, this painful toil would become trials that would refine our spirits to the point that they would be acceptable to glorify God again once more. However, it was God, not man, that decreed that painful toil would ensue due to man's sin; and over this he has no control and cannot avoid it.

The colour yellow is therefore associated with this divine mechanism and attests to this itself, being divine in nature.

Yellow is also associated with the third person of the Trinity – the Holy Spirit, because it is the Spirit of God that is associated with fire, which is yellow. The most stunning example of this is when the disciples, newly orphaned from their master Jesus, gathered in an upper room to worship and pray at Pentecost, when the Holy Spirit came and each:

> "saw what seemed to be tongues of fire that separated and came to rest on each of them." (Acts 2:3, NIV)

Blue

The third and last primary or 'divine' colour is blue. Blue is the eternal presence of the Word and healing power of God.

Per Numbers 15, verses 38-41:

> "Speak to the children of Israel...and put upon the fringe of the borders a ribband of blue: And it shall be unto you for a fringe, that ye may look upon it...And remember, I am the LORD your God..."

Blue is also the colour of the Star of David, seen on Israel's flag, and represents the eternal presence of Yahweh. We have the last stage here, where through the eternal power of God and by faith in Him, we are healed of all sin.

Again, though, notice that eternity and supernatural healing are not matters over which man has control. God is eternal in nature, and can heal disease in an instant in a word. Likewise, the colour blue, which attests to these divine features, is itself divine in nature.

As the other two primary colours represent God the Son and God the Holy Spirit, blue, by deduction, must represent God the father, and it does. He sits on a lapis lazuli (blue) throne and His feet rest of an expanse of sapphire (blue) stone, which is as clear as the sky[23]. He also commanded the ancient Hebrews to fix blue tassels on the corners of their garments, to remember the commandments of the law[24], which were handed down to Moses, from a stone which is believed to be carved from the pavement under God's feet emanating from His throne (and therefore of blue sapphire). These laws were provided by God Himself. We can see this from Exodus 24, which states:

> "Moses went up...and...saw the God of Israel. And under His feet as it were a paved work of sapphire, clear as the sky itself." (Exodus 24: 9- 10); and

> "I will give you tablets of stone, and the law and commandments which I have written." (Exodus 24:12)

The only stone that is mentioned being (blue) sapphire, and so it is inferred that Moses obtained the law as pure caved sapphire. Once taken down from the mountain, the tablets are placed in the ark of the covenant, which is the representation of the presence, or the throne of God on earth. Therefore, the sapphire stone and its laws remain close to the throne of God in heaven and on earth at all times.

This is given some further weight in Louis Ginzberg's publication: "Legends of the Jews"[25], which states that:

> "Moses departed from the heavens with the two tables on which the Ten Commandments were engraved and they were made sapphire – like stone"

Now Ginzberg was a Jewish scholar of high standing, having received an honorary doctorate from Harvard, having taught in the Jewish Theological Seminary at New York all of his life, and he took a particular interest in the 'scientific study of Judaism' or 'Wissenschaft' as it is known. He was called upon as an expert to defend Judaism in national and international affairs and was a Talmadist (which has its roots in oral tradition handed down from generation to generation, which the Jews were past masters at practising with acute accuracy).

It seems clear from Jewish tradition and the circumstances we glean from the Bible that Moses brought two tablets of pure heavenly crystal-clear sapphire, upon which legal precedents for the instruction of mankind were engraved by God Himself. Those were pretty valuable objects!

When we mix the divine, or primary colours, we obtain other colours which have a consistent biblical application

I set out a couple of examples of primary colour mixtures to show how, even here, colour appears to have a consistent relationship to divine attributes.

Blue and yellow:

If you mix blue and yellow, you get green. In the spiritual, you mix trial/purging (yellow) and blue (the Word or Power of God), we get green (the colour of immortality and resurrection – a totally healed state). Jesus faced His trials and was resurrected, according to the prophetic Word of God and His power to do so. As we saw from the table above, the colour green is seen in Rev 22:2 as a colour of healing:

> "and the leaves of the tree are for the healing of the nations"

We also saw how Aaron's staff budded green leaves and almonds and was placed in the ark with the tablets of the eternal law,

45

which signifies both a symbol of resurrection and of eternity, as we showed in our table above.

Red and blue:

If we mix red and blue, the result is purple. In the spiritual world when we take red (flesh) and blue (Word or power of God) the result will be purple (royalty or priesthood). Flesh being guided by the eternal word of the Lord creates a royal priesthood[26].

To recapitulate, Noah, looking at the rainbow saw seven 'divisions' in colour as a sign for man that God would never destroy the earth again by flood. However, it meant so much more. For anyone with a knowledge of the spiritual significance of colour would have been able to read the entire story of creation, redemption, purification and separation from sin, healing from the effects of sin until bestowed a crown of glory as part of a royal priesthood again to reign with God for eternity, thus fulfilling Revelation. 5:10:

> "And hast made us unto our God, kings and priests: and we shall reign on the earth."

The colourful prophetic voice of the Holy Spirit - Aaron's breastplate and the twelve tribes of Israel

Colour progression and symbolism can be seen within Aaron's breastplate and the foundation Stones for the new Jerusalem that represent the twelve tribes of Israel. There is less certainty about what the colours represent and their association with particular tribes, so the following is certainly not a scientific observation. It makes interesting reading, nonetheless.

The breastplate consisted of a tablet of twelve stones of different colour, each representing one of the twelve tribes of Israel. Mamonides, the noted Jewish rabbi, described the stones as being

46

laid in four rows of three across, with the first stone, being the tribe of Reuben, being also engraved with the names of Abraham, Isaac and Jacob; whilst the last stone, which represented the tribe of Benjamin, was engraved also with the words: "the tribes of God"[27]. This order does not appear to be agreed upon by all scholars, however.

The breastplate was accompanied by the Urim and Thummim. Nahmanides, whose full name is Rabbi Moses ben Nahman Girondi, so shortened to the acronym Ramban for short, was a twelfth century scholar and lawyer from Girona in Spain. He explained that the Urim and Thumim were inserted into the pouch formed by the breastplate of jewels and a backing section behind the breastplate. This is where the Tetragrammaton, or 'ineffable name of God' would be placed, next to Aaron's heart, so that the names of the twelve tribes of Israel, plus the name of God and the High Priest's heart were adjacent to one another which was important when doing business with God. Aaron would therefore act in love when enquiring of God about Israel, in this process.

But Exodus 28:30 also states that into the breastplate of judgement should be inserted the Urim and Thummim, next to Aaron's heart, so that Aaron can bear judgement over children of Israel over his heart before the Lord continually. Now Ramban stated that "Urim" is taken from the word: "light" and this is because the Urim would cause individual letters of the tribal names of the Jewish tribes of Israel to light up. However, "Thummim" is taken from the word: "completeness" because if these letters that lit up were put together and read correctly, the answer given would be the full, true and complete answer to the enquiries of the Lord by the High Priest. This process is much like the way Christians read the Bible today, asking the Holy Spirit to 'highlight' certain words or passages within the reader's mind, to obtain revelation.

Rabbi Chaim Richman wrote as follows in his publication, the Holy Temple[28]:

> "The Kohen Godal [which is the High Priest] would stand facing the ark of testimony, and the questioner stood behind him, facing the High Priest's back. The questioner did not speak aloud but posed his question quietly, to himself, like someone who prays in silence before his Creator. The High Priest **enveloped by the spirit of Divine inspiration**, gazed at the Breastplate and, by meditating upon the Holy names of God, was able to receive the answer through a prophetic vision. **The letters on the stones of the Breastplate would light up and shine forth with a bright luminous light to spell out the answer to the question.**"

That the breastplate lit up came in useful when carrying out divine judgement upon the enemies of Israel, as Josephus Flavius, the Jewish historian, explained. These stones shone brightly when going into battle – a sure sign that God had instructed the Jews to purge the enemy and would provide His assurance of victory:

> "...for Adonai declared beforehand, by those twelve gems which the High Priest wore on his breast and which were inserted into his breastplate, when they should be victorious in battle; for **so great a splendour shone forth from them before the army began to march that all the people were sensible of Adonai's being present for their assistance.**"[29]

So then, here is another example of the light of God issuing a word to the High Priest, much as the light of God by His word created the universe and everything in it. When His light shines forth, the material world is changed.

The details of the order of these stones in four rows of three, is taken from the Bible at Exodus 28:17:

1   Ruby, Topaz, Beryl
2   Turquoise, Sapphire, Emerald
3   Jacinth, Agate, Amethyst
4   Chrysolite, Onyx, Jasper

The mapping of a particular stone to a tribe is uncertain, however, but Josephus the Jewish historian states that they were ordered according to the birth of the tribal chiefs. In the picture of the New Jerusalem, the foundations of the city of God are made with stones representing the twelve tribes of Israel, which scan exactly to the Exodus list.

Whatever the correct order of tribes and stones, it is without doubt that the stones and their colours were chosen at God's instruction to embody certain traits about the tribes and these representations have eternal value, being embedded in the very foundations of the New Jerusalem.

Joseph's coat of many colours – a hint of the Holy Spirit

Again, this is speculative, but interesting. The translation for this coat of many colours is debatable. The Hebrew phrase to describe this coat is "kethoneth passim" and has been translated as a coat of many colours, but might equally be a coat of long sleeves[30] or a long coat with stripes. The Septuagint translates the passage as 'many coloured'. Whatever the academic view, it is likely that this coat stood out, as Joseph was clearly distinguished by it and it looked like nothing else commonly used by his brothers or others around him.

But consider the analogy from the symbolism drawn from his story, and a very strong picture emerges of a different sort of coat.

In Genesis, his father Jacob (formerly Israel) gave him this coat. The Bible translation tells us that it had many colours on it, and it was given by a father to his son. In the guise of this hero of our story, Joseph is double crossed by his brothers, who left him to die. They were jealous of him, because he was born to his father's beloved first wife, Rachel, and so his father doted on him to the exclusion of others. His character irritated his brothers, and he towered above his siblings showing his precocious gift of special divine insight – the interpretation of dreams. They despised it, and him. Yet Joseph, who is saved by his brothers from the burial pit they put him into, only to be sold by them for twenty pieces of silver to passing Ishmaelites, ultimately ends up in Pharoah's household.

Here he rises far up the chain of influence, because of his gift of dream interpretation, helping Pharoah avert disaster; and with this new-found power as the King's Right Hand Man, he returns to save these two-timing double-crossing brothers from their own doom – and keeps intact the progeny of Israel (Jacob), with his magnanimous forgiveness. Read all about it from Genesis 37...

The parallels with the life of Jesus Christ are startling. A man, given up for dead, denied by his own (Peter and the cock crowing) and betrayed by another (Judas, for thirty pieces of silver); is crucified after the betrayal, but rises from the dead, is exalted to the right hand of God as the King's right hand man, and returns to provide his magnanimous forgiveness to undeserving sinners – being the whole of Israel (and those grafted in).

Yet it is the coat with which I am fascinated.

Jesus' earlier life records His baptism, in which the Holy Spirit, in the form of a dove, is sent down from heaven where He resides with the Father, to rest on Jesus. Jesus is then affirmed by His Father, with the words:

"This is my son, whom I love. With Him I am well pleased." (Matthew 3:17, NIV)

This statement about Jesus and His father in heaven reflects the special relationship that Joseph had with his own father Jacob. With the Holy Spirit now having been bestowed by the Father as a dove, Jesus takes up His ministry of forgiveness and redemption of mankind.

Likewise, Joseph's coat was bestowed upon him by a loving father, as part of the special relationship between them. The coat is clearly analogous of the Holy Spirit. Joseph stands with the Holy Spirit as a former 'remez', a Hebraic textual hint as it were, of the ministry of Jesus Christ, who comes to save his twelve disciples and the whole of Israel (for he came first to the Jews) and all those grafted in subsequently. Joseph came to save his twelve brothers, being the whole of the progeny of 'Israel'.

As the coat is analogous of the Holy Spirit, it can be contended that it was not a coat of many colours, but a coat of seven colours. It is clearly a sign of the Holy Spirit; clearly a sign of the rainbow power that surrounds the Lord as depicted in Ezekiel 1:28 and a sign of the covenant relationship that God has with His people. And he wore this coat like Aaron would wear his priestly robes and the breastplate (close to his heart in order to determine the Lord's will); and he spoke the truth as it was given to him, by the imagery sent to him by the Lord when he wore his coat, just like Aaron would do when he observed the lighted breastplate.

It seems that Joseph wore a rainbow. Joseph was clothed in light – the light of the Lord.

So, colours, what they mean for us and how they represent the Trinity, are important in understanding something about God.

Let us now turn from light and colour to another medium, and another creative characteristic of the Lord: sound. But we look at sound in the context of what we have learned from light and colour.

4. The sound of Heaven touching Earth

"In the beginning was the Word,
and the Word was with God,
and the Word was God."

(John 1)

In this chapter, we look at the relationship between colour and sound. Some time is spent on the primary colours, to show that there is more than a causal relationship between their biblical use or reference, and aspects of the Trinity. God tells us something about Himself by using colours.

Earlier, we saw that Newton discovered that light was in fact composed of seven different colours. But Newton went further than that, suggesting in his book 'Optiks' his Sophist belief that different colours are assigned to different musical notes.

In other words, Newton believed that light and sound are interrelated. Furthermore, if colour tells us something about God, it follows that if sound and colour are interrelated, sound must also tell us something about God.

We know that there are seven different visible colours, but we also know from musicians that there are seven different musical notes. As every school child knows, these are Doh Ray Me Far Soh La Te, finishing up with Doh again to complete the octave. There are seven different notes and the number seven is often described as the perfect number, or God's number, stemming initially from the time line for creation as being seven days. It is stated in the bible that God created everything in 'six days', resting on the seventh, as a signpost, or hallmark of His, so that we would recognise that it was Him who did it.

Newton's proposal that each colour has a musical note ascribed to it is quite extraordinary at one level. Why could colour have anything to do with sound? What a mad or, alternatively, quite brilliant statement.

We know that light vibrates at a particular frequency (and Newton could not have known that at the time). So, if one could hear that part of the spectrum, we could therefore 'hear' light vibrating at a particular frequency. That sound is often crowded out, however, by the plethora of radio and other **waves** that make up the wider light – electromagnetic spectrum.

(The 'wave' has some importance for Christians. It is interesting for Christians who have a relationship with God The Holy Spirit that they often feel the Presence of the Holy Spirit as a wave – like electricity pulsating through them. Given the Spirit's relationship to light, this is to be expected and should not be surprising. It is important for Christians to 'hear' the Holy Spirit, so that He is able to interact with and inform their lives constantly. This is not myth, as for Christians, it is practised fact).

We can explore the extraordinary correlation between light and sound further, as propounded by Newton. He showed in his 'colour wheel', that is used by artists the world over, that there are three primary colours. As we know from the earlier chapter, these colours are the:

> First in the rainbow: red
> Third in the rainbow: yellow; and
> Fifth in the rainbow: blue

We learned that these colours cannot be formed from a combination of any other colour, so are 'primary' or 'divine'. So, in a sense, these three colours are a reflection of the Trinity, God as three persons and each of these persons is a distinct person in His own right and cannot be reduced to a simpler state. And we can see from the Bible that these three colours were already known to be representative of the Trinity around two thousand years ago, before they were known to be 'primary' or unable to be reduced further.

Furthermore, one can create white light using just these three primary colours, since the other four are combinations of the three primary colours.

To remind ourselves again, we learned that the following colours represent an aspect of the Trinity:

> First – Red – represents Christ's blood
> Third – Yellow – represents the fire of the Holy Spirit; and
> Fifth – Blue – represents the righteousness, or royalty of the Father

We saw in the last chapter that the bible is consistent in its use of colour by reference to the Trinity. To support this contention, I now consider a variety of different biblical references which attest to that.

Jesus and the colour red

The potter and clay (Oudem)

Frequently throughout the Bible references are to be found which relate to life in the context of clay, and life being formed as pottery is formed by a potter on a potter's wheel.

In Psalm 64:8 (NIV) it says:

"Yet, O Lord, you are our father. We are the clay, you are the potter; we are all the work of your hand."

Here, we are compared to a potter moulding and making us as if like a piece of crafted pottery under the influence of the potter's careful, skilled hands.

And in Psalm 31:12 (NIV) it says:

"I am forgotten by them as though I were dead; I have become like broken pottery."

Here, dead flesh is like broken pottery.

The passage set out in Matthew 27:7 confirms that the potter's field is called the field of blood because it is purchased as a burial place for strangers – and is of course where Judas hanged himself following his betrayal of Jesus. His intestines fell out, which meant he spilled his blood. Blood is of course red.

Now, the Hebrew word 'Oudem' means red clay, and it is the root of 'Adam' who was formed from the dust of the ground; but later references to men being formed in the Bible are to being formed out of clay, by a potter. But this word 'oudem' has its root relationship to 'Adam' meaning 'man'. So, we have clay, speaking of earth, out of which man – Adam – was formed, by the potter, who is Jesus Christ (or the second Adam as He is also known[31]), as he made the heavens and the earth and everything (including Adam) in it:

"For by Him (speaking here of Jesus) all things were created." (1 Colossians 1:16, NIV)

Blood is life and blood gives life

In Romans, we learn that sin entered the world, and death

because of sin (Romans 5:12) and as Romans 3:23 says, "All have sinned and fall short of the glory of God" so that as Romans 5: 12 continues: "so death passed upon all men, as all have sinned"

But the Hebrew believed that life was contained in the blood of animals (Leviticus 17:11). A substitution could be made by the giving of another's life for the sin of a human. As this verse continues: "I have given you the blood on the altar to purify you, making you right with the Lord. It is the blood, given in exchange for a life, that makes purification possible." Red blood for blood.

The red heifer sacrifice

This sacrifice is highly symbolic as a foreshadowing of Jesus Christ's sacrifice. The cow was a red brown colour, and never had a yoke placed on it, so was unburdened and symbolically pure. A pure red heifer is an extremely rare animal to find, so it was symbolic of the uniqueness of Christ. It was required to have no blemish in its skin (as Christ was pure and blameless), meaning that it should not have more than a single hair follicle of a different colour to red on its skin. Since Christ died, there has never been found another pure red heifer, but with His imminent return, another is now expected by Jews who believe that the Messiah will prepare the final one. The pure heifer is expected to be burned completely, then its ashes are to be mixed with waters of remission, which can then be sprinkled on sinners to purify them.

At the wedding at Cana in Galilee, Jesus' first miracle was to turn water into wine. But this was not any old water. It was the water of remission to which ashes of a burned red heifer had been added. We know that he used such water as John says: "Nearby stood six stone water jars, the kind used by the Jews for ceremonial washing, each holding from twenty to thirty gallons." Jesus then turns this into choice wine; the Chateau Petrus of Israel; the very best wine, as noted by the guests. This was to show Israel that he was the replacement sacrifice and that His sacrifice trumped that of frequent ritual cleansing. His was a once and for all sacrifice by red blood, pictured symbolically by the colour of red wine, that trumped the red heifer sacrifice and fulfilled its foreshadowing.

Red rope of Rahab:

The book of Joshua tells of an intriguing story of a prostitute from Jericho called Rahab, who hid two spies from Shittim on behalf of the Hebrews. She was told by the King of Jericho to hand them over, but instead lied and explained that they left before the city gate was closed, and that she did not know which way they had gone.

She informed them that she had heard of the Hebrews' mighty God, and of His great and mighty deeds, and that He had given Jericho – 'this land' – over to them. So in return for hiding them, she asked to be shown favour when the siege was completed and asked for a 'sure sign'[32] that she and her family would be spared death. The men made an oath that will only be binding if, when they entered the land, the scarlet cord that they give to her was shown tied in the window through which she was to let them through. That oath provided protection for anyone held inside the house. Should anyone leave, or should she spill the beans about the spies, then the men would be released from their oath.

This story has remarkable resonances with Noah's ark, a space of safety in which a single family was kept alive when all around lost theirs 'outside the building'. It also has strong echoes of the Passover, in which sacrificial lambs' blood were daubed on the door frames of the Israelites' houses and in so doing, the angel of death passed over their houses and sought penance from Egypt instead. But above all, it has a remarkable similarity, and points forward to, a new covenant promise that God makes to all who believe in His son, Jesus, when Jesus spills His own blood on the cross – that all who are covered by the blood of the lamb are saved by Him.

This red cord binding then is symbolically significant in pointing to the person of Jesus Christ and His death for all on the cross.

Red Sea 'baptism':

The story of the Exodus is a story of emancipation of an entire nation under bondage of an anti- Christ character – the oppressive Pharaoh. Here, in order to flee evil and tyranny, Moses faced a moment of impossibility – crossing a sea. In faith, he raised up his arm across the sea, and it parted, allowing the entire nation to escape across it. This sea, the so called 'Red Sea' made room for the whole nation of Israel to pass through, but engulfed the whole of the 'evil' army of the raging Pharaoh that were in hot pursuit. This was the biggest single event that needed to happen for the entire of Israel to reach the promised land thereafter.

One theory as to why the Red Sea is so termed, is because there is an annual bloom of Trichodesmium Erythraeum, a bacterium which turns it red and processes certain necessary nutrients which assists the indigenous sea creatures who dwell there to survive. But it has been known as the Red Sea for thousands of years, though some contend that part of it to the North is in fact called the 'Reed Sea', but it still seems to exist within the overall basin of what is the Red Sea.

The symbolism points forward to Jesus' death on the cross. Here, God makes a way for man to pass through death and to reach a promised land the other side of death. In the transition, evil is put to death, leaving a believer clean from sin. Sin is buried in an abyss by Christ who takes it there and 'travels' with man by raising man up with Him to take Him, saved, to the promised land. The process can only take place because Jesus' blood has been spilled in the process.

The whole transition is a baptism. 'Baptism' means, literally, 'immersion'. Clearly the Israelites went through a deep sea and so were 'immersed' symbolically within it (though not actually covered in the waters). They thereafter came out 'free from bondage' on the other side. The process is cleansing, in that it frees the immersed thing from stain. In this case, it is the Israelites who are freed from their 'evil' bondholders, the enslaving Egyptians.

In the case of the death of Jesus Christ, Christians who believe 'on' Jesus are immersed with Him into His cleansing death, through which His blood is figuratively spilled over us, to 'wash us free from sin', and sin is left deposited in the depths of the abyss, or hell, in the process.

The Red Sea crossing, then, strongly points to Jesus Christ and His finished work on the cross.

Holy Spirit and the colour yellow

In Genesis 8:11, we learn that Noah sends out a dove who after several attempts brings back a freshly plucked olive leaf. Olive oil and the dove are symbolically related thereafter. Olive oil is yellow and was used to anoint Israel's spiritual leaders (Aaron – Exodus 29:7) and Kings (Saul – in 1 Samuel 10:1). A good example can be found in Judges: "But the olive tree answered: 'should I give up my oil, by which gods and men are honoured...?" There are many references to anointing oil in Exodus, another being verse 29:21: "Take some of the...anointing oil and sprinkle it on Aaron...Then he...will be consecrated."

Exodus is enlightening. The lamp (as we have spoken of earlier), being a symbol of light, is a representation of the Holy Spirit. The Lord commands Moses to bring an offering to Him, which includes: "Olive oil for the light" (Exodus 25:6) and later the Lord states: "Command the Israelites to bring you clear oil of pressed olives for the light *so that the lamps may be kept burning*" (Exodus 27:20). These lamps were to be kept burning in the Tent of Meeting [the Lord], before the Lord from evening till morning. The symbolism is strong – the light of the Holy Spirit remains constantly burning before the Lord, even in the darkness. This is also set out in numerous Old Testament references to the Israelites being guided by a pillar of fire from the Lord during the night. One place this is recorded is in Psalm 78:14. Returning to our lamp, one can see that it uses yellow oil and burns with a yellow flame – all symbols of the Holy Spirit.

This brings us to another representation of the Holy Spirit: fire, which is of course yellow. There follow some biblical references to the 'fire of the Lord', which attest to the relationship between fire and its colour, the Holy Spirit, and the refining properties of fire:

The Lord appears as fire

Exodus 3:2 – "There the angel of the Lord appeared to [Moses] in flames of fire from within a bush and spoke to Moses. Moses saw that though the bush was on fire it did not burn up". This is very similar to the spiritual fire that appears annually at Easter at the church of the Holy Sepulchre in Jerusalem, symbolising Christ's resurrection. It is a fire that burns and can be passed across hair, flesh and other objects and does not burn any of them up. It is also worth noting here that Moses heard the Lord from a 'speaking fire'. As stated earlier, the Holy Spirit speaks to Christians like a song; like a tune. There is a fascinating reference in Deuteronomy 4:12 which says that "The Lord spoke to you out of the fire. You heard the sound of words but no form; there was only a voice" It is from the fire of the Holy Spirit that He speaks.

Exodus 24:17 - "To the Israelites the *glory of the Lord* looked like a consuming fire on top of the mountain". Here again, the Lord (by His spirit) appears as a fire.

Fire is refining:

Numbers 18:17 - "Sprinkle their blood on the altar and burn their fat as an offering made by fire, an aroma pleasing to the Lord."

Numbers 31:23 - "...and anything else that can withstand fire must be put through the fire, and then it will be clean."

The fire of the Holy Spirit engages with people personally:

Acts 2:3-4 - "They saw what seemed to be tongues of fire that separated and came to rest on each one of them. All were filled with the Holy Spirit and began to speak in other languages as the Spirit enabled them."

The Father and the colour blue

We saw in the previous chapter on 'Colour' that blue represents God the father. God the father sits on a lapis lazuli (blue) throne and His feet rest on an expanse of sapphire (blue) stone, which is as clear as the sky.

He also commanded the ancient Hebrews to fix blue tassels on the corners of their garments, to remember the commandments of the law, which He gave directly to Moses.

The Ark of the Covenant, which is where the tablets of the law rested as provided by God the father Himself, was to be covered in a cloth 'entirely of blue'[33], as was the altar[34], and the veil for the temple of the Holy of Holies, into which pictures of Cherubim were woven[35]. Cherubim guard God the father Himself, as we see from the description of the four cherubim that travel with God's throne, in Ezekiel 1.

As blue progresses along the spectrum into purple, we see that purple signifies Kingship:

"He put a purple robe on Him...and began to salute Him: "Hail, King...." (Mark 15:17-18)

However, there are plenty of references to blue and purple both signifying kingship as well, such as King Ahasuerus' white and blue linen palace curtains[36]; Mordecai's royal apparel of blue and white and garment of linen and purple[37]; and the lamentable loss of kingship of the King of Tyre (an apotheosis of Satan) in which the writer states that once, before his fall, he was clothed in blue and purple[38].

The point, then, of spending some time on colour within a chapter on sound, is to demonstrate that God is consistent in His symbolism for the use of colour and that each primary colour does indeed consistently point to a particular person of the Trinity.

The artist's point in using primary colours in painting

When a person observes a religious painting, they see the active use of these primary colours as the artist tries to capture the spirit or essence of these characteristics of redemption or purging fire, holiness and royalty. He is trying to draw the viewer into a relationship with the picture, using the most emotive sensory buttons he knows he can push. The paintings of Michelangelo Buonarotti (see the Holy Family with the Infant St John); Jan van Eyck (see God Almighty); Rogier van der Weyden (see the Crucifixion Diptych); or even Massaccio's Crucifixion all attest to this. These artists understood the *power* of those colours perfectly well. That power engages our *emotions* and causes us to respond in kind with the painting. Good painting is popular, precisely because it speaks to us deeply at a level we may not understand entirely, but our spirit does.

The academic artist's book on 'Art and Visual Perception' by Rudolf Arnheim shows this quite brilliantly in chapters VI and VII on Light and Colour, respectively. Arnheim points to the work of Ernest Schachtel who suggested that humans react to colour *emotionally*: "Ernest Schachtel...has suggested that the experience of colour resembles that of affect or emotion....An emotion is not the product of the actively organising mind. It merely presupposes a kind of openness..."

Revelation, not solely reason is the way to truth

For a Christian, that is a fascinating concept. It is more important for them to receive revelation from the Holy Spirit than it is to rely on personal reasoning – i.e., not via an 'actively organising mind'. The very suggestion that emotion in response to colour presupposes that it bypasses logic, or organisation, and shows an openness to it in some way is also an extraordinary parallel with the way in which the Holy Spirit dialogues, interacts and informs Christians. (They may not even be aware of the manner by which the Holy Spirit does this). The wise use of colour, then, is very powerful, and we are wired to appreciate it in the way they it was intended to be appreciated, by the Creator Himself.

The Gospels only mention *man's reason* twice, and both times, exercised without God, in a derogatory way:

> Jesus gently chides His disciples when they consider how were to provide bread for feeding the four and five thousand the: "O you of little faith, why do you reason among yourselves because you have brought no bread?" (Matthew 16:8),

and:

Jesus recognising that Pharisees, who were criticising Him for forgiving sin had used reason and not the revelation brought about by their hearts and so said: "<u>Why do you reason about these things</u> in your hearts?" (Mark 2:8)

According to God, it is only good to use man's reason alongside His own, for He says:

> "...let us reason together..." (Isaiah 1:18)

Yet as we have seen, revelation is always better:

> "Trust in the Lord with all your heart and lean not on your own understanding...Do not be wise in your own eyes" (Proverbs 3:5-7),

and as the Lord wishes to reveal great things about His kingdom to His followers, He states:

> "Eye has not seen, nor ear hard, nor have entered into the heart of man the things which God has prepared for those who love Him. But God has revealed them to us through His Spirit. For the Spirit searches all things, yes the deep things of God." (1 Corinthians 2:9-10)

Therefore, painters, in using these colours in their proper representative sense, are communicating with our very souls at the deepest level and in a way consistent with biblical teaching.

Little wonder that their paintings have stood the test of time. We are wired to appreciate them.

The 'sound' of colour

We have shown that the biblical Trinity is represented by the first, third and fifth colours in the visible spectrum and so, if one could 'hear' these frequencies as notes, it would be interesting to hear what they sounded like. Now the Lord is perfect and is three persons in one God. Whilst Augustine wrote many volumes trying to explain that mystery, it must be true to show that if notes represent the Trinity, then they should work together harmoniously and not dissonantly.

It says in Ecclesiastes 4:2 that a cord of three strands is not quickly broken. Clearly the spelling tells us that this is not talking about musical notes! However, it can also be shown that a chord of three notes is not easily 'broken' either.

That is because if you take the frequencies of the first, third and fifth notes in a scale, you get a major chord, which is of course, harmonious!

A perfect chord is made up of three major notes, which in turn correlates precisely to the three light frequencies or 'sounds' of the primary colours.

As a website commentary says: (gootar.com),

> "if you could actually 'hear' the extremely high frequencies the red, yellow and blue (primary colour) light waves are vibrating at...you would hear a major chord.
>
> If you could 'see' the sound of notes in a major chord relative to the same 'rainbow scale' used by light...you would see notes and chords in primary colour just the way they are used in [a] chord diagram..."

The fascinating opening verse in this chapter is from the most mystical of all disciples, John, provides a large amount of helpful information about God.

God is described as a Word: a vibration, a resonant outpouring. It says at the start of John's gospel that: "In the beginning was the Word, and the Word was with God and the Word was God." This Word poured out of the Lord as stated in so many places in the Bible to create the world and life within it. [Jewish belief 'Heh'= word of creation]

John explains that the Lord was quite scientific in His use of sound:

> "All things were made through Him, and without Him nothing was made that was made."

This Word, this sound, created absolutely everything. In fact, as described in one place, this Word poured forth to create the dwelling of God Himself in our midst, for John goes on to say:

> "and the Word became flesh and made His dwelling among us"

Cymatics

How does God create such complex forms using sound? It appears that the science of cymatics – creation of form using sound, can provide us with a few suggestions.

If you go to YouTube, you can easily see video clips showing experiments where students place grains of sand on a stretched skin and then place a sound generator under and next to the skin. At defined intervals, the sand separates into geometric shapes, increasing in complexity in response to the use of higher frequencies. This is a demonstration of the science of cymatics.

Indian Shamans understood the power of this sound. They used to shout words at certain frequencies at dust and create shapes. They believe that certain sounds heal. Eastern Mystics believe in a sound mantra that resonates at certain frequencies and reacts with our soul and being to bring about a numinous intervention. Sound and religious practice appear to have a long history and therefore sound is worthy of some investigation.

It appears that sound can create very complex and beautiful shapes. Many animals and even viruses exhibit cymatic sound shapes. So, the humble five pointed starfish can be created identically using sound. The twin spiral of a daisy head replicates a cymatic twin spiral, and even a fossilised Trilobite can be replicated cymatically[39]. Tortoise shells have been shown to replicate cymatic sound shapes, as many of them look identical to Chladni shapes[40] as observed by the German photographer Alexander Lauterwasser. It seems even infamous crop circles obey the science of cymatic shapes, suggesting that some may have been created by sound waves[41].

From the previous chapter, we learned that light and sound are related, and that both have special, common frequencies at the first, third and fifth note or colour in a sequence. It would seem natural that the act of creation is a relationship between sound and light.

The question is: which came first, the chicken or the egg – sound or light? (The answer has to be light, for God is light. Or is it? God who is light used the sound of His voice to create the light of the sun. - Genesis). This remains a circular mystery.

It is probably better to say that light and sound have co-existed for eternity in the eternal person of God.

The watery Lord

It would take a complex interweaving of different sounds to create complex objects and forms, in order to permit the creation of man and the world around us. If this is how God created, then there must be evidence of complex sounds used by the creator in the manner in which he speaks. We are bound to ask whether the Bible makes clear that God speaks using a complex voice.

Well in fact the answer is quite astonishing, because it reveals that God does not always talk as humans do. God can talk with a polyphonic voice, whereas humans talk with a homophonic voice.

It says in Ezekiel 43:2 that "His voice was like the roar of rushing (or many) waters". The Bible doesn't just state that once. It also affirms that he speaks like that in Revelation 1:15 as well.

The sound of water moving down a stream, or over the edge of a waterfall, or even of waves breaking is a constant draw to the human psyche. Have you ever wondered why? I am fascinated by water. I sail, dive, swim and spend my life by the beach. I know the reason for this. When water moves, it reminds me of something I must miss. *The sound of water speaks to my spirit. The reason for that is simple: the sound of water moving is a constant reminder of the voice of my Father.* When you next stand close of breaking waves and marvel at the power, the beauty and the form they create, I hope you will reflect on these words, because they come straight from the throne room.

And the Lord not only *speaks* with the sound of rushing (or many) waters, as the Bible makes constant analogies between God and nature of 'divine' water. John, the New Testament mystic, notes the following:

(John 4: 13-14): "Whoever drinks of the water of this well

69

will thirst again, but whoever *drinks of the water I shall give him will never thirst*....the water I shall give him will become in him a fountain of water springing up into everlasting life".

(John 7: 37-39): develops John's theme about Jesus and water: "If anyone thirsts, let him come to me and drink. He who believes in me, as the scripture said, out of his heart will *flow streams of living water.*"

Water, a sign in creation of God and His kingdom, which quenches thirst, is being used figuratively as an analogous, but poorer example of the water of the Holy Spirit. The water of the Holy Spirit similarly quenches thirst, but in this case the thirst for meaning, hope, and a satiated eternal life in all its fullness.

Water, an agent for cleansing, is also used by God to show how death to a sinful life and rebirth into a cleansed new creation is performed by the agency of the Holy Spirit. Following Jesus' own baptism in water, the heavens were opened for Him and the Holy Spirit came down and rested on Jesus like a dove (Matthew 3:16).

Finally, there is the stream that proceeds from the throne of God. This is a curious use of water, as in this case, there is no attempt to be analogous to the Holy Spirit. This stream starts ankle deep, which appears strange given that the shallowest depth is nearest to the proximity of God. For this reason, it is probably not figurative, but an actual prophetic statement about a reality that will exist here on Earth upon the return of the Lord as he settles onto His throne in Israel. This literal river is caused by the returning Lord and its purpose is literal healing and literal eternal life given for the nations. Its purpose is to reverse the curse of death by sin through Adam in Genesis (see Revelation 22:3). This water, then, has a function concomitant with the Holy Spirit: water and spirit conjoined in a holy outpouring and an expression of a healed earth, just as God originally intended and created it to be.

So, just as the Holy Spirit heals, so this water will heal the nations. It flows to the Dead Sea and will cause the sea to be healed from its barrenness. Salinity will give way to the crystal clarity of pure water that is described so poignantly in Revelation, and many trees will grow along the banks of the river as it flows towards that sea (see Ezekiel 47, Joel 3:18, Zechariah 14:8 and Revelation 22:1).

As water is used so often in a divine sense, the use of the description: "rushing waters" when talking of the Lord's voice is therefore a quite deliberate, important and informative detail that cannot be overlooked. The characteristics of rushing water are creative, renewing, purifying and therefore tending to perfection, and life giving. Likewise, the Lord's voice is creative, pure, perfect and life giving.

When God speaks, matter bows to His command. That sound or rather, *those watery sounds* cause changes in matter. The sound that the Lord speaks with provides many frequencies at the same time. They can both melt a mountain like wax (Psalm 97:5) and can build solar systems.

The Lord's voice covers all parts of the audible and presumably inaudible spectrum. It is therefore quite possible to suggest from cymatics that the frequencies used can permit shapes to take the forms that we see around us.

The creative effects of light and sound together: Sonoluminescence

The interplay between light and sound is also fascinating and gives us a glimpse into the divine world. Sonoluminescence was discovered in 1934 in the University if Cologne. In the

71

experiment, ultrasonic sound is beamed at a bubble that is 'cavitated' (formed) and then suspended in developer fluid, and which then collapses into itself creating light and intense heat. It does this with a regular pattern. **Over 20,000 Kelvin has been measured; and a million degrees Kelvin has been postulated, which would cause nuclear fusion**, being the creative reaction at the heart of life giving stars like our Sun. The light given off is intensely bright given it comes from a tiny bubble, measured at between 1 and 10 milli-watts.

The point that I am interested in is that this experiment shows that *sound can create light.* In the Bible, the *Ancient of Days speaks into nothing using this voice of rushing waters and commands*:

> "Let there be light, and there was light" (Genesis 1:3)
> "Let there be lights in the firmament of the heavens" (Genesis 1:14)

So then, we might say that the God who exists as light, uses the sound of His voice to create light: the light of fusion- filled stars in the universe! It is quite an incredible concept.

But there is also another experiment that shows that light can create matter. In 1997, twenty physicists from Stanford University proved 'creatio ex nihilo' – creation from nothing. They created particles of matter from pure light. To do this, the scientists pumped an enormous amount of energy (virtually the run rate of power supply for the USA) but for a fraction of a second into a billionth of a centimetre. The energy was focussed into a laser beam that was only half a millimetre long but contained two billion-billion photons. They sent this beam around a particle accelerator, and an electron beam in the opposite direction and let them collide. Some of the electrons caused the photons to kick back into others, creating positrons – over 100 were observed over several months. Now, positrons have mass. (Science Daily 18 September 1997).

So, it is true then. Light can create matter, and so it would be entirely in order for God, who is light, to order matter into existence:

> "In the beginning, God created the heavens and the earth." (the opening statement of the Bible, Genesis 1:1)

Creation as an expression of the science of God

Really, we might wish to complete this chapter and the beginning of Genesis, using slightly different words, to express it scientifically. It is said that the Bible is a pauper with words, so this *could* be written:

> "God, the I AM who has never not existed, a person of light, and who is more powerful than the residual energy in all of the universe (measured at up to 300 million suns per cubic centimetre), collided light brought forth from Himself, with itself, and used electromagnetism that is contained within God, to create matter and hold it together. Simultaneously, God issued an instruction in a multitude of frequencies like the sound of rushing waters which, together with His light, caused such intense heat that this newly created matter underwent fusion and form."

In so doing, the universe was brought into existence.

It has taken thousands of years of experimentation to have begun to understand the depth of Genesis chapter 1, verse 1. That the universe has been brought into existence is without doubt; but perhaps now we can suggest that science supports the biblical creation account, *given what we know about God, his nature, and the science related to light and sound.*

5. The Senior Senior Wrangler

"It is the glory of God to conceal a matter,
but the glory of kings is to search out a matter"

(Proverbs 25: 2)

Whilst John Herschel matriculated from Cambridge as Senior Wrangler (which is the top student of his year) his son, Sir William James Herschel, followed an altogether different career that led him to the discovery of the usefulness of fingerprinting. Had they been alive today, both of them will have appreciated the following observations set out in this chapter, I am sure.

Fingerprints – a unique identifier

Fingerprints are both unique in nature and permanent, and when William James served during the British Raj as an officer for the Indian Civil Service in Bengal, he began regularly to use fingerprints as a way to secure obligations in contracts for those who could not read or write. He used his own fingerprints taken at various stages of his own lifetime, to prove their permanence.

In due course the system was introduced to Sir Edward Richard Henry of Scotland Yard and Henry introduced a classification system for fingerprinting that has been used ever since.

Herschel discovered that a person has been given a unique identity that no one else shares: his or her fingerprints. It is so secure that even smart phones now use it for logging-in. That identity is part of a person's special mark that sets them apart from anyone else alive.

Fingerprints – a signature hint of God Himself

As you might expect, a biblical view of this sort of thinking would suggest that if we are created in the image of God, then God Himself might have 'fingerprints', being His own unique characteristics, that show that He has left His hallmarks behind for those of us who are willing to search for Him. And as it is the glory of Kings (us) to search out a matter, the answer may lie just below the surface of scripture – just beyond the realm of the immediately obvious.

The following is a summary of much research that does not belong to any particular author, but I provide attribution, and quote references for their work. The section compiles the excellent work done by many individuals in different fields. I add some of my own observations and my own family history and colour to these contributions.

Ivan Panin

Ivan Panin was a Russian émigré, born in 1855, who became a Harvard mathematics scholar, but also a lecturer on textual criticism. These two skills were to be brought together spectacularly for him, in so doing, transforming an atheist into a firm believer. Being well known in his time, newspapers headlined his conversion. At 35 he discovered that there was a mathematical harmony within the Greek construction in the New Testament. He discovered this on seeing a purported 'mistake' in John's gospel. There was an extra 'the' that appeared in the original Greek that did not appear in translations.

The Greek appeared to say:

> "In the beginning was the Word and the Word was with *the* God and the Word was God."

75

Translations miss out the second use of the word 'the', to read:

"In the beginning was the Word and the Word was with God and the Word was God."

It appeared extraordinarily incongruous to him that this word 'the' should appear before 'God' in one case (for no apparent reason) and not in the second use of 'God' within the same sentence. So, coupled with both mathematics and textual skills, his enquiring mind eventually discovered that the use of the apparently superfluous 'the' was entirely necessary to complete a number sequence without which it would fail.

He began to look further and found number sequences all over the bible, including within the original manuscripts written in Hebrew. As there are no symbols for numbers, Greeks and Jews use the letters of their respective alphabets to define numbers, and the value of words is given as the sum of all the numeric values of the individual letters in that word.

He found patterns relating to the numbers 7, 8 and 9 throughout the bible.

For example, in the opening verses of Genesis the number 7 occurs numerous times, and numerical patterns can be seen within the accounts of Jesus lineage, birth and resurrection. Patterns of sevens occur throughout the bible (and we have seen seven spirits of God, being the Holy Spirit, for example). Even biblical mention of the number '7' throughout the bible is a multiple of seven.

Jesus' number is 8. His name in Greek has a value of 888. The various titles by which He is known are divisible by 8. The name 'Saviour' and Peter's expression: "the Christ" both have numeric values divisible by 8.

Rather than simply a superstition, the number 13 does in fact appear to be associated with Satan. Various names by which he is known are divisible by 13, from the Serpent to the murderer. .

Panin publicly asked that his exceptionally carefully documented work, running to tens of thousands of pages, be challenged by critics; and thereafter made the same appeal throughout the world's papers. No one has been able to rebut his work. It stands as a testament to the truth contained in the bible.

When one bears in mind that the bible was written over millennia, by geographically and socially disparate peoples, the fact that it remains totally harmonious and contains within it a hidden mathematics, points to a single, outstanding reason – it must have been inspired by God Himself. For it says in the bible:

"All scripture is God-breathed[42]"

That statement can be comprehensively proved through mathematics. No single person is or can be responsible for writing the bible or bringing it together, and the statistics are too overwhelming for this to have happened by chance. The bible attests to itself and God's fingerprints are all over it.

Fibonacci

Leonardo Pisáno Bigollo, an Italian who lived during the twelfth and thirteenth centuries, is best known for his work distributing the Hindu-Arabic numeral system throughout Europe. Now Leonardo Bigollo was also known as 'Fibonacci' and a peculiar number sequence is named after him, although he never discovered it. He only referred to it in his book 'Liber Abaci' (Book of Calculation). It was already known throughout India by the 6th Century (Wikipedia).

Fibonacci wrote out the sequence, which takes the first number,

1, and adds the preceding number, 0, to it to create the next in the series, which remains as 1. Thereafter the same rule applies, so 1 + 1 = 2. The next number is 2 + 1 = 3; the next is 3 + 2 = 5; and so on.

The simple series begins as follows:

1, 1, 2, 3, 5, 8, 13, 21, 34, 89, 144, 233, 377, etc.

Whilst Fibonacci listed out the start of the sequence, the "golden ratio", as it has become known, which is representative of this sequence, appears to have been used since Egyptian times in building the pyramids. It has also possibly been used by the Greeks in building the optically perfect Parthenon in Athens (see e.g. www.goldennumber.net). However, the parlance 'Divine Proportion' (as it is also known) appears to have been coined by Leonardo da Vinci in the 1500s in describing some geometric solids. This ratio then appears to have been taken up as a tool in painting, to provide perfect balance and proportion to paintings during the Renaissance.

Much has been made of da Vinci's 'The Last Supper' and his Mona Lisa, which both use this ratio. Albrecht Durer's 'Melencolia I' also used it, as did Michelangelo in 'The Creation of Adam' and countless other artists from Van Gogh to Whistler. Even architects like Le Corbusier have used it. Whole books have been devoted to the use of mathematics in art and architecture. This ratio is now known as the 'golden ratio', 'golden section', 'golden mean', and other similar names.

If this ratio appears to convey perfection in design and creation, it would be interesting to see what use is made of this ratio, if any, by the God of the Bible. One could contend that as God is perfect, His perfection could be observed in creation as 'hallmarks' – His fingerprints if you will. It would therefore be extremely interesting to see if God uses any form of 'Divine

Proportion' in creation. It would also be extremely interesting to determine whether God's use of a perfect ratio is the same as that discovered 'later' by man, from the Fibonacci sequence.

Mathematics states that two quantities are in the golden ratio, 'Phi' if:

"their ratio is the same as the ratio of their sum to the larger of the two quantities."

This ratio works out to be roughly 1.618 or 5/3.....

Biblical use of the Golden Ratio

When we look through the Bible, we see that there are various places where the golden ratio or 'Divine Proportion' can indeed be found in the use of objects that God instructed to be made; and also in certain biblical numbers. Its use appears to be quite frequent.

1   The ark of the covenant – God's mobile home on Earth

The Lord gave strict instructions to Moses in Exodus 25:10 to build an ark out of acacia wood to a set measurement, which was:

"two and a half cubits long, one and a half cubits wide, by one and a half cubits high"

The ratio of 2.5:1.5 (or 5/3) is 1.6666, which with such crude measurements is close to Phi.

2   The altar of the Lord – the table of sacrifice to the Lord
The Lord also gave strict instructions in Exodus 27:1 – 2 to build an altar of similar wood:

"three cubits high; it is to be square five cubits by five cubits wide"

Again, the ratio 5: 3 is 1.6666 – approximate to Phi.

3   Noah's Ark Genesis 6:15 requires that the ark should be constructed as follows:

"The length of the ark shall be 300 cubits, the breadth fifty cubits, the height 30 cubits."

Again, the end section shows a 5:3 ratio – 1.6666 – Phi.

Now the objects we see mentioned above have to do with proximity to God's Presence, which provides a further interesting 'hallmark' as it were, of the divine use of this ratio. From salvation of mankind through the righteousness of the line of Noah in Noah's Ark, to the temporal presence of God within the ark of the covenant itself residing with man, to the sacrifice of the lamb represented by the altar for sacrifice, we see symbolism representing Jesus Christ and His eternal desire to rest with mankind.

Phi, then is a representation of Jesus Himself, and as the person responsible for all of creation, we see His 'fingerprints' in the shape of this number, absolutely everywhere. There are of course other divine numbers, like the number 3, representative of the Trinity of God the Father, God the Son and God the Holy Spirit; or 7, which is representative of the perfection of God, and of the Holy Spirit who exists as seven spirits of God. But Phi is another such number, though its mention is less explicit within the Bible.

"The heavens declare the Glory of the God; and the firmament shows His handiwork" - Psalm 19:1

Some work has been done by the Institute of Creation Research ("ICR") to show that much planetary motion observes Fibonacci numbers. So, beginning with Neptune and moving towards the sun, taking some of the planets, and comparing the number of days that each planet takes to circle the sun with the planet next closest to the sun, there are ratios using Fibonacci number throughout as shown in an extract below from the table the ICR prepared. Remember the Fibonacci sequence uses the following numbers: 1, 2, 3, 5, 8, 13, 21, 34...etc. See how these numbers are incorporated in ratios of days to circle the sun, relative between planets, as shown in the last column:

Planet	Days to circle the sun	Ratio of days compared to next planet	Fibonacci sequence numbers used
Neptune	60193	1/2	1 and 2
Uranus	30688	1/3	1 and 3
Saturn	10670	2/5	2 and 5
Jupiter	4332	3/8	3 and 8
Mars	687	5/13	5 and 13

At a basic level, the Trinity itself also reflects Fibonacci numbers (three persons, one God).

The smallest things in the universe also obey Fibonacci numbers

From DNA - the stuff of life which has measurements of 21 "angstroms" in width and the length of one full turn in its spiral is 34 "angstroms", to the structures of atomic nuclei, creative Fibonnaci numbers are used.

ICR goes on to describe many flower petal and leaf protrusions around a plant's stem are similar in design to many of these

81

planetary ratios, citing, among many, that the elm has a circumference arc of petal dispersion of half the way round the stem; whereas a poplar has 3/8ths. Petals in flowers appear to respect Fibonacci numbers, so that the Michaelmas Daisy has 89 petals whereas an Aster has 21 petals.

Arrangements of chapters and the order of books in the Bible

Max Day showed that even the arrangement of the books of the Bible seem to follow a Fibonacci format[43]. This format follows a 'UCCOO' format, or a 'Unique', 'Complementary x 2', and 'Opposite x 2' format, throughout the old and new testaments.

It is a little complicated, so I hope I have faithfully represented Max Day's work well in setting out the following. The Unique, Complementary and Opposite expressions are as follows:

The first part of Fibonacci sequence starts with zero: 0+1=1. 1 stands in isolation and is unique as it is the addition of nothing. It is therefore described as 'Unique' (U)

The next two number pairs are 1+1=2; and 1+2=3. The number 1 is common to both number pairs and the first addend to both number pairs. The number 2 is the addition of 1+1 and the number 3 is the addition of 1 + 2 and 2 and 3 are described as 'Complementary' (C) as 1 appears as the first addend in each.

The next two numbers pairs are 2+3=5 and 3+5=8. The number 3 is the second addend for the first pair and the first for the second pair. So, the number 3 sits in opposite positions, so the characteristics of 5 and 8 is that they are said to be 'Opposites' (O) of each other.

Therefore, the Fibonacci format for the first five numbers is UCCOO. This format can be seen throughout the Bible by reference to each of its books. A book is either unique, or complementary or opposite to the one next to it. The following is taken from Max Day's pioneering discovery work via JHS Publishing Ministries on this biblical format. He wrote of this exhaustively in his book 'Secrets of the Kingdom Bible Revealed' and his work can be found now in an updated document entitled: "The Golden Ratio Format of the Bible". He shows that the format can be seen to work down to sentence construction within books in many cases, and the very order of books of the Bible themselves, giving some credence to a view that we have the full canon of books available to us.

Some examples of his work are given:

In the book of Acts, the following can be seen to bear out the Fibonacci format within chapter construction:

U – Chapter 1.1 – Jews of the diaspora believe Peter's testimony and therefore Jesus' resurrection C – Chapter 1.2 – Sanhedrin rejected testimony of apostles regarding Jesus' resurrection

C – Chapter 1.3 - Sanhedrin rejected testimony of Stephen regarding Jesus' resurrection

O – Chapter 1.4 – God elected Jews of the Diaspora to be saved

O – Chapter 1.5 – God elected Gentiles to be saved

And book construction in order of chapters and book order follows suit:

U – Genesis 1.1 – God chose Old Covenant Zion Peoples out of all nations to serve Him

C – Exodus 1.2 – God led those people out of Egypt to Mount Sinai

C – Numbers 1.3 – God led those people from Mount Sinai to Promised Land

O – Leviticus 1.4 – God taught chosen people of Zion how to worship Him under Old Covenant

O – Deuteronomy 1.5 – Moses taught chosen people of Zion how to serve God under Old Covenant

And this can be seen throughout the Bible, although the order reverses at equidistant points so that if you see two rounds of UCCOO appearing then the next sequence starts with an O, it will invariably be two rounds of OOCCU.

But why did God choose Phi (amongst other numbers which Ivan Panin revealed)?

Creatio ex nihilo – means "creation out of nothing". The sequence starts with a zero to represent 'nothing' and adds 1 to represent 'something' or 'creation'. The symbol for Phi is a zero with a line, or a '1' dividing it. Symbolically, unity, represented by the number 1, splits nothing and creates something out of it in an ever-expanding sequence. Add 1, or God, to nothing, and you get 1. Add God (1) again and you get 2. But as www.goldennumber.net makes clear, the very clever bit is the relative difference, or ratio between the numbers. We have seen that Phi is 1.6180339887... and absolute Phi is eventually reached when the Fibonacci sequence ends at infinity.

When the Fibonacci sequential numbers 2 and 3 are divided, we get 1.6666..., but later in the sequence, when 233 and 377 are used, the approximation to Phi is more accurate, at 1.618026, and so on. Therefore, at eternity, the fullness of Phi is reached. And God is eternal, so His fullness cannot be understood except in the context of eternity.

The sequence is the gospel in numbers

Representing this biblically, and in relation to us – being 'works in action', we have God, who created something out of nothing. That 'created' something fell and is not perfect. But as we are transformed from Glory to Glory, our approximation to perfection increases until we are received into eternity, with God, as immortals once again. Putting this together with the Fibonacci sequence, we have creation of something out of nothing. The first part of the journey we see that there is a rough representation of God's image in Phi (as we have fallen), but slowly, throughout the life of the sequence, and therefore over our own lives, this improves to become a better and better representation of Phi – God's number, until at the point of immortality, eternity, it is indeed 'Phi' and we are unified in perfection with our creator once again.

The Bible is so obviously full of examples using this ratio, and it has the gospel written into it. Furthermore, creation itself has these hallmarks of the King embedded into it. Creation points to the Fibonacci sequence, because the Fibonacci sequence appears to be God's own fingerprint.

Conclusion

This genius in the use of mathematics in creation and within the construction of the bible shows a very fine mind indeed. John Herschel was Senior Wrangler of Cambridge University and excelled in mathematics, but this codified sequencing and the mathematics written into prose of various different genres within the textual construction of the bible by independent human beings surpasses anything of natural origin. Whoever wrote it; whoever influenced these disparate human beings to write such a remarkable series of interlinked accounts takes the prize - the 'Senior Senior Wrangler', in fact.

85

We see the involvement of a similar designer genius represented in the manner in which the Big Bang occurred. Again, had this designer-genius varied the rate of His expansion in the first moments of the first second of the Big Bang by eye-wateringly small differences, we could not have come into existence and neither could the universe have done so either. A genius of mathematical design by a genius mathematical designer is also written into the entire fabric of the entire universe.

When, as a child, I learned of my grandfather's fingerprint discovery, I wondered why, if we had somehow evolved, it was necessary for humans to have individual identifying marks like fingerprints. Evolution does not require unique identifiers like fingerprints at all: what possible purpose can they serve for Evolution? But then, fingerprints show just how much God carves 'uniqueness' into every single one of His creations. And I am thankful that it was given to my family of believer scientists, to discover the uniqueness of them.

This creator God ensures that His own signature is written into His artistry and handiwork. Any artist ensures that he takes care of each creation of his as though it were his most special. And to show that each is different, and special, it must have different characteristics, to make each as unique as the Lord Himself. And one of those hallmarks of unique identity is the humble fingerprint. It is entirely consistent, therefore, with a unique creator God that has His own unique identifiers, for each of His creations to similarly have unique identifiers, as after all, we were made in His image[44].

6. Hard wired

"So God created man in His own image;
in the image of God He created him;
male and female He created them"

(Genesis 1:27 NKJV)

According to the Bible, mankind looks like God. That's both females and males. So, the image that Ezekiel sees in Ezekiel 1:26 of God as 'a likeness with the appearance of a man', and Daniel sees in his vision in Daniel 7: 9: "I was watching in the night visions, and behold, One like the Son of Man ...", appears to confirm that we are all a bit like God in appearance.

But it doesn't end there.

God also said, at Genesis 1:26:

"And God said, let us make man in our image, according to our likeness: and let them have dominion over the fish of the sea, over the birds of the air, and over the cattle, and over all the earth, and over every creeping thing that creeps upon the earth."

He made us as His stewards to look after His creation. And because He had created the earth and its creatures according to His own design, according to aspects that reflected *Himself*, He could feel confident that a being (us), made in His likeness, would do likewise. He allowed us, made in His image, to have dominion over all the earth and everything in it. Sadly, Satan crept in to try to take that promise away for a while, but God has a plan for that.

But God had us in mind for His purposes before a single thing had been created:

"...just as He chose us in Him before the foundation of the world...." (Ephesians 1:4)

And we were created for Him and to bring Him as our creator, glory:

"Everyone who is called by My name, whom I have created for my glory; I have formed him, yes, I have made him."

We learned from the chapter called "The sound of Heaven touching Earth" that man was made from dust or clay. Scientists have shown that every element contained in clay is contained in man. In the November 1982 edition of Reader's Digest, a scientist from the NASA Ames research centre was quoted as saying that: "the Biblical scenario for the creation of life on earth turns out to be not far off the mark". In fact, to put it another way, in terms of the scenario in Genesis, man can be made from clay.

We were also created to have relationship with each other and with God and to have that eternally. Having created man, God recognises that because He exists in perpetual relationship as a Trinity of persons, being God the Father, God the Son and God the Holy Spirit, and as He created man in His own image, as they are like Him, and experience his emotions[45], that:

"it is not good for Man to be alone. I will make him a helper comparable to him."

Man gets woman as his helper and co-equal. And the Lord also says:

"I have loved you with an everlasting love..." (Jeremiah 31:3)

88

God loves man with all of His might and forever, and shows that He is aching for relationship, because we were created for relationship. If we were created for relationship, then it would be unsurprising that God designed us to be sensitive to His calling on our lives, and His promptings. This is why I find the prospect of a God gene so interesting, as it suggests that we were created, by God's own design, to worship Him.

The so called "God gene" began its emergence in 1958 with the discovery by Nils-Åke Hillarp of 'secretory vesicles'.

If we read Wikipedia, we might learn that the God gene hypothesis proposes that a specific gene VMAT2 predisposes humans towards spiritual or mystical experiences, as postulated by Dean Hamer, a geneticist who wrote the 2005 book: "The God Gene: How faith is hard wired into our genes."

This is what is quoted from Wikipedia:

> "The God gene hypothesis is based on a combination of behavioural genetic, neurobiological and studies. The major arguments of the hypothesis are: (1) spirituality can be quantified by psychometric measurements; (2) the underlying tendency to spirituality is partially heritable; (3) part of this heritability can be attributed to the gene VMAT2 (4) this gene acts by altering monoamine levels; and (5) spiritual individuals are favoured by natural selection because they are provided with an innate sense of optimism, the latter producing positive effects at either a physical or psychological level."

All that may be true, or just some of it.

It is notable that John Polkinghorne, the respected scientist and

89

Anglican priest dismisses the idea of a god Gene in that it somehow 'defines' our experience of God, and to some extent I agree with that. He says:

> "The idea of a God gene goes against all my personal theological convictions. You can't cut faith down to the lowest common denominator of genetic survival. It shows the poverty of reductionist thinking"

Walter Houston, chaplain of Mansfield College, Oxford and theology fellow is cited by Wikipedia as stating that religious belief is wider than a person's constitution, being related to a wider range of exogenous factors such as culture, tradition and character, so that everything is involved. I would agree with that too.

Finally, Wikipedia cites Hamer, The God Gene author's response, where he says that having a God gene would not be incompatible with the existence of a *personal* God:

> "religious believers can point to the existence of God genes as one more sign of the creator's ingenuity – a clever way to help humans acknowledge and embrace a divine presence."

And I agree *partly* with that statement in that it is clear to me that with the addition of "personal God" some doubt is cast on whether God really exists outside human experience, being only 'personal' to the person experiencing sensations of the numinous.

Whether or not a God gene might assist in predisposing us to the things of God, it does not take away from our choice as to whether we turn the spiritual radio on or not. If VMAT2 exists and predisposes people towards faith in something, then they will put their hope and trust in *something*. People put their hope and faith in drugs, money, ambition and all sorts of things besides. Surely VMAT2 does not therefore predispose the type of faith in which a person places their hope? Just a quick look at the world and its many problems tells us the answer to that one! So, one must be better off choosing faith something good, or *someone* good – God!

Yet, if we do make that choice, we find our bodies are hard wired through VMAT2 to respond to God's call on our lives. God's design for improving our hard wiring exists as well. Did you know for example, that scientists now understand that fasting can regenerate the entire immune system? Sarah Knapton, science correspondent for the Telegraph, reported on 5 July 2014 that:

> "Fasting for as little as three days can regenerate the entire immune system, even in the elderly, scientists have found in a breakthrough described as "remarkable". Although fasting diets have been criticised by nutritionists for being unhealthy, new research suggests starving the body kick-starts stem cells into producing new white blood cells, which fight off infection.
>
> Scientists at the University of Southern California say the discovery could be particularly beneficial for people suffering from damaged immune systems, such as cancer patients on chemotherapy. It could also help the elderly whose immune system becomes less effective as they age, making it harder for them to fight off even common diseases.
>
> The researchers say fasting "flips a regenerative switch" which prompts stem cells to create brand new white blood cells, essentially regenerating the entire immune system."

Indeed, a calorie restricted diet involving 'fasting' for five days appears to "slow down ageing, add years to life, boost the immune system and cut the risk of heart disease and cancer, scientists believe"[46].

Fasting is an order for Christians (which obviously should be done only under proper supervision and medical oversight). It does not provide a choice to fast with an 'if' in Matthew 6:16, but uses a word 'when' to suggest that all Christians should do this:

> "And when you fast, do not look gloomy like the hypocrites..."

The reasons why the Lord requires us to fast are many-fold, but amongst some of the most important are to endure temptations and shore up defences against temptations. In Luke 4:1-2, it says:

> "Jesus, full of the Holy Spirit, returned from the Jordan and was led by the Spirit in the desert, where for forty days He was tempted by the devil. He ate nothing during those days..."

The biblical record showed that the devil never once returned to try to tempt him ever again. In Mark 9:29 NKJV, a demon is cast out only by prayer and fasting – a healing act. So, the point of this is to demonstrate that biblically, it was recognised that fasting could lead to a shoring up of defences and even healing. It is quite amazing therefore, to find that even after as little as a three day fast, the body itself responds to a fast in a physical way by producing more defensive white blood cells. How could this effect possibly have been known two thousand years ago? But it is simply a fact: the science has yet again followed the theology and proved its truth.

But the Bible, in telling us to fast, is offering a fundamental solution to hard-wiring our brain to eradicate bad habits. Jesus, and therefore we, can learn that resisting the devil causes him to run from you and not to return. Therefore, it would be appropriate to consider that if we resisted some bad habit for forty days, which has caused 'needs' in our bodies, may well break the habit completely, in the sense that our brains have been re-wired to resist dependency.

Lent, or the New Year's resolution, both traditionally times for giving up a food or habit, requires us to 'fast' from the thing for forty days, as it is well known that this diminishes dependency. Even secular websites talk of breaking dependency from resisting temptation for a period of time. So, this does something to our minds.

Bill Johnson, the pastor of Bethel Church, Redding, California, has written a book entitled: " The supernatural power of a transformed mind", which takes up a theme proposed by Paul in Romans 12:1-2:

> "By the mercies of God...present your bodies as a living sacrifice...Do not be conformed to the pattern of this world, but be transformed by the renewing of your mind, that you may prove what is that good and acceptable and perfect will of God."

And that could not express it better. By prayer and fasting, resisting the stuff of sin such as certain bad habits, will invariably see our minds becoming renewed, rewired, for better things, and healed, as it were. And we see the proof, as the passage says, by developing practices that show a transformed mind: those habits are broken and we step more and more into freedom or, to put it biblically, "we are transformed from glory to glory".

In the converse, we also now know that bad habits and unhealthy lifestyles are very bad for our genes. Whilst it has been known for some time that eating lots of fruit and vegetables and exercising frequently is good for people, this works at a molecular level as well.

One study found that eating well turns off genes that puts people at a higher risk of heart disease. In other words, a genetic defence against heart disease is created by eating well[47]. Another exercise using mice on treadmills showed that stem cells, that can become many different cell types can be prompted to become bone and blood cells as opposed to fat cells by exercising frequently[48]. We are quite literally 'what we eat' and 'what we do'. Our life choices really do affect our genes.

We can see this in many other examples, which include[49]:

Firstly, a reduction in prostate cancer tumour growth through eating a plant based diet with low fat. In the test, 48 genes crucial to cancer growth were more active, but 453 genes were less active in producing the proteins for cancer growth. Blood tests for prostate cancer improved and tumours shrunk.

Secondly, the slowing of ageing. Again, a plant based diet showed that the enzyme that produces telomerase, an aging enzyme produced by genes, is slowed by eating well.

Thirdly, over the course of a year, heart disease patients saw 143 genes involved with promoting inflammation in inflamed blood vessels decrease activity through eating differently. Under the control, those patients who continued with the same standard diet saw no genetic improvement.

Epigenetics: our kids are affected by our life choices

The new field of Epigenetics looks into the link between lifestyle,

94

habit and even finances on our genetic makeup.

In an important article by Chris Bell, a correspondent writing in the Telegraph dated 16 October 2013, we learn that famine caused by food shortages in Holland from blockades during World War II not only affected the adult population, but also affected their offspring when tested years later. It seems that the effects of prenatal exposure to famine predisposed those babies to an ongoing increased risk of health problems, as their immune systems were more fragile and, despite eating well, they also remained significantly underweight.

The genetic shock had been passed on.

In Chris Bell's words:

> "...it seems you are what your mother ate. How much your father drank, and what your grandma smoked. Likewise, your own children, too, may be shaped by whether you spend your evenings jogging, worrying about work, or sat (sic) on the sofa eating Wotsits".

It seems that aside from diet, Epigenetics can show how exposure to toxins, stress, and even shocks can affect the genetic legacy we pass on to children. It seems then that certain disorders such as diabetes can point to markers that were left in the code several generations back. DNA can self- repair when sections are missing, but this is not always so, and these particular markers have been left to pass on through the generations.

Chris Bell points to a statement made by one David Crews, who explains: "It's as if the exposure **three generations** before has reprogrammed the brain" when considering the exposure that the chemical revolution of plastics, fertilizers and detergents had on the Forties generation. (See the biblical reference to 'three

95

generations', below).

It's not just physical characteristics, but also behavioural – and I would therefore contend, spiritual or emotional characteristics that are passed down too. Rats who show love to their young cause the young to cope with stress better in their later life than those who are not shown that love, and so the imprint is physiological. But these characteristics are not solely confined to animals. Audrey Hepburn put her later depression down to malnutrition in her earlier years in the Dutch Netherlands.

These good and bad factors actually give rise to blessings, or woes, to future generations. We are highly responsible then, for how we steward ourselves, as what we do now affects the inheritance we pass on.

And yet, thousands of years ago, a loving and all-knowing father, God Himself, said quite simply:

> "I, the Lord your God am a jealous God, visiting the iniquity of the fathers upon the children to the third and fourth generations..." (Exodus 20:5 NKJV)

> ..."but showing love to a thousand [generations] of those who love me." (Exodus 20:6 NIV)

The Lord did try very hard to warn people. If they veer off the path He had planned for their good, this will happen. If they stay cleaved to Him, not only will this not happen, but in fact the blessings outweigh the curses in lorry loads, and for many, many generations.

We are, says the Lord, a temple for Him and His dwelling. It says in 1 Corinthians 6:19-20:

> "did you not know that your bodies are temples of the

Holy Spirit, who is in you...you are not your own. You were bought at a price. Therefore, **honour God with your bodies.**"

This includes sexual relationships. It is quite impossible for sexual disease to be transmitted across the human population if everyone stuck to the biblical example of one partner for life:

"Therefore, a man shall leave his father and mother and be joined to his wife, and they shall become one flesh." (Genesis 2:24, NKJV)

This was His good design. But we have ignored it and have borne the consequences. He really tried to warn us. Thousands and thousands of years before we ever had the technology to prove that He was just plain right, all along. We were created perfect. But we just had to eat *that* apple...

Now, remember this chapter when you read the next chapter concerning evolution.

7. Evolution:
Was the Origin of Species intelligently designed?

This chapter and the one following are both different to those that have preceded them.

With previous chapters, we were able to turn to grand statements made by God or made about God, uttered thousands of years ago, and to show, by modern science, that these statements can be trusted. That is because we are able to turn to things that existed in the past that have not changed and can still be measured today.

But with evolution, we cannot do that. Evolution speaks in terms of processes that have taken millions, or even billions of years, to accomplish. Therefore, as no one was in existence at the time certain life forms supposedly came into being, we cannot be sure precisely that they came into being when evolutionary theory states that they did.

"Macro evolution" cannot be proven, to the extent that it speaks of the emergence of species that developed from simple organisms. Anyone who says it can, is selling you something. But neither can young earth and universe theory, either.

However, we can show that many of the scientific arguments for Evolution are flawed, and by some margin. The theory is broken, at least at the so called 'macro evolutionary' level. By 'macro evolution', we are talking about a totally new species developing from one that preceded it. There is also 'micro evolution', by which we mean that many species can be shown to adapt to environmental and exogenous factors. This book does not argue with that. In fact, there is no reason to disbelieve micro evolution, as it can quite patently be seen in the adaptation of modern species to their environments today.

But the big-ticket item – macro evolution, is a broken theory, and if that is broken, then that leaves few theories left, one of which the secular agenda refuses to teach in schools and universities. This banned theory says that an intelligence directed creation. And that intelligence means "God".

Faith and trust

I have deliberately left this chapter until now, because it was important for me to be able to show you how truthful the Lord is about a number of things He said, or that have been said about Him in the Bible, before asking you to trust Him with what is said in the Bible about creation.

As nothing can be categorically proved one way or another regarding creation, it has to be taken to some degree on faith, so we need to understand a little about what we mean as Christians by 'faith'.

Paul, that fabulous soldier for Christ said:

"Now faith is being sure of what we hope for and certain of what we do not see" (Hebrews 11:1, NIV)

But faith is blind, isn't it? Or is it?

Informed, evidence based faith, not blind faith

Nicky Gumbel is the vicar of Holy Trinity Brompton. He is the person who has been the principal face of the world-recognised Alpha course, with attendance estimates approaching 30 million at the time of writing. Yet he was also once a successful Cambridge-educated barrister. Evidence is important to him. He discusses the parallels between the faith and the consideration of evidence in the conduct of criminal trials. When he was involved in criminal trials a point would be reached where the judge asked the jury to consider their verdict. He says that the judge would direct them not to find the defendant guilty: 'unless they felt sure. Every such verdict', he writes 'was an act of faith. The jury was not there at the time the crime was committed. They had to believe the evidence. Faith and being sure are not opposed....St Augustine wrote, "God does not expect us to submit our faith to Him without reason, but the very limits of our reason make faith a necessity"'[50].

Now, we weren't around when Jesus rose from the dead. We weren't around when God created the Universe and the Earth, so we have to look to evidence, much like the jury does, in criminal trials.

So, I have endeavoured to build up your faith in previous chapters. But your faith will not be unrewarded regarding creation, as I support statements made about creation with circumstantial evidence, although I give some room for manoeuvre on timelines, for scientific reasons; but I refute macro - evolution.

Evolution is 'not subject to the scientific method'

Certain biologists claim that biology – and hence evolution alongside it, should not be subject to the 'scientific method' of induction, or proof from repeatable testing. That is because evolution cannot be answered by repeat testing, under controlled conditions, because evolution is attempting to reconstruct history which may never repeat itself. Whilst this is a fair point, if evolutionary biology cannot be subjected to the scientific method, then however sympathetic one might be to the cause, it is little more than an interesting art form, like 'ancient history', and we all know how inaccurate that can be! For example, we all know the well-known aphorism: "history is written by the victors". This might be interesting, but is surely not the complete picture!

The truth is, that when biology, and particularly evolution, is put under similar scientific scrutiny, pitching it against what we do now know, as scientific fact, it cannot bear the weight of evidence against it. It doesn't stand the test of the trial. There is something disquieting about being 'required' to accept a theory as fact when it cannot be, or has not been, proven.

Having believed the conventional story about evolution and the age of the universe for many years, I came across snippets of news from time to time that seemed to fly directly in the face of conventional wisdom. Chief amongst those was the fossil record.

This caused me to look further and I unravelled more and more evidence that seemed to point in a very different direction, so I began to smell a rat: and this was before I was a Christian. It began to feel to me that there was a silent agenda. It made me look further still.

The god of Evolution requires great faith

Let us be quite clear: as evolutionists cannot prove that the universe is ancient, they too are appealing to you to trust them in faith as well. If you are happy to believe them, you have, in effect, assumed faith in a different religion, for it is certainly not science or fact, but a series of assumptions and theories.

The theory of Evolution undermines belief in a creator God and ultimately a God of miracles

It is notable that Jesus Himself knew that people would struggle

101

to believe, even when they saw His miracles. He said to Nicodemus:

"If I have told you earthly things, and you do not believe, how will you believe if I tell you heavenly things?" (John 3:12)

In other words, Jesus could see, 2,000 years ago, the problem with prevailing human culture, then and now. There are many people who have chosen not to believe the physical things that Jesus says He did, like the creation of the universe, and of the heavens, the seas, and all of the animals and vegetation in a miraculous set of periods that the Bible describes as "six days".

It is unsurprising then, that if they do not believe that he did those things, they will hardly believe in the spiritual things that he taught, for example, that he raised Lazarus from the dead. (Luke 16:30).

I know of the common view that the first 11 chapters of the bible are seen as 'myth' because there is nothing outside of the bible, so it is believed, to attest to the truth of the stories contained in those chapters. This includes the so called 'myth' of the Tower of Babel. Yet we now have steles that evidence the very words and existence of the "Tower of Babel" itself (see later). So, the story is far more than mere 'myth'. Without faith in His word, being the very gospel itself, which is the power of God for the salvation of everyone who believes[51], scriptural authority is undermined, because even Jesus upheld the entire Old Testament[52].

Jesus Himself taught that biblical creation included the creation of mankind

We need to regain and believe this fundamental truth of the physical origins of the earth from the Bible. We cannot pick and choose, as otherwise we call Jesus Himself a liar, because even He preached it:

"From the **beginning of creation, God made** them [man and woman] **male and female**" (Mark 10:6)

Evolution assumes that millions of years elapsed from the emergence of the first organisms to mankind and generally accepts an age for the Universe of 13.8 billion years. Jesus doesn't quite extend His teaching to comment on time itself. But His statements could be implicitly understood by us to mean that the earth and indeed the whole of creation must be younger than the evolutionary account because mankind, the last of the Lord's creations was created along with everything else at the 'beginning' of creation. He does not teach that living things developed from other living things over millions of years in evolutionary terms, but were instead individually created. 'God made them'.

We now turn to a consideration of evolution, and of the age of the earth and universe.

<u>The Great Debate between two well-known scientific gladiators – Herschel and Darwin</u>

According to Gregory Radick on Herschel, Darwin's theories "gave no indication of the Creator's foresight[53]".

He says that Herschel believed that "men of science were committed to discovering secondary laws, not primary laws. Darwin acknowledged that God, the primary cause, may well work by secondary laws; but he did not see why he had to include reference to God in his explanations of these secondary laws any more than astronomers [such as Herschel, no doubt] had to in explaining how the planets circle the sun. (It is possible that Darwin gave tacit acknowledgement to God in primary laws in order to put his position forward on secondary laws, as opposed to holding a firm belief a fortiori in God's involvement).

Radick continued that Herschel did not object to Darwin introducing secondary laws, but to the character of secondary laws he introduced. For Darwin, variations were in no sense preordained. The fact that an organism might need a particular variation did not increase the likelihood of it getting that variation. To make matters worse, selection looked equally indifferent to the good of individuals, including humans"[54]. Radick explained that Herschel "warned that to ascend to the 'origin of things, and to speculate on the creation, is not the business of the natural philosopher"[55] (i.e. scientist).

Darwin, however, ended his Origin with a statement that: "there is grandeur in this view of life, with its several powers, having been originally breathed into a few forms or even one." According to Radick's account, Herschel pressed Darwin on this point with its single oblique reference to God's original involvement, as it gave no indication of "the Creator's foresight"[56].

Herschel stated:

> "We can no more accept the principle of arbitrary and casual variation of natural selection as a sufficient condition, per se, of the past and present organic world, than we can receive the Laputan method of composing books (pushed à outrance) as a sufficient account of Shakespeare and the Principia. Equally, in either case, **an intelligence, guided by a purpose, must be continually in action to bias the directions of the steps of change – to regulate their amount, to limit their divergence, and to continue them in a definite course[57]"**

Now, whilst I am grateful to Radick for suggesting that Herschel

104

objected to Darwin's theory as it had dissociated the Creator (God) from foresight in his secondary laws, it is in fact difficult to read in Herschel's account that he attributed this intelligence to God, as opposed to any other creative agency.

Herschel, a man of moderation; a man who was if anything a principal pioneer of the inductive method of science (as opposed to the logic-based deductive method that preceded it) was hardly going to provide an absolute reconciliation with numinous matters about which inductive proof was unlikely to be forthcoming. He trod a careful pathway, keeping an open mind and ensuring his faith did not intermingle too closely with the rapid forward movement of the frontiers of science.

Herschel kept his powder dry.

But in my personal view, there is no other logical or reasonable explanation for an 'intelligence that can design' other than the Creator Himself. If an intelligence is involved, given the universal magnitude of that intelligence, really there can be few realistic contenders for that position other than God. And whilst Herschel left the door open for the possibility that a new species might appear as a result of the law of natural selection and not direct divine intervention, it does seem apparent that he believed in some interventionist creative agency, that continually biased the steps and direction of change.

Darwin had this to say to Herschel:

> "the point you raise on **intelligent design** has perplexed me beyond measure....one cannot look at this Universe with all living productions and man without believing that all has been intelligently designed; yet when I look to each individual organism I can see **no evidence of this**. For I am not prepared to admit that God designed the feathers in the tail of the rock-pigeon to vary in a highly

peculiar manner in order that man might select variations and make a Fan-tail."

So, according to Darwin, the universe when viewed on a macro scale, 'might look designed', but when considered more intimately, it appeared to be lacking such evidence.

Thus commenced the great debate on evolution versus intelligent design.

Herschel believed that an intelligent agency was intimately associated with species creation and direction. Darwin did not. But Herschel was no religious fundamentalist. For example, he could readily believe in a creation older than 6,000 years, which is what Christians had hitherto believed:

> "Time! Time! Time! - we must not impugn the Scripture Chronology, but we must interpret it **in accordance with whatever shall appear on fair enquiry to be the truth for there cannot be two truths**. And really **there is scope** enough: for the lives of the Patriarchs may as reasonably be extended by 5,000 or 50,000 years apiece as the days of Creation to as many thousand millions of years."

As Herschel's account above makes clear, he had no truck with adjusting biblical time lines. After all, as his friend Sir Charles Lyell would seek to demonstrate in his influential work: "Principles of Geology" that the world itself was not 6,000 years old, and that prevailing scientific evidence therefore tended to support a proposition that the planet was far older.

In fact, Herschel's own family had also toyed with evolution for some time, as the next account of the visit of Charles Darwin to John Herschel at the Cape of Good Hope, to share Darwin's views and discoveries, makes clear.

<u>Herschel: the inspiration behind Darwin's Origin of Species</u>

Darwin looked to Herschel for his inspiration in writing his *Origin*. I am indebted to B Warner[58], who has set out a good account of Darwin's meeting with Herschel at the Cape of Good Hope in 1836. John had published his book: "A Preliminary Discourse on the Study of Natural Philosophy" six years earlier and this had been a profound influence on the young Darwin. Herschel himself had speculated about evolution just a few months earlier, and so would have been a natural point of contact, and in Darwin's view, an essential contact, to discuss the *Origin*.

Darwin was returning from his travels on board the famous ship Beagle, and he arrived at the Cape in Simon's Bay on 31 May 1836.

Now Darwin made a number of studies whilst he was at the Cape, but his goal was Herschel. He had written that:

> "During my last year at Cambridge, I read with care and profound interest Humbolt's 'Personal Narrative'. This work, and Sir J.Herschel's 'Introduction to the Study of Natural Philosophy', [sic], stirred up in me such a burning zeal to add even the most humble contribution to the noble structure of Natural Science. No one or a dozen other books influenced me nearly as much as these two."
> [59]

The day before he met Herschel, his excitement was bubbling over:

> "Tomorrow morning I am going to call...on Sir J. Herschel....I have heard so much about his eccentric but very amiable manners, that I have high curiosity to meet

107

the great Man."[60]

He was at first disappointed with Herschel, but not with Herschel's beautiful wife, Lady Herschel!

> "...He was exceedingly good natured, but his manners, at first, appeared to me, rather awful. He is living in a very comfortable country house, surrounded by fir and oak trees, which alone, in so open a country, give a most charming air of seclusion & comfort. He appears to find time for everything; he sh[o]wed us a pretty garden full of Cape Bulbs of his own collecting; & afterwards I understood, that every thing was the work of his own hands. What a very nice person Lady Herschel appears to be, in short, we were charmed with everything in & about the house."[61]

The meeting was for Darwin the most significant for a long time – high praise for a man who had travelled much of the globe in search of evidence to support his new theory. Darwin's views on Herschel's strange manner tempered, as he later said: "He never talked much", "but every word he uttered was worth listening to"[62]; and "I felt a high reverence for Sir J. Herschel...."[63]

As Warner suggests, evolution was not far from Herschel's own mind, and it is probable that this was very much the subject of their mutual discussions, spartan though they may have been. However, whatever Darwin had taken from their conversations, it seems that privately at least, John Herschel remained circumspect about Darwin's own personal views on evolution.

Warner says[64]: "By a remarkable coincidence, in the months before Darwin's arrival, Herschel had been thinking about evolution of animals and plants. Thoughts on evolution ran in the family – his father, William Herschel, had tried to determine from his own observations whether stars possibly evolved from gaseous nebulae, or vice versa, and had suggested that if rates of change could be measured then the dates of origin could be found. John Herschel had continued to work towards this, and early on expressed his justifiably cautious attitude towards evolution in general:

> "...however completely a scale of graduation between a multitude of individuals existing simultaneously may be made out, this affords <u>no ground whatsoever for supposing any one among them to have been passed, or be capable of passing, through all the other states, or for concluding them to be in a course of progress from one state in the series to another</u>. There are infinite varieties in the modes and forms of animal life, from man down to the lowest orders; and some naturalists would willingly establish a progression among them, beginning with the simpler, and going on to more complicated forms; <u>but so long as no progress can be seen to go on – so long as for generation after generation every animal succeeds to all the imperfections of its parent</u>, the utmost that we can admit is, that such a formative nisus may have once existed, and acted in the progressive manner supposed, but that <u>all such progression has long since ceased in the present state of nature</u>."[65]

In short, even if there was some sort of evolution that once existed, there was nothing to suggest that evolution had support in the observable natural realm in that present day. Indeed, the offspring, if anything, inherited all the problems of the parents. The case, it seemed, remained to be proved.

His statement now seems almost prophetic in its correctness these days as I will consider shortly.

But Herschel did give credence to evolution of all states existing in the heavenly realm in a later edition of his Treatise on

Astronomy, suggesting that all states of celestial creation could be observed at the same time. Stellar evolution, though, is a very different proposition from species evolution.

He also made some further observations from his botanic collections and drawings, which suggest he could sense a relationship between different plants, though one would hasten to inject caution here, as John Herschel would not make a leap between relationship and begetting another species from such observations:

> "...I am nothing of a Botanist – but with one feature it is impossible not to be struck – namely, that when you find a species which fills up as you fancy a wanting link between two others – it does not merely fill it, but does so with the superaddition of some new characters – or some analogy with a 3rd species which the others do not offer."

Herschel made these comments 23 years before the theory of evolution had been published, and decades before the principles of inheritance had been established.

As Herschel had 'form' on the subject of evolution, and had in some senses mentored Darwin, when Darwin finally published his opus magnus Origin of Species in 1859, he was keen to hear what his mentor had to say, so he sent him an advance copy.

But there was a pregnant silence, which very much perplexed Darwin.

Herschel appears contemptuous of Darwin's Law of Natural Selection

Eventually, Darwin heard through others what Herschel's thoughts were, namely an excoriating comment that this law of natural selection was nothing more than the *law of higgledy piggledy*. In other words, "confused".

Herschel believed not only that a guided and purposeful direction continually in action was required for progress between species, but he was also circumspect that if evolution cannot be seen to have occurred, then one should not jump to any conclusion that it in fact occurs.

This is perhaps the biggest legacy on the subject from 'Herschel the moderator'. Whereas Darwin might have been quick to leap to conclusions from his secondary laws, Herschel was not tainted by such a disease. He suggested that ultimately evolution can only advance from theory to fact and therefore be believed if it can be seen to have in fact occurred.

And there it has been left between the two, and there the issue has remained stuck for two centuries.

For reasons that modern science can reveal, I am deeply proud of my grandfather for his views. It now seems that that the evidence points to a design and a designer, and so indeed does it point to an intelligence. It was right to have taken a circumspect view all along.

Evolution's repugnance: God has been sacked

What was perhaps challenging for Herschel was that Darwin's theory contended that an intelligent designer was irrelevant, as the law of natural selection rendered intelligent design (and thus certainly God), to the bin.

But Herschel was to some extent the instigator of his own misfortune. As the popular 'heir to Francis Bacon', he had himself insisted and influenced Darwin to follow a system of pure scientific induction, or: "the inductive philosophy of science", as it was then called. Thomas Jefferson, perhaps borrowing from Plato and Socrates, himself also once said: "we are not afraid to follow the truth wherever it may lead"[66], and Herschel enthusiastically bought into that belief. Therefore, if the science tended to suggest one thing, then it must be followed to its natural conclusion, however awkward this might be for the scientist. Whilst initially supported by very few, some years later Darwin's theory began to gather support as evidence of an older earth and fossil discoveries appeared for two centuries to support his views.

The debate continues, even now, and Darwin and Herschel remain inseparable. They are buried next to each other at Westminster Abbey; somehow battling the debate out for eternity; carefully overseen by another neighbourly bedfellow: Isaac Newton.

8. Evolution's evolution

The case still remains to be proved

As we learned from the last chapter, Herschel believed not only that a guided and purposeful direction continually in action was required for progress between species, but he was also circumspect that if evolution cannot be seen to have occurred, then one should not jump to any conclusion that it in fact occurs. He was in effect saying, gently, that the case remains to be proved.

Inductive science once pointed to an older earth

The evidence Darwin and other scientists were unearthing then seemed to be pointing in a different direction from the biblical account.

Aside from Lyell's geological findings, rumblings of an ancient creation and an older earth than proposed by the biblical account had been encouraged by John Herschel's own father William, not least through his discovery of Uranus.

The discovery had inspired William's peers to consider that lights in the sky no longer hovered somewhere over the earth, but actually existed in deep, deep space. This set creative minds alight such as the writer John Bonnycastle, who published his book in 1786 entitled "Introduction to Astronomy in Letters to his Pupil". He states that: "This discovery [of Uranus]...may produce many new discoveries in the celestial regions, by which our knowledge of the heavenly bodies, and of the immutable laws that govern the universe, will become much more extended..."[67]. This "extension" appeared to him to point to a universe of at least 2,000,000 years old, based, he contended on

113

the findings of the best astronomers of the time.

By the time that John Herschel had matured as a scientist, there was plenty of speculation from romantics and scientists about the age of the universe; and that it was much, much older than the received biblical wisdom that creation occurred only 6,000 years ago.

A universe of 6,000 years old, or 13.8 billion years old?

We now turn to the subject, some of the various theories for the age of the heavens (universe) and of the earth. We consider these theories and some science which provides some context for them.

Myth?

The first 11 chapters of the Bible are often taught, even by Bible scholars, as 'myth'. A myth is not necessarily untrue, but scant independent evidence exists to support the story and so it is ranked as 'myth'. The first 11 chapters of the Bible take us from the creation story, through the Flood and Tower of Babel epics to the decision by Abram to leave his country to seek a nation for himself. As myth by its nature could have elements of truth contained within its story, it is a fruitful and legitimate enterprise to consider what truth we might find from sources externally in support of the biblical account.

The idea of a young earth and universe comes from what people think Jesus said about creation, the time lines given in the Bible and from creation theory based on the Bible. The latter provides a link between six days of creation as set out in Genesis and 6,000 years of the earth's theoretical existence taken from the chronology of successive biblical lifetimes.

In Genesis chapters 1 and 2, the narrative tells us of how God made the heavens and the earth and all the creatures in "six days" and then by Genesis 2:2 God rests from 'all His work' for another day.

The story is often cited in these modern times as allegorical, or mythological, as opposed to factual, and is based on other ancient mythological stories of creation extant at the time which preceded Genesis. It is difficult for people to accept that God created everything within six days particularly when so much of our world and universe looks so ancient. By taking that view, those who find a young earth difficult to accept are minded to somehow barter a difficult peace between evolutionary science and the biblical account to enable them to come to some half way house solution between the two.

<u>The problem for Christians: God says He did it in six days!</u>

But the problem for bartering believers is that God directly attests to the six-day creation Himself in Exodus. A tension, and sometimes a guilty sense of compromise can arise for Christians, as they are required to deny that a six-day creation existed in order to 'fit in' with the prevailing view of science; or at least the version taught within most classrooms. To accept an old universe, and evolution, one has to deny what God Himself said; or to put it a slightly different way, if what God said cannot be trusted as the cast-iron truth in respect of this most important of themes, then frankly how will anyone trust God with other things He says he did, like healing people, or the promise for believers of an eternity with Him as immortals?

There is an account where God *speaks directly* to confirm the "six-day" account of creation, as opposed to the Genesis account which is really a narrative *about what God did* over the course of a so-called six-day time frame.

In Exodus 20, the chapter starts by confirming:

"And God spoke all these words:"

God then thunders some powerful words from the top of Mount Sinai, where He is seen descending in fire; where thunder and smoke billow forth and the whole mountain trembles; flashes of lightning are experienced; and the sound of a trumpet (traditionally always the sound of angelic intervention) increases in volume.

Whilst the imagery of a volcano might spring to mind, the carefully described biblical account that states that fire comes down, as opposed to ascending from the mountain, and that a trumpet is heard, makes a volcano an improbable explanation. When God then spoke, it is clear that the whole of Israel could hear Him, so His voice, given from the top of a mountain, must have been both authoritative and very loud indeed.

When He spoke, His narrative confirmed that he made everything in 'six days'.

To assist Christians to lay aside a sense of 'guilty compromise', it becomes important to look into what God may have meant when He said, and then confirmed, that He made everything in six days. However, God didn't just give this narrative to Christians or believers, He also intended for the whole world to listen to and take seriously that He made everything in six days. What is meant by 'six days'?

God addresses not just believers, but those who practice the dark arts and sciences as well

Rabinnical literature has it that Balaam the sorcerer mentioned in Numbers 22-24 could hear all of this as well, as all kings trembled at the sound of this mighty voice that shook the foundations of the earth. Irrespective of the truth of this account,

116

it is possible then, that the biblical account of God thundering His law to all of Israel was <u>intended to be heard by all lands and peoples</u> reasonably proximate to Mount Sinai. He intended to explain what standards must exist for the world; that the Israelites were His chosen people, and that He was indeed the <u>all-powerful, creative God</u> of the universe who miraculously created all things within six days. God here comes down to earth and intervenes powerfully; whereas all other tribes seek to reach their Gods in heaven by scaling heights (like the Tower of Babel, for example).

So then, taking God at His word, what support exists for a younger universe and earth? And what might God mean by 'six days'? Let us now turn to some of the theories and consider them in the context of some prevailing science.

<u>The theories: young earth chronology</u>

There is some support that, from the start of all creation, only 6,000 years have passed. This is from Bishop James Ussher who in 1650 finished his tome: "The Annals of the Old Testament." His endeavour was to try to bring scholarship to the biblical chronology and he amassed a library of 10,000 volumes of ancient books and manuscripts in the process from which he took his stance. He begins his book:

> "In the beginning, God created heaven and earth, which beginning of time, according to this chronology, occurred at the beginning of the night which preceded the 23rd October in the year 710 of the Julian period."

Ussher helpfully adds a side note in his margin, which explains that this is a 'Christian' time of 4004 BC.

Christians already understood that the earth and the heavens were created roughly 4,000-5,000 years before Christ, from the very timetabling provided by the Bible.

As for the earth itself, Shakespeare quoted that it was almost 6,000 years old in "As you like it"; and Johannes Kepler, the astronomer, gave a date almost 4,000 years BC for creation.

For me, Ussher's chronology is a reasonably compelling account of the age of creation and of the earth, all of the methods that support a young earth, as it has some basis in reasoned fact that can be easily understood. But this doesn't entirely detract from 'creation theory', which has some basis in science as well.

The theories: Creation theory attests to a similar 6,000-year timescale, perhaps less rigorously

Whilst the chronological summation of ages and dates (however done) provides for a very young universe, there is also a second timescale provided from creation theory which comes to the same conclusion. I naturally resist creation theory, because it takes as a concept that a day is equivalent to 1,000 years, when the use of that phrase may not be directly intended to refer to the creation time frame (see next paragraph).

This theory develops along the following lines. There are 6 days of creation, and according to Psalm 90:4, "a thousand years is like a day...". This Psalm may just be hinting at the timelessness of the Lord's own existence, rather than giving a specific meaning to what a day, or 1,000 years means, so it could be dangerous to interpret Genesis in that light. But in spite of these detractions, there is in fact some scientific validity to a comparison between 1,000 years and a twenty-four-hour day which I set out later.

The theories: Rabbinical support for an old universe (and hence earth) exists – but it is not rigorous

One interesting account by a Jewish Rabbi Yitzak deMin Acco

118

believed that the name of God included the age of the universe within it. This 42-letter name of God related to 42,000 divine years between creation and the coming of man. As a year is 365.25 days long (a leap year in every fourth year makes up the additional day), then as 1,000 years is a day for the Lord (from Psalm 90), this means that a divine year is in fact 365,250 years long. Therefore, the time between creation and the advent of man is approximately 365,250 x 42,000 = 15.3 billion years.

The obvious problem with this is that it bears no relationship to any other form or use of 'year' in the creation account nor does it involve '6' in its calculation. For example, on the basis the biblical time frame of six days of creation, this would either make the universe, according to divine or earth years, either 252,000 or 2,191,500 years old depending upon your point of view. It is not a compelling argument.

The theories: expansion of the universe from inception

Against this, 13.8 billion years is the time given by most scientists for the approximate age of the universe. This is determined by measuring the rate of expansion of the universe and extrapolating back in time to the point of the Big Bang. Some calculate it to be as old as 15.3 billion years.

We now turn to some considerations about both a younger and an older origin.

Creation theory – there *is* some validity in science

Regarding creation theory, as we stated earlier, there is some scientific basis to consider a direct comparison between a day and a thousand years. It all depends on one's perspective: that of God, or that of man. By taking these different viewpoints, it may provide a different perspective on what a 'day' might mean in primordial biblical terms at the point of creation.

If we now turn to the formula for Einstein's theory of Special Relativity, we learn that there is a relationship between speed and time. Einstein proposed that time slows down as speed increases, to the point where it reduces to nothing once one is travelling at the speed of light[68].

The theory of Special Relativity was tested by Joseph Hafele and Richard Keating in 1971. They used two similar atomic clocks, one based on earth and one based on an airliner that travelled twice around the earth. The airliner flew eastward, then westward, then landed. The times, which were consistent between the two clocks before the airliner took off, were different following the flights, and upheld the prediction of Special Relativity. The time on the atomic clock based on the airliner lagged behind that of the stationary clock.

Now, God is light (see chapter entitled "God is Light"), and the speed of light[69] is 186, 000 miles (or almost 300 million metres) per second. At that speed, time slows to nothing. (Go past it, and the theory is that time begins to reverse!)

As God is light, it would be logical to conclude that He could clothe Himself with attributes that uphold the laws governing light – correct? Let's look at Einstein's theory to assist us once again.

The formula for Einstein's theory of Special Relativity provides that:

"time at rest is equal to time at motion divided by the square root of 1 minus 'v squared divided by c squared', where v is velocity and c is the speed of light."

We can see that if we take the time at rest as 1,000 years (and use the convention of 365 days as a year for these purposes), and

1 day as the time at motion, it takes the speed of light to 'convert' 1,000 years into a day...

Putting this into plainer English, if we assume that as God is light, He can experience a different timeframe, related to the speed of light. According to Einstein's theory of Special Relativity and creation theory, seen from Earth, a day of the Lord's hard work would look like 1,000 years of waiting around to us, on earth.

As we saw above, the bible says that 1,000 years is like a day to the Lord and the bible appears, according to science, to show consistency, as God says He is light. God's experience of time is *different to ours and the bible suggests that this is the case.*

God is light but also omnipresent which can support an *older* creation

Until now, nothing has outpaced light, so the prospect of omnipresence – a person who exists in or can go to places that not even the oldest light has reached yet, was pure faith or fantasy, depending upon your perspective.

However, the bible says that God is not only light, but also that He is omnipresent. He is not limited by the speed of light to go to the farthest reaches of the universe. He is already ahead of it, being in all places at once. This means he can look back to where the earliest light has reached and see the end from the beginning, or even determine what events (caught in space time) are yet to happen, because He is 'already there'. This perhaps explains how God is able to provide accurate biblical prophecy (see the chapter on Prophecy fulfilled), because He alone has the ability to see the end from the beginning.

In science, we now have a couple of glimpses as to how this might happen.

The latest tests in CERN now demonstrate that neutrino particles can indeed outpace light. As CERN has shown us that the speed of light can now be exceeded[70], this does not make the bible untrue or say anything less about God being light (with an implicit implication that He is somehow 'restricted' to characteristics associated with the speed of light, as we shall see shortly). God is not only light but also omnipresent. We now see that physical laws now uphold the truth that, as there is something faster than light, it is indeed possible for God's omnipresence to be able to be more readily acceptable to us all, since we hitherto believed incorrectly that the speed of light was a fundamental unchanging universal constant.

Yet there is a more elegant scientific solution emerging. This may suggest another way in which God, who is light, can avoid the need to take into consideration the limits of the speed of light in order to be in all places at once, and to know everything at once. It has to do with 'quantum entanglement', which we considered earlier. Reported in the New York Times in 1997[71], the news story told of a Swiss experiment where two photons of light nearly seven miles apart both reacted immediately to stimulus applied to only one of them. This was many orders of magnitude faster than a signal transmitted by light could cause the other photon to react. In fact, no signal between the two was sent. It is as if the other photon 'knew' what had happened to the first photon and reacted similarly. The scientist was quoted as saying: ""In principle, it should make no difference whether the correlation between twin particles occurs when they are separated by a few meters or by the entire universe".

This surely has profound implications for our understanding of God. If photons (light particles) know what each is doing wherever they are in the universe, it follows that our God of light can control all of the universe at the same time. Yet as time has a relationship to speed, including the speed of light, it follows God will know the limits of where light has reached emanating from any particular point of light in His universe, so He can see the end from the beginning. For God, being light has advantages: it makes Him indeed omnipresent and omniscient!

So then, Einstein's theory is perhaps not the final word on speed, time and God's omniscience. But Einstein's theory can assist us in showing how time, experienced by God, could be different to time experienced by us.

This omnipresence available to God, and His ability to experience a different timeframe from us, could also potentially imply that the periods of time we experience here on earth are far, far longer than the Lord's experience of one of His God 'days' – much more than 1,000 years possibly. The biblical account of 'six days' might be in fact six incredibly long periods of time, due to the probable maths associated with God's omnipresence. This assists some sort of reconciliation between the biblical account of creation and those long-time periods put forward by some scientists for the age of the universe and the earth, but it does not imply that the evolutionary process is supported by the bible.

The evolutionary *process* is clearly off the table.

The changing nature of time

There is another point of interest to make in this section, and that concerns the subdivision of light from darkness by the Lord, at creation. Notice that He subdivided not once, but twice:

> Day 1: "In the beginning God created the heavens and the earth....and God said, "Let there be light"...and God divided the light from the darkness." (Genesis 1:1 – 1:4)

> Day 4: God made two great lights – the greater light to govern the day (sun) and the lesser light to govern the night (moon)...and to separate light from darkness."

123

(Genesis 1:16 -1:18)

Is it possible, therefore, that the nature of time changed between day 1, and the second time He divided light from darkness by means to the sun and moon, on day 4? It is not a completely preposterous suggestion!

Whilst the use of the word 'day' does not change throughout these opening words of Genesis, making this idea a little unlikely, the manner by which light is divided from darkness *changed*. We are told in the context of the second division, that the sun and moon and stars have been created specifically as a means to measure time[72]. This was not so during the first division.

One is bound to ask why not? Did the nature of a day change or were we simply given a way to measure it?

Our 24-hour time periods have been measured by reference to the rotation of the earth around the sun, as God intended. Days became 24-hour time periods from day 4, but this *may* not mean that days were 24-hour time periods for the first 3 days of creation. They might have been different in some respect. If so, this might assist us greatly to resolve these theological and scientific tensions. After all, we have shown scientifically that the biblical saying that for a God of light, a thousand earth years is indeed a day for God, and yet if God is not restricted by the speed of light (and He is not as He is omnipresent), then it follows that many millions of years are like a day to Him as well. Therefore, two statements about God on Day 1 and Day 4 show how time can be experienced by Him differently in the context of the same 'day' in human terms.

In fact, it may be more correct to say that the Lord's day has not changed[73], but earth's experience of a day has. This would mean that the use of a day may remain static when seen from God's perspective, but our experience of the length of that divine day changes. Revelation 21 explains that where God resides, there is *only day and no night*, so there is some biblical perspective to this statement.

The effect of a massless God

There is one other effect that comes from Einstein's theories. As mass accelerates towards the speed of light, it requires vast and eventually infinite energy to get it to accelerate to a point where it attains the speed of light, and therefore the speed of light can never be attained by an object that has mass.

However, we have shown that light can exist as either particles (photons) which have mass, or in waves, which have no mass (of themselves). We have seen how the theory of quantum entanglement suggests that light may 'choose' in which state it wishes to operate. Man was created as mass-spirit, and God is spirit but can choose to adopt mass, as we see from the accounts of the risen Jesus eating with fellow disciples. We also see Jesus in His risen spirit form (massless) during the transfiguration, so it is clear that He can exist in both ways. These differences are important in the context of physics. Where God is spirit (which we assume has no mass), it follows that God may travel at the speed of light or indeed beyond, since He is not restricted by physical laws governing mass[74]. Therefore, it is quite appropriate to suggest that 1,000 years or longer is a day unto the Lord, since God is not restricted by physical laws governing mass and the speed of light. Our human mass-spirit existence suggests we could not do this however.

Pillars of an old universe and earth and of evolution challenged

It seems that the light exceeding-speed of the simple neutrino may lend support to a much older universe after all, even in biblical terms. But whether or not the humble neutrino may show support for an older universe, it does *not necessarily mean or follow that the universe is in fact that old.*

Now evolution requires an old earth. However, creationism or intelligent design does not *require* a young earth, but biblical chronology and the heavy implication given by the statement from Jesus that mankind was created at the start of creation[75], suggests that the earth is still younger than the many billions of years suggested by the expansion theory for the universe drawn from science.

We must therefore undertake a consideration of the pillars of evolution, and of the assumption that the earth and universe around it is old, against some of the other conflicting evidence.

Atheists philosophically require an older universe

If the foundations of atheistic evolution are shaken considerably, then atheists have nothing, and that is what scares them, as this is what the Lord says about His creation:

> "For since the creation of the world God's invisible qualities – His eternal power and divine nature – have been clearly seen, being understood **from what has been made, so that men are without excuse.**[76]"

The Lord infers that they live in rebellion, because His work is quite clear – and it is. But without their own faith in atheism, they only have the Bible, which is the very thing they resist. For atheists, so says John C Lennox, atheistic evolution is a philosophical necessity[77].

I turn to John Lennox, who has provided so much of the important data for this part of the chapter. Lennox is Professor of Mathematics at the University of Oxford and Fellow in Mathematics and the Philosophy of Science at the Green Templeton College. He has challenged the atheists Richard

Dawkins and the late Christopher Hitchens and brings mathematics into the scientific debate to assist in demolishing any realistic prospect of the Evolutionary argument succeeding.

Melanie Phillips of The Spectator recognises his work as:

"An excoriating demolition of Dawkins' overreach from Biology into religion".

There follow a number of excerpts from his book: "God's Undertaker. Has Science buried God?"

<u>Fossil record: there are no missing links to demonstrate evolution</u>

Darwin had it that species developed by natural selection. The fossil record has been trumpeted for generations as one of the most powerful evidences for evolution. Family trees have been drafted, showing the evolution of animals from simple to more complex species, until eventually we get to the most sophisticated evolution of all, human beings.

But the Lord does not state that about His creation. Genesis says that He made each animal independently.

On closer inspection, it appears that this fossil record is not joined up at all. Missing links are, err....missing!

This demonstrably remains the case after centuries of finding and analysing fossils. Indeed, each time the Palaeontologists and bone rattlers dig up another so called: "missing link", it turns out to be a different species and not an incremental change from an existing species!

Mark Ridley, a zoologist concludes that in 1858 Darwin could not give a single example of a missing link or evidence of

127

evolutionary change. No wonder Herschel felt confident of his comment that until animal evolution can be observed, he supposed (rightly) that it did not exist in the present. No single example exists today either.

John C Lennox points us to the comments to Palaeontologist David Raup of the Field Museum of Natural History, which houses one of the world's largest collections of fossils, who says that after collecting about a quarter of a million fossils, 'we have fewer examples of evolutionary transition that we had in Darwin's time."[78] Niles Eldridge of the American Museum of Natural History admits that: "We Palaeontologists have said that the history of life supports [gradual adaptive change], knowing all the while that it does not."[79]

When a species appears in the fossil record, it does not change much[80]. It appears to be static, then disappears from the record and other species emerge. Some scientists have suggested that this is the way evolution works – by leaping between species (as the gradual change model is clearly flawed!) However, there is absolutely no evidence whatsoever for a leap between species either. Not a shred; and whilst scientists can postulate and position themselves, unless evidence exists, it cannot be put forward as science, but merely theory. The trouble is that evolution is being taught as science.

It is said also that fossils take millions of years to fossilise. But many dinosaur fossils contain well preserved soft tissues. One example is a dinosaur T Rex that has been given a date of 68 million years old. Dr Mary Schweitzer observed within the bone some blood vessels, containing red blood cells and protein fragments. Scientists have trumped up an idea that this is some unrecognised form of fossilisation previously unseen that preserves blood cells and proteins over tens of millions of years, when in fact a far more obvious and elegant answer is likely: the beast is not actually that old. Egyptian mummies show that preservation of blood cells is possible at 3,000-4,000 years old[81].

The preservation of soft tissues is also seen in a squid, unearthed at Trowbridge, in Wiltshire, England in August 2009. The find gave rise to an article by Frank Sherwin, MA who, writing for the Institute for Creation Research, says that: "...physical evidence of very young-looking biological materials from supposedly ancient fossils continues to accrue from around the world, and from various depths under the earth."[82] The article cites a find of a '150 million-year old squid' with an ink sac intact, found within rock. "It is difficult to imagine how you can have something as soft and sloppy as an ink sac...inside a rock that is 150 million years old, quote Sherwin from a Dr Phil Wilby of the British Geological Society. Creationists see this as evidence of more recent burial and preservation.

Further, so called 'living fossils' can be seen, whereby animals that are with us presently, such as crocodiles, horseshoe crabs, vampire squid, clams, and dragonflies amongst others, all exist, without change, over so called 'millions of years', despite different or changing environments and supposed nature-changing mutations. Microbes and DNA can be extracted successfully from supposedly ancient remains. The article concludes: It would seem that many scientists are putting the cart before the horse – embracing long ages before they consider the physical evidence that shows otherwise.

Stability of carbon 14 and of collagen

In fact, collagen and carbon 14 have been measured in reasonable quantities in fossil remains. Yet both decay much sooner than the millions of years attributable to the age of tested fossils, leading to the inevitable conclusion that either collagen and carbon 14 do in fact survive for millions of years, or fossils are simply a lot younger, and definitely no older than 1,000,000 years at the extreme.

Polystrate fossils – prejudices ageing through sedimentary layer-counting

The ageing process is sometimes supported by sedimentary evidence, whereby age is calculated by determining how many layers of sediment there are covering a particular object such as a fossil. Sadly, polystrate fossils blow much of this thinking apart. These include tree fossils that cross many sedimentary layers, and if sediment really did settle slowly, the top of the tree would have rotted very quickly, leaving only a stump visible, but often the whole tree is preserved intact, yet traversing many layers[83]. This rather puts into dispute Sir Charles Lyell's contention that uniform processes took place over millions of years to cover these fossils. The obvious alternative answer appears to involve catastrophe – namely the biblical flood.

It appears that billions upon billions of fossils were all laid down in the same layers of rock worldwide and few fossils have been found forming since then.

Here are some additional observations about fossils, by Dr Kent Hovind:

First:	The earth has trillions of fossils
Second:	Most animals today have been found in fossils
Third:	Fossils are not seen forming today in significant numbers
Fourth:	Fossils often have well preserved internal organs indicating rapid burial, to prevent rot
Fifth:	Many fossils show stress and instantaneous burial, with some showing a meal still within their mouths
Sixth:	Fossils can be found traversing different layers of rock that have been given different ages by millions of years

130

Seventh: Rapid fossilisation, (contrary to scientific belief, as opposed to proof – my emphasis) can occur quickly. An example is given of a fossilised pickle found in a jar made between 1930 and 1960.

Therefore, given all of the above, the conclusion of the so-called fossil record has to be that there is no record as such, but that most fossils were laid down in catastrophic conditions at a relatively recent point in time, which is not millions of years old. The evidence simply does not support ancient origins.

It is just as likely that these fossils were laid down during the flood of Noah, some 6 thousand years ago, which provided catastrophe, perfect sedimentary conditions and instantaneous death.

Evolution cannot explain the requirement for instant working mechanisms – the humming bird

Creationists point to the humming bird, by way of example.

It has a wing that beats at least 50 times a second. It requires a specialist light weight body; it has to be able to adjust rapidly in mid-air by a plant, send out a proboscis long tongue via a long, thin beak able to probe into the depths of a plant, and yet it also has to have the capability of migrating thousands of miles. It also has a refractive body of colour, not a pigmented colour. This is incredible and designed.

If this evolved, then we need to find the immediately preceding species from which it evolved. Did this mythical intermediate monster climb up the plant, loll its rather club-fisted tongue into some plant and work out that it needed to mate with something subtler for the job – perhaps an ant eater? Or did it think itself into a better form, perhaps fasting for a few generations as it couldn't eat properly? The suggestions are of course absurd, because there is no immediately preceding species. As this cannot be explained by evolution, evolutionists have come up with a different theory – equally absurd – that species take a jump from one to another! Therefore, the example I have given of my mythical monster that wishes it were a humming bird is resolved at last! One day his species woke up and...as if by magic it was indeed a humming bird. We can all now rest easy. They have resolved the problem!

Both solutions put forward by evolutionists require extreme, but blind faith. We are required to believe that either animals came from other types of animals gradually, or they leaped forward into totally new species. If you wish to believe the evolutionists, you will have to do so on uninformed faith, as they will not be able to give you any proof of this ever having taken place. Yet the Lord provides distinct proof of His individualised creations in the fossil record, and there is no proof of graduation, or of leaping between species. They are all simply individual.

Evolution cannot explain the requirement for instant working mechanisms - the cell

Darwin wrote to Herschel:

> "One cannot look at this Universe with all living productions & man without believing that all has been intelligently designed; yet when I look to each individual organism I can see no evidence of this..."[84]

I would contend that Darwin did not have the means to look deeper into the cell, but if he had, I think it would have altered his statement considerably.

The bacterial cell, in its simplest irreducible form, is still mind-blowingly complex. Its chemical structure is the same as that of all other living beings, employing the same genetic code and translation as for human cells. There is nothing 'primitive' about cells. There are no earlier stages of evolution. A cell is a cell and always has been. It is composed of incredibly complex and intricate parts such as 'nano' motors, like the flagellum, that causes the bacterium to swim. This motor has all the components of a motor, being a rotor, stator, bushings and a drive shaft. Whilst incredibly complex, they cannot be reduced to something simpler and so cannot have evolved from something more primitive, because without all very complex parts having been ever present, they would never have worked in the first place. Plenty of other examples of complex, yet irreducible systems also exist, which all provide very strong evidence that they could not have evolved. In fact, the well-known Atheist philosopher, Anthony Flew changed his view and published a book entitled "There is a God", precisely because the cell was so irreducibly complex, it could not have been caused by evolutionary processes, but only by an intelligent designer – God. If only other atheists would see such sense as well!

In his day, Darwin did not have the means to consider the cell more intimately. Had he had such means, he would not have been able to account in evolutionary terms for the cell, because it did not evolve. It had to have been created intricately by a very, very clever designer, as there is simply no other possible, rational explanation. It could not leap into existence. A cell cannot work unless it is completely a cell from inception.

John Lennox sets this account out in fine detail in his book "God's Undertaker". He begins to show the mathematical improbability of Dawkins' statement in his book "the Selfish Gene". Dawkins states:

> "At some point, a *particularly remarkable molecule was formed by accident*. We will call it a replicator...to create copies of itself."

A remarkable accident indeed: a molecule made up of many proteins that could bring about life by replicating itself, just like that!

Lennox considers a simple protein involving construction from 'only' 10 amino acids. The correct natural form for this protein would be the 'L chiral' form and the probability of getting 100 amino acids in the right order is 1 chance in 10^{30}. That's one chance in 10 with thirty noughts after it. That is tending towards completely impossible, which is an arbitrary definition (but is sometimes defined as 1 chance in $10^{50})^{85}$.

So, with 'statistical impossibility' in mind, this statistic is amplified further when we consider how amino acids are put together to form proteins used to build cells. It is not just as simple as inserting energy into a mixture of amino acids and watching the chain grow. The amino acids must be organised. The chance of all amino acids being organised in the correct order is about 1 chance in 10^{130}, which is impossibly small and beyond the arbitrary definition of 'impossible' by many, many times – 80 more noughts, in fact. That is for a single protein. Life requires, says Lennox, hundreds of thousands of proteins which statistically amounts to about **1 chance in $10^{40,000}$**. Lennox shows that the statement made by Dawkins that somehow remarkable things like this happened by accident is simply impossible.

Completely and utterly impossible.

Dr Henry Morris of the Creation Institute agrees and, having mapped out his calculations, concludes:

> "Lest anyone think that a 200-part system is unreasonably complex, it should be noted that even a one-celled plant or animal may have millions of molecular "parts." ...the chance that any kind of a 200-

component integrated functioning organism could be developed by mutation and natural selection just once, anywhere in the world, in all the assumed expanse of geologic time, is **less than one chance out of a billion trillion**. What possible conclusion, therefore, can we derive from such considerations as this except that evolution by mutation and natural selection is mathematically and logically indefensible!"[86]

These sorts of impossibilities show that such arguments suggesting that cells and life just sprang accidentally into existence are risible and lead to one conclusion only: that cells, and hence life, is a matter of intricate and careful design. There is no other logical or reasonable explanation.

Epigenetics revisited

Darwin would have us believe that changes in species takes place over millions of years, yet the new science of Epigenetics has already shown quite quickly that genetic change (but only for the worse, incidentally), happens in just a couple of generations.

I have found nothing to show that we can somehow improve our genetic code to become something more than we are – like a type of Eugenic master race that are more than simply human beings, by morphing into a different species. I have found evidence to suggest that within our species, our genetic code can become more tolerant – an example being 'lactase persistence' – the persistence into adulthood of an enzyme that allows humans to digest milk (from cows), but it is a far cry to suggest that this adaptive micro-evolution to exogenous factors can be extended into macro evolution between species. Many humans do not remain lactose (milk) tolerant into adulthood.

I have found evidence to show how ill effects on our bodies can be slowed or reversed, pointing to an ability to attain our *original* state again (see last chapter). Therefore, and with reference to that last chapter, the Lord's statement that man's iniquity will be visited on the third and fourth generation, yet blessings can flow for a thousand generations is consistent, in so far as it suggests that we maintain our balance in the perfect *original design* as humans, by obedience to God's will, but our rebellion (sin) causes this *original* state to become damaged, for a while at least.

The universe points to design and not random processes

The universe exhibits impossible statistics for random formation. There are forces such as the nuclear strong force and electromagnetic force that exist within matter; and if the ratio of the nuclear strong force to the electromagnetic force had been different by one part in 10^{16}, then no stars could have been formed. Similarly, the ratio of the electromagnetic force constant to the gravitational force constant must be fine-tuned as well. Increase by 1 part in 10^{40} and small stars will exist only; but decrease by the same amount and only large stars exist. We need both for a functioning universe: large ones as furnaces and small ones to sustain a planet with life. Again, the tuning is of such a fine degree that only a skilled designer could have possibly brought it all about.

Within the first micro second of the universe's existence, had the ratio of expansion to contraction forces been altered by 1 chance in 10^{55}, expansion would have been too rapid and no galaxies would have formed or too slow and rapid collapse would have followed.

There are even higher statistical impossibilities that even these, and when considered in isolation, each is remarkable.

The end of the universe may be equally well designed

On 7 December 2014, the Telegraph correspondent Michael

Hanlon considered how the earth might end. Item 6 on the agenda was headed: "God reaches for the Off Switch". It stated that the numbers governing the fundamental forces and masses of nature – seem fine-tuned to allow life of some form to exist.
The article quoted Sir Fred Hoyle (an atheist), who believed that the universe appeared to be 'a put-up job'.

Intriguingly, however, was the next paragraph:

> "More recently, the Oxford University philosopher Nick Bostrom has speculated that our Universe may be one of countless "simulations" running in some alien computer, much like a computer game. If so, we have to hope that the beings behind our fake universe are benign – and do not reach for the off-button should we start misbehaving.

> ...According to Bostrom's calculations, if certain assumptions are made then there is a greater than 50 per cent chance that our universe is not real. And the increasingly puzzling absence of any evidence of alien life may be indirect evidence that the Universe is not what it seems.

Taken together, these observations are astounding, for the Bible says:

> "Our light and momentary troubles are achieving for us an eternal glory that far outweighs them all. So, we fix our eyes not on what is seen, but on what is unseen. For what is seen is temporary, but what is unseen is eternal" (2 Corinthians 4:17, 18)

So, the spiritual dimension is not ephemeral and is more real than the material dimension. The material dimension – the known universe – according to Bostrom apparently disappears at the flick of a switch, when he cites that God hits the 'off button'. It is interesting that Revelation explains that:

"The heavens receded like a scroll being rolled up, and every mountain and island was removed from its place." (Revelation 6:14)

This may not be a perfect translation, however, as J. Richard Middleton suggests in his book "A New Heaven and a New Earth"[87]. He suggests that actually the imagery may be more like the sky, (or in my view, heavenly dimensions) being split apart to allow God's judgement to be carried out on corrupt heavenly powers. This appears a more honest reflection of the true heavenly realm breaking into this artificial realm that is sustained by God's light.

Whatever the truth of a heavenly annihilation, it seems that science does make room for an unseen realm to be more real than this material realm. Whether atheist scientists they are prepared to relinquish their pride and recognise that God said: "I told you so" is a personal choice, but the evidence that concords with the biblical account of things is now so overwhelming that it really narrows the gap across the chasm of the leap of faith to a simple hop.

God is in charge of any possible demise or remodelling in any event. Professor Brian Cox has stated on television that the universe will turn back into energy in billions of years' time. However, according to Bostrom, God may well hit the 'off button' to eradicate or, as I prefer, redeem and remodel it, which may easily take place before it turns back into energy, just as He switched it on in the first place.

Carbon 14 dating is unreliable and points to a younger earth

I turn to an excellent chapter in a book written by Mike Riddle[88], which explains some of the problems associated with Carbon 14 dating that can sway the readings to a significant extent and in all cases strongly point to a younger earth. Carbon 14 dating is best used to date once living (organic) things, whereas inorganic things like rocks produce unreliable results since they were not living, though may contain some once living matter (such as fossils in sedimentary rock for example).

Carbon 14 dating relies on the fact that Carbon 14 decays at a constant rate whereas another isotope, Carbon 12 does not. Consequently, the measurement of the ratio of Carbon 12 to 14 is taken and compared against what is expected when an organism was living to determine the age of an organism, given that Carbon 14 has a half-life of 5730 years.

Cosmic rays constantly renew Carbon 14 in our atmosphere by bombarding atoms that split and Carbon 14 results from this process. This Carbon 14 combines with Oxygen to form CO2, and that is absorbed by plants and by eating plants, animals. The ratio of Carbon 12 to 14 is constant in all living things.

When an animal or other organism dies, it no longer takes in Carbon 14, as it no longer absorbs CO2 (plants); or eats them (animals), so Carbon 14 is no longer being topped up.

To date that creature an assumption is made about the ratio of Carbon 12 to 14 and that ratio is assumed to be constant at 1 trillion (C12) to 1 (C14). The more C12 to C14, the longer the organism has been dead.

Mike Riddle explains that unfortunately there are many reasons why this ratio is very unreliable.

> First: Even if the ratio was indeed constant, the methods used can only provide accurate readings up to 80,000 years and beyond that instruments do not exist that can produce reliable results. Thus, it is not possible to obtain

a date of millions of years from Carbon 14 dating.

Second: If the ratio has not been constant, even this period of 80,000 years may be in doubt. Doubts are cast in the following ways: The rate of C14 production from cosmic rays has altered significantly over time. This makes knowing the amount of C14 in an organism difficult of impossible to know accurately over time and cause significant dating problems. The ratio of C12 to C14 has not yet reached 'equilibrium' and it takes 30,000 years to reach 'equilibrium' meaning that the earth cannot be that old. This factor was ignored when Carbon 14 dating was accepted widely.

Third: The magnetic field of the earth used to be far stronger. This means that fewer cosmic rays can reach the earth's atmosphere, so that there was less Carbon 14 produced historically. "The field has always freely decayed.... The field has always been losing energy despite its variations, so it cannot be more than 10,000 years old."[89] Earth's magnetic field is fading. Today it is about 10 percent weaker than it was when German mathematician Carl Friedrich Gauss started keeping tabs on it in 1845, scientists say."[90]

Mike Riddle concludes that "If the production rate of 14C in the atmosphere was less in the past, dates given using the carbon-14 method would incorrectly assume that more 14C had decayed out of a specimen than what has actually occurred. This would result in giving older dates than the true age.

Fourth: Noah's flood killed all known organisms, other than a few fortunate animals and humans on Noah's ark. The dead bodies produced oil and gas and indicates a vast amount of living organisms and vegetation the size of which we do not have in existence today. This would have further diluted the ratio of Carbon 12 to Carbon 14, with estimates at around 500 times weaker than today. Therefore, any age estimates using 14C prior to the Flood will give much older dates than the true age. Pre-Flood material would be dated at perhaps ten times the true age.

Fifth: RATE group findings. In 1997, a group of scientists decided to review Carbon 14 dating techniques, as they were alive to some serious provable anomalies. Ten coal samples were taken that conventionally would have been dated to hundreds of millions of years old based on standard evolution techniques, contained significant measurable amounts of Carbon 14 in all cases – yet C14 has a half-life of 5730 years and should not have been detectable for specimens that old and diminishes for ages of around 100,000 years old. The amount of carbon showed that these specimens could be aged at around 50,000 years old, but using a flood type of ratio, would be nearer around 5,000 years old, which is biblically accurate.

The conclusion is that Carbon 14 dating techniques can be seriously inaccurate given the assumptions which may well be wrong, throwing calculations of ages out and providing an impression that specimens are far older when they could in fact be far younger.

There are accounts of evidence that do not sit well with older earth theory which emerge from time to time, and seem to call evolutionary theory into question[91]. Whether these (contained in endnotes) are easily dispelled will always be a subject which will arouse much passion, but there is a certain logic to them, such as the low degree of saltiness of the oceans (4%), which become increasingly salty each year and therefore give rise to questions as to how they are not more salty given the supposed 'ancient' age of the earth; to the degree of helium content of rocks, which presupposes a much younger timeframe than billions of years; and the dispersal rates of stars within galaxies that suggest that they should have moved out of their galaxies a long time ago had the universe been that old.

Together, the suggestion is that the Earth and the universe are much younger than the account of 13.8 Billion years old; and the evidence even supports a creation account of a few thousand years in many cases.

The presumed age of the universe and earth, which is what is taught as a theory at school (but without giving room for an alternative) is based on a range of assumptions about an unobserved past that cannot be proved. This leads to the vast lengths of time required to support the evidentially flawed theory of evolution. Whilst having shown that the humble neutrino may support the possibility of an older creation, when set against multifarious challenges that support a younger creation, it seems that we must view an old creation with just as much scepticism.

The risk: that the biblical account of creation may be in fact true

God is the only person who claims to have been a witness to creation and its progress and all of time since, because He was there at the time, doing it. No one else has been there throughout, to observe it. (Even evolutionists have to confess they weren't round then at the start, either!).

On page 18 of Lennox' book, "God's Undertaker", a survey undertaken in 1916 by one Professor Leuba on 1,000 American scientists, is quoted as showing that in a response rate of 70%, 41.8% believed in a God who answered prayer and in a personal immortality; and 41.5% were agnostic. In 1996, the response

142

rate was slightly smaller at 60%, of whom 39.6% showed a belief in a divine being, and 45.5% were agnostic, which is remarkably consistent over almost 100 years.

Therefore, a very healthy proportion of randomly chosen US scientists DO BELIEVE IN A DIVINE BEING.

They are in good company. Aside from my own relatives, the following notable scientists were men who believed in God, who are quoted in the endnote[92]. They do not all necessarily believe in Intelligent Design, but they are believers nevertheless.

This is a pretty prodigious list of some of the most famous names in science. It lends credibility to suggest that if such great minds are comfortable with the existence of God, we can be too. Some of the most prestigious names also rejected evolution and accordingly this gives confidence to those who, having read the evidence against evolution, wish to reject it as well.

Conclusions

The evidence suggests that:

> First: There is some validity to the statements that 1,000 years is like a day to God, because God is light and there is a direct relationship between the speed of light and time as shown through Einstein's theory of Special Relativity;

> Second: As God is omnipresent, this implies that He exists in places beyond which light has ever reached, so that in applying a speed greater that the speed of light to Einstein's theory of Special Relativity, a day to God may seem like many thousands (and possibly millions or of even billions) of years to us. It makes no logical sense to limit the statement under 1 since God is eternal in

143

nature;

Third: High dispersal speeds of dwarf galaxies and the few supernovas that exist point to a universe of only a few thousand, not billions of years, however;

Fourth: The fossil record, flood evidence and physical characteristics of the earth (magnetic field decay, saltiness of the sea, soft flesh found in some dinosaur discoveries and other matters) seem to point to a younger not older earth;

Fifth: Carbon dating and geological 'layer dating' are unreliable, but the extent to which carbon 14 and collagen has been found in fossils suggest that they are much younger than the dates often attributed to them; and

Sixth: Biblical statements, including those attributed directly to God and Jesus appear to support a young earth and creation.

Therefore, whilst item 2 above does provide a mechanism to support the existence of an older universe and earth, as discussed in this chapter, it does not follow that creation is in fact that old. Plenty of physical evidence exists, including evidence often erroneously cited in support of evolution (such as the fossil record) that shows that a younger creation than 13.8 billion years appears more reliable.

Science and creation – a more fruitful partnership

There are some obvious tensions in the Bible with what evolutionary scientists think they know. In Genesis, God says he created living things in this order (interjecting the sun):

Day 1 – **light and darkness;**
Day 2 – division of sky/heavens from waters of the earth;
Day 3 – dry land, seas, grass, herb yielding seed, fruit trees;
Day 4 – **moon and sun;**
Day 5 – water based creatures, birds, whales; and
Day 6 - land based animals including cattle, creeping things and beasts of the earth and then man followed by woman – from Adam's rib.

Now, evolution suggests that the sun was in existence before green plants; land animals before whales; and creeping things before birds.

Thus, in terms of time and chronology the two appear totally irreconcilable. But if creation was undertaken in six 24 hour days, then it is not necessary for the sun to appear before plants were created, because actually plants can easily survive a night or two in darkness. And even if these periods were far longer than 24-hour earth days as we contended earlier, as God created light from day one, then though the sun was not created until day four, plants could have survived under the previous light system (whatever that was).

But I leave it to you therefore to conclude what you believe, having read this chapter!

The Bible tells us clearly that Jesus Himself was intimately involved in the act of creation:

> "In the beginning was the Word, and the Word was with God, and the Word was God. He was with God in the beginning. Through Him all things were made; without Him nothing was made that has been made." (John 1:1-2)

> "The Word became flesh and made His dwelling among us" (John 1:14)

It was Jesus who was the Word made flesh and dwelt with us, just over two thousand years ago, so John states clearly that Jesus Himself carried out all of the creation when He was with God, and whilst being God (which He is as the Second person of the Trinity).

Perhaps we may make even faster progress if we begin to study God's word, as He so obviously has so much to show us – us, who wish to be obedient, for He only intended us to use our reason in conjunction with His oversight and direction:

"Let us reason together" (Isaiah 1:18)

When we tried to use our reason in isolation originally, we took our eyes off Him and it got us into trouble (Eden, snake, carnal knowledge, fall). When we seek revelation from the Lord and apply our reason with Him, amazing things follow for as John Herschel said:

"All human discoveries seem to be made only for the sole purpose of confirming more and more strongly the truths that come from on high and are contained in the sacred writings."

And this has to be exactly right, for as that scientific book of Job also says:

"But now ask the beasts, and they will teach you; and the birds of the air, and they will tell you; or speak to the earth, and it will teach you; and the fish of the sea will explain to you. Who among these does not know that the hand of the Lord has done this..." (Job, 12:7-9)

Job holds that the sacred writings are <u>evidenced by His creation</u> – and Herschel was right in that it is even biblical for us to test

146

His creation and see more and more clearly His skilful hand at work within it. Jesus designed it and now maintains it by His light (see chapter on "God is Light").

Perhaps we might make more progress if we stop resisting God, and turn to Him and His Bible to seek more insights, as it seems increasingly obvious that so much science confirms "more strongly the truths that come from on high and are contained in the sacred writings". It has been said that: "Science is catching up with the Bible". John Lennox provided a precious quote for the Christian Alpha Course series of videos that 'we are thinking God's thoughts after Him'. Nothing could be truer.

I conclude with an appeal to you and to scientists everywhere to work with the Bible, and to plumb its deepest truths. Isaac Newton did it; John Herschel suggested science upheld it, numerous other notable scientists believe the biblical account as well, and that must be reason enough for all of us to do likewise.

9. Physical evidence

I turn to look at architecture and archaeology – the stuff of buildings. Architecture can evidence that a particular historical statement might in fact be true if it can be found that those places were in existence at the required time. This might be understood from engravings, pictures, and words inscribed on buildings, and from an understanding of the building's function relative to others. Archaeology can additionally unearth circumstantial evidence of a particular biblical story, hitherto uncorroborated.

Either has its limits, though. They can never point to the existence of God, however, and nor can they provide direct evidence of the intervention of God, even if an ancient description can be found to support an event stated by the bible to be under God's command such as, for example, the Flood or Mosaic plagues. But one of their most useful features, is silencing scoffers who, in their naïveté assume that because something has not been found, the Bible is unreliable in its account of the matter.

It is after all, only a fool who would suggest that all that there is to be found has been found by now.

Ever since the first city was built, by Cain which was called Enoch (Genesis 4:17), after his first son, there has been evidence left behind for us to find and review. The Bible speaks of many cities, temples, boats, dwellings, watercourses, monuments, walls and other constructions that have variously been built, sieged, burned, or even left standing. It also speaks of kings and kingdoms outside of Israel's own, and many of these kept records in scrolls, parchments, tablets and even inscribed on their architecture.

Taken together, biblical and extra-biblical writings can and do point to the truth of biblical accounts themselves as they relate to real history, so they must be considered to address an age-old hurdle:

"Well, you can't believe in the Bible, because it's all myth."

This is an uninformed statement, when an ounce of study has been applied, as archaeologists will tell you – believers or otherwise. Many archaeologists have first taken a Bible to determine that such and such a place or person existed, and have thereafter taken their trusty spade, to find out that in fact the Bible provides a very good historical record of places, people (such as kings and patriarchs), events and even dates. Without it, the world would be much poorer if only from an historical perspective. It cannot be all myth. In fact, the rate at which archaeological discovery is now producing new finds of these ancient biblical accounts is attesting ever more strongly to the Bible's accuracy.

Yet, to return to our scoffers, some quite vocal noises have been made over the years regarding the fallibility of the Bible, precisely because such evidence had not been discovered, at that particular time. These are dangerous statements to make if one is seeking to keep one's reputation intact, for it only takes one cast-iron discovery for a jester to be made out of a biblical nihilist.

Scoffers, the Age of the Enlightenment and the seismic discovery of Nineveh

Following the Age of the Enlightenment, and the man-centred power of the Industrial Revolution that followed it, many people scoffed at the biblical references to the city of Nineveh. There is a story concerning a British archaeologist called Austen Henry Layard who had to work against this tide of cynicism. In Arnold Brackman's book 'The Luck of Nineveh', the following account is given of the difficulty Layard faced, and of his excellent eventual triumph over the torpid voices of dissent:

"In 1817, when Austen Henry Layard was born, there was no tangible proof that Nineveh, the seat of the Assyrian Empire, which reputedly had endured longer than any empire before or since, ever existed. For that matter, there was no evidence that there ever was an Assyrian empire" (Foreword, p. vii).

"In the Old and New Testaments Nineveh is mentioned twenty times, and in the Old Testament there are 132 references to Assyria... An increasing number of sceptics, however, their religious faith diluted by the spectacular scientific breakthrough accompanying the first stirring of the Industrial Revolution, sneered at tales about Nineveh and treated it as a legend that belonged to an age of fables. For them, there had never been a Nineveh any more than there had ever been a Troy" (pp. 12–13).

Then one day, Layard eventually discovered Nineveh. You can see the valuable finds in museums all over the world. The evidence is clear and irrefutable. Layard overcame; and we remember and honour his discoveries. No one remembers his archaeological critics. Upon his discovery, they became instantly like sand blown away in a storm.

A similar criticism has been given about the Kingdom of Solomon, as there is a paucity of evidence at the moment. However, much evidence is now emerging of Old Testament finds, as we shall see below. Beware scoffers.

Healing pools

An excellent example is given of the healing pool at Bethesda. Until 19th century (a time of increased cynicism about the truth of the historicity of the Bible), scholars attempted to argue that John's gospel in which this pool of healing is mentioned (John 5:2), was written later than previously thought, because no one had found such a pool. It was therefore contended that it was written by someone without first-hand knowledge, and must be in any event only 'symbolic' in nature. (David Couchman, 'The Pool at Bethesda in Jerusalem', Focus Publishing, 2010, p1).

Then in the 19th century, a pool fitting the biblical description was found in Jerusalem. (James H Charlesworth, Jesus and Archaeology, Wm B Eerdmans Publishing, 2006, pages 560-566. Whether or not it was in fact the exact pool, the fact that such a pool existed made red faces of any critics, because such a pool described in John could have existed. It has in fact taken over 100 years to fully understand the nature of the find, and we can now be sure that this pool has been identified. Why? Because John attests to an unusual feature of this pool, that cynics consigned to invention: it had five porticoes.

The Biblical Archaeology Society has revealed on 6 January 2014:

"...when this site was excavated, it revealed a rectangular pool with two basins separated by a wall—thus a five-sided pool—and each side had a portico."

But there is a wonderful story about this and similar healing baths, that according to footnotes in the Revised Standard Version of the Bible, an angel stirs up the waters as they are stirred, before anyone enters, so that the first person who enters gets healed. (See "The Puzzling Pool of Bethesda where Jesus cured the Crippled man", Urban C. Von Wahlde, Biblical Archaeology Review, sept/Oct 2011).

151

This perhaps explains why the crippled man in John's account complains to Jesus that by the time he can get to the pool, "someone else steps down ahead of me." (John 5:7). Jesus heals him. Since the Bethesda pool was discovered, another pool at which Jesus performed healing has been discovered in June 2004, namely the Pool at Siloam (John 9:6-7). It was located near the City of David, a long way from where it had hitherto been believed to have been located[93].

Both pools appear to have been 'mikveh' or ritual bathing sites, leading us to believe that Jesus deliberately chose them to show His power of healing and cleansing over the Old Testament rituals that predated Him, much as He did at His first miracle when He turned water into wine at a wedding in Cana in Galilee.

These are two finds that help support the stories about Jesus we read in John's gospel. It seems that they could have taken place after all, in places that we now find do exist, and in so doing, they raise these biblical stories from fanciful myth, to something more substantive than that. For after all, had there never been any pool, we would be bound to concur that there was no substance at all to the story. Now, at least, there is at least the possibility that the story did occur, and at the time it was said to occur, in the first century AD, because we now know where it could have occurred.

With these two examples to hand, let us cast the net more widely and turn to a number, and these are by no means exhaustive, of the countless archaeological examples of the truth of the historical accounts set out in the Bible. One could write books on this alone, and space permits me to cite just a few.

The Flood

I spend some time on this as it is often contested. The biblical account of the Flood that came upon the earth is set out in Genesis 6 and 7. This flood occurred about 4350 years ago and Genesis is quite clear that it covered the whole of the earth and its purpose was to wipe out all living things (Genesis 6:7 and 6:17).

It is important therefore that we can determine that there is evidence that such a flood took place and that it covered the whole of the earth. It is also important to be able to show that this flood could have killed all life. For that we might turn to the fossil record.

Fossils are able to be created in recent times. They do not have to be, as claimed, millions of years old. Provided living things are covered quickly, and under some pressure, fossilisation can occur.

We have seen this in the chapter on Evolution. It is perfectly acceptable, therefore, for fossils to have been created from the Flood process. This process uses an extreme event to wipe out and drown all life, moving much sediment during the process, so that living things are buried in their own mass graves of mud and debris, much like the dramatic pictures show us from the tsunami coverage of Banda Aceh, in 2003. Fossils do not occur from dropping to a sea bed, or dying in the open. There has to be a catastrophic 'covering' event in the model of the flood, for fossilisation to occur.

Polystrate fossils

As we are not aware of many such examples happening in history, it seems that most fossils will have been laid down 4,350 years ago. There are few reasonable alternative explanations. As stated earlier, one of the strongest pieces of evidence that both contradicts accepted fossil theory and at the same time makes the case for massive, worldwide flooding, is polystrate fossils, such as trees.

These tree and plant fossils can be observed in sedimentary rocks on all continents, particularly near coal seams (former forests). The interesting thing about these fossils is that they often cross several strata that we have all been led to believe constitute a timeframe of millions of years! This is difficult for palaeontologists who believe in older world theory to explain, since these fossils clearly call into question the science of dating using layering.

Since when was it possible that a tree was covered by sediment over a process of millions of years, without most of it rotting? Yet, perfectly preserved, traversing layer upon layer of stratification, are these tree fossils. They were covered quickly, in fact. Some of these trees are over 80 feet long! In Joggins, Nova Scotia are some good examples, that can be found in strata spanning some 2,500 feet. Whilst some are perpendicular to the strata, others are not, and more often than not they do not have their roots attached and are, more often than not, found individually. The clear evidence points to trees having been separated from their roots by some violent sideways force, that has removed them from their original habitat in which they supposedly grew in numbers, and deposited them elsewhere, burying them in the process.

Short period sedimentation is possible

Sedimentary layers can be produced in days and hours, not millions of years, and so can whole canyons. These processes permanently change the landscape and can be completed in many cases in exceptionally short time frames. Two examples serve to make the point, though they do not of themselves determine that all sedimentation occurs in such a way. They just serve to show that sedimentation as a 'science' for ageing is highly flawed and one person's estimate of millions of years may well be millions of years off the mark. The actual age, if we were given it, could equally be thousands of years or even just days.

Mount St Helens

Mount St. Helens erupted on 18 May1980. The volcano used to comprise a symmetrical cone about 3,000 meters above sea level. The eruption removed approximately 400 metres from the summit in a vast explosion. It left a massive crater and destroyed the surroundings, which looked like a nuclear bomb had scorched them.

Mount St Helen's erupted three times, and provided so much residue that sedimentary layers, hundreds of feet thick, were produced very quickly. Many sedimentary layers varied in their production. For example, one was produced in an avalanche style speed process producing thousands of different layers only 25 feet thick. The final eruption produced a hot lava flow which mixed with the nearby river, the Toutle and turned into a muddy scouring agent that ripped out the surrounding rock to produce canyons 17 miles long and 140 feet thick. It diverted the course of the river, and all of this was achieved in a few hours.

Now, one wishes to make comparisons with other canyons, as this one is now referred to as the little Grand Canyon. It did not take millions of years to produce, but hours. It cut through rock in hours.

Palouse Canyon, USA

Another example will serve. Palouse canyon, in Eastern Washington is 400 feet deep and in places is 500 feet deep. The canyon is made of solid basalt, and was carved in 2 days by the action of a sluicing flood lake, Lake Missoula[94].

The author, Michael J Oard, who has written a book entitled: "The

155

Missoula Flood Controversy and the Genesis Flood", provides this example:

"The flood overtopped a ridge north of the Snake River, rapidly cutting a narrow canyon 500 feet deep. The modern Palouse River that used to flow west into the Columbia River before the flood now takes a 90-degree left-hand turn south and flows through the canyon carved by the flood. This is called a water gap in which a river or stream flows through a barrier instead of flowing around it. If a geologist did not know about the Lake Missoula Flood, he would have suggested one of three main speculations on the formation of water gaps. But it was formed in the Lake Missoula flood. The Lake Missoula flood provides an analog for the thousand or more rivers over the earth that now flow through mountain barriers, sometimes through gaps much deeper than Grand Canyon. The river should have gone around the barrier, if the slow processes over 'millions of years' model were true, but these water gaps through transverse barriers can be cut rapidly during the Genesis Flood."[95]

The point in citing two examples is to demonstrate that layering and the erosion of canyons can take place exceptionally quickly and has, in fact, happened. The Palouse Canyon case suggests that it could be an 'analogue' (model) for the 'thousand or so rivers over the earth that now flow through mountain barriers', which suggests that the model is widespread globally.

Therefore, because this potential exists, layering and erosion are not reliable examples for dating purposes, if seeking to prove that the age of the earth is dated in the millions of years. The age of the earth could be far more recent if much of the sedimentary composition and erosion took place in violent, but short events as described. Similar debates suggest that the Grand Canyon was created by the receding flood waters from the Noahic flood and possibly further erosion from sluicing lakes created as a result of the flood to the east of the canyon. Whilst interesting, however, these arguments are nowhere near as compelling as the mount St Helens example for volcanic sedimentation and erosion, because it shows that such an event does in fact occur, and was observed in real time.

So, having put into question the age of sedimentary layering based on millions of years of a relatively uniform depositary process, it seems appropriate to return to the depositary action of the Flood that took place, according to the Bible, which it seems, is perfectly capable of having occurred only 4,350 years ago, according to the sedimentary record. We see that there is evidence of a massive flood having occurred, contained in writings the world over.

Other texts evidencing a massive flood
The Epic of Gilgamesh

The Genesis flood story can be seen also in the Epic of Gilgamesh. The tablets on which the story is found were fired, it is believed, in 1850 BC. The ancient Sumerian gods mentioned in the tablet stories bring the date back to about 2150 BC. These stories were probably handed down by oral tradition until they were inscribed in Akkadian Cuneiform text. The discovery of these tablets was made upon finding the Temple library of Nabu and the royal library of Assyrian king Ashurbaminal (669-633 BC) in Nineveh.

People often state that the Bible plagiarised the Epic of Gilgamesh, but it could be equally likely that the Hebrews have their own version, since the event affected all people.

Robert Goh (Chinese Memories of Noah's Flood, www.across.co.nz), writes:

157

"In fact, over many parts of the world, there were other ancient peoples who had similar stories [to the flood]. Similar stories come from southern Asia, the South Sea islands, and all parts of the continent of America..."

Flood stories from other cultures

The Greeks had several versions of a myth in which a king Deucalion and his wife Pyrrha escaped from a great flood by floating in a chest that finally landed on a mountain. They took refuge on Mt Parnassus (in central Greece not far from Delphi) and, at Zeus' command, cast stones which became a new race of human beings.

An Indian myth from the 6th century BC tells how the hero Manu was advised by a fish to build a ship as a means of escape from the coming flood. When it came, the fish towed the ship to a mountain top.

Excavations at Ur in Iraq by Sir Leonard Wooley in 1929 may have confirmed the ancient belief of many nations when he discovered a layer of clay 3m deep which was apparently deposited by a great ancient flood.

It seemed to echo the story of a great worldwide flood as recorded in a Babylonian clay tablet, the Epic of Gilgamesh, written over 2,500 years ago. According to that epic the hero and sole survivor Utnapishtim landed on Mount Nisir (in Kurdistan, upper Iraq).

The Flood and the foundation of the Chinese nation

Today a surviving Chinese legend of an extensive ancient flood vaguely revolves around the person of a goddess Nukua who supposedly ended the flood by patching up the blue sky with five-coloured stones...

Only the character "boat" and its eight passengers seems to remain as a constant reminder of what had happened long, long ago."

That is one person's research and collation of stories. But I find the author of the next more compelling still, with its direct comparisons between the Noahic one God religion and that of the first Chinese religion.

This is by Hieromonk Damascene, Fr. Damascene, from the St. Herman of Alaska Monastery in Platina, California, on Ancient Chinese Theology in the Light of Genesis, June 2004. In his three-part series of articles, to which I am indebted for the following account, he explains that the earliest account of religious worship in China is found in the Shu Jing (Book of History of Book of Documents), the oldest Chinese historical source.

Paraphrasing his article, we read that this document aged around 2230 BC records that the Emperor Shun "sacrificed to Shangdi", the 'supreme ruler', the single, ancient God of the Chinese, in a ceremony called the "Border Sacrifice" celebrated twice a year.

The ceremony was conducted from at least 2230 BC to 1911AD when the Manchus fell. The worship of the one true God, Shangdi, was eventually obscured with other pagan deities, but still continued as the one true God faithfully served by the Emperor into modern times.

The oldest Border Sacrifice text dates from the Ming Dynasty performed in 1538 AD, based on existing ancient records of the original rituals. The Emperor was the high priest, and the only one able to undertake the rituals, which began:

"Of old in the beginning, there was the great chaos,

159

without form and dark. The five elements [planets] had not begun to revolve, nor the sun and the moon to shine. In the midst thereof there existed neither forms for sound. Thou, O spiritual Sovereign, camest forth in Thy presidency, and first didst divide the grosser parts from the purer. Thou madest heaven; Thou madest earth; Thou madest man. All things with their reproductive power got their being."

There are obvious and stunning parallels with Genesis. In the Chinese ritual, we see Shangdi as the single Creator of heaven and earth, and in Genesis, we recall:

"In the beginning, God created the heavens and the earth. The earth was without form and void, and darkness was upon the face of the deep" (Genesis 1: 1- 2).

Other parallels in language are remarkable. Compare the Chinese version:

"Thy sovereign goodness is infinite. As a potter, Thou hast made all living things. Thy sovereign goodness is infinite. Great and small are sheltered [by Thee]. As engraven on the heart of Thy poor servant is the sense of Thy goodness, so that my feeling cannot be fully displayed. With great kindness, Thou dost bear us, and not withstanding our shortcomings, dost grant us life and prosperity"...,

...with Isaiah:

"But now, O Lord, Thou art our Father; we are the clay, and Thou our Potter and we all are the work of Thy hand" (Isaiah 64: 8).

The author concludes that both ceremonies are drawn from the same, single source. This is particularly marked with the description of the origins of their respective religions.

The Noahic Flood occurred around 2500 to 2350 BC. After wiping out the whole earth, only Noah, his wife, his three sons, and their wives, totalling 8 people, survived. When Noah touched dry land, he offered a sacrifice to God, in Abrahamic fashion. Noah also took some animals on the ark for sacrificial purposes.

As just over a century later evil became rampant once again, races were scattered by God and peoples of one language were scattered, now speaking many languages at the incident that took place at the Tower of Babel in about 2247 BC, he explains.

Fr. Damascene then notes that it was after this point that Chinese history commences. It appeared to him that the original people of China had travelled from Babel and that all Chinese people came from this root. In fact, there is a group, represented in Genesis 10:17, called the Sinite people, and the possibility arises that they are one and the same. The first (Xia) dynasty began around 2205 to 2000 BC, giving plenty of travel time. As Noah lived centuries after the flood, it provided plenty of time for his cultural mores to be passed on to this travelling band of Sinites, including the creation, fall, and the flood.

It is not surprising therefore, he contends, to find Noah's religion imported, and stories of the Flood, but the question remains whether there were any stories of the flood having occurred in China itself.

The Shu Jing, or Book of Documents was written in about 1000 BC and was based on material from the Shang Dynasty, which began in 1700 BC, 200 years before Moses, the writer of Genesis. Therefore, some 500 years passed from the beginning of China until the written record of its history was recorded.

161

Damascene notes that the "first thing that students of Chinese history learn is that Chinese history began with a Flood. This is not surprising, since we know that ancient peoples from all the continents of the world have a story of a Great Flood which covered all the earth as a judgment on man's sin. In many cases, the details are remarkably like the details recorded in the book of Genesis. The Aboriginal peoples of Australia, for example, speak of a global flood and how only eight people escaped it in a canoe."

Damascene notes what is said in the Shu Jing records:

"The flood waters are everywhere, destroying everything as they rise above the hills and swell up to heaven."

But this flood was the remnant of the Noahic Flood, since:

"the Shu Jing only begins with Chinese history...[so]...this statement does not refer to the global Flood, but rather to the local flooding that was caused in China by the remnants of the Great Flood....after the Great Flood, some of the land was not yet habitable because the flood waters were still inundating the land...The time between the Flood and the founding of the first Chinese dynasty was as little as 143 years, and we would expect that huge pockets of water would have been on the land at that time, which are not there today...These leftover Flood waters made parts of the land uninhabitable. At that time, according to Chinese history, there were the first righteous Chinese Emperors, Yao and Shun: the first emperors to offer the Border Sacrifices to Shangdi. To a man named Kun given the task of ridding the land of the flood waters, but he was not able to do so. It was not until Kun's son, Yu, devised a new technique to channel the waters out to sea that the land was eventually made habitable."

Yu the Great cut a channel into the sea to clear these remnant flood waters, taking nine years to do so. He became a hero because of this amazing feat. As a result, Shun turned the rulership over to Yu. Yu became emperor, thus beginning China's first dynasty, the Xia. After that, China's dynastic culture lasted almost another four thousand years.

It seems then that the flood is recognised in national literature across most of the world. This includes the Hindus from India; the Greeks within the Mediterranean; the Chinese in Asia as explained above; the Mexicans towards Central America; the Algonquins of North America and the Hawaiians midway across Pacific Ocean. If we assume that Noah's provenance rests somewhere within a wide region representing the Northern Afro-Asian lands (which one extrapolates from the demographic map of peoples who speak Hamitic languages that supposedly descended from Noah's son, Ham), then we can see that stories of the Flood were widespread far beyond those lands, traversing vast oceans and other continents. It is therefore inconceivable that the Noahic Flood did not take place.

Josh McDowell, in his book: "The New Evidence that Demands a Verdict", makes some interesting textual observations regarding a comparison between the Sumerian and Babylonian accounts of creation regarding myth, which we can as easily impart to the story of Noah in Genesis. He suggests that a myth does not imply that the subject matter described is untrue, but merely that it has been embellished over time to become 'mythologised'. Literary progression moves from an unadorned elegance to something that becomes more accreted so that the true historical version is hidden under layers of adornment. In the Ancient Near East, he states,

> "the rule is that simple accounts or traditions give rise (by accretion and embellishment) to elaborate legends,

163

but not the reverse."[96]

This is extraordinary. McDowell suggests that although the Epic of Gilgamesh was written before Genesis, Moses sought to strip the embellishments and adornments away to reveal the true account under the myth and superstition that had arisen over time, and which had raised an historical account to fanciful fiction.

By inference, Genesis is the more reliable account, being simpler, and in respect of the story of Noah, Josh McDowell makes these additional observations. He says that:

> "there are good reasons to believe that Genesis gives the original story. The other versions give elaborations indicating corruption. Only in Genesis is the year of the flood given, as well as dates for the chronology relative to Noah's life....[by comparison to Babylonian accounts] The cubical Babylonian ship could not have saved anyone. The raging waters would have constantly turned it on every side. However, the biblical ark is rectangular – long, wide, low – so that it would ride rough seas well. The length of the rainfall in the pagan accounts (seven days) is not enough time for the devastation they describe...The Babylonian idea that the waters subsided in one day is equally absurd....[In the Babylonian account] the hero is granted immortality and exalted. The Bible moves on to Noah's sin. Only a version that seeks to tell the truth would include this realistic admission."[97]

Thus, whilst we are assured that the account is recorded worldwide, by textual analysis we are better assured of the truth of the biblical version. This does not significantly add to the general premise of what I am trying to portray, namely, that the Bible is reliable and records truth. That we can see from the highest point of observation: namely that most other cultures had the same catastrophic event happen to them as well.

As we can be reasonably confident about the truth of this event from different historical accounts, the subject with which we started this section, namely the Flood process, attests also to fossilisation, as the purpose of the Flood was to wipe out all living things[98].

Anything contemporary with Noah will have died, in a very short period of time, without the normal process of decay happening to it, and buried under many feet of sediment. We know from polystrate fossils, which otherwise would have decayed, that the thickness can be measured in tens, if not hundreds of feet. We also know that animals that die and drop to the ocean floor, for example, do not undergo fossilisation and preservation in a manner consistent with a catastrophic event like the Flood. Because the Flood was worldwide, we would expect to see laid down millions upon millions of fossils...which would all come from the same era, but covered in hundreds of feet of sediment, varying in thickness dependent upon the nature of their habitat (e.g. a rock vicinity or sand); altitude at which they lived, and other factors. We would not expect to try to date the age of fossils that were laid down under a different thickness of sediment caused by a worldwide flood differently, simply because they were covered with, say, 50 feet of sediment as opposed to a hundred.

The Bible, however, provides us with a date for the Flood, and therefore the date when all such animals laid down in this process, lived. It was just a few thousand years ago.

The plagues of Egypt

There appears to be some scant archaeological evidence for the ten plagues from outside of the Bible. William F. Albright, the famous American Archaeologist, considered that the water-trough found in El-Arish which shows heiroglyphs detailing darkness is evidence of the ninth 'plague' of darkness. However, this is an area of archaeology that may yet reveal more evidence over time as the increasing efforts of archaeologists find more.

Discovery of red sea chariots

There appears to be some archaeological support for the crossing of the red sea, from dive exhibitions undertaken around 2000 which resulted in findings of chariot wheel shaped corals and a golden wheel on which no coral has grown. These have been found on the red sea floor at a narrow point of crossing through the sea. This is at Nuweiba. Nuweiba was once known as "Nuwayba al Muzayyinah", or 'the waters of Moses' Opening', which is encouraging enough. Metal detectors were used and found that this gave rise to metal readings.

On the Saudi side, the army was left dead there too, presumably from the surge of water drowning them as it smashed together and lapped up the sides. Wheel shaped coral was again found off the shores of the Saudi side, in accordance with the biblical record. These represent the shapes of four and six spoked wheels that can be seen drawn in ancient Egyptian pictures.

Nuweiba beach could house the whole of Israel's two million occupants as they waited to cross. The added advantage of the Nuweiba position is that there is an underground ridge here traversing the void between Saudi and the Egyptian wilderness that causes the bottom to be shallower than the rest, which otherwise would not have been passable. The covering here, unlike other areas, is silt, or sand which can be walked over easily. Other sites suggested for crossing have mud.

There are also red granite pillars which have been placed either side of the crossing (though one appears to have been removed by authorities). The Bible says that Solomon placed them there.

166

They were allegedly found (1978 and 1984) lying on their sides and the base of one is now set in concrete. The column on the Saudi coastline contained Phoenician letters which mention Mizraim (Egypt), Solomon, Adom, death, Pharaoh, Moses, and Yahweh. There is of course some speculation that these may be modern replicas – so it would be a majestic find if actually ever authenticated.

There is nothing yet definitively proven, but the findings so far are encouraging and suggest that the site may have been located.

Tower of Babel

It seems that the tower was likely to have been a ziggurat, many of which can be found for example, in Iraq, and are thousands of years old. The point which historically deserves mention about the biblical Tower of Babel story is that it makes specific reference to the world speaking one language[99], so if there is evidence that the world did indeed speak one language at a point in time, then this story may also prove to be accurate. Dr Quentin Atkinson, of the University of Auckland, published two major studies in 2011 showing that the origins of all of the world's languages points to a single source. His research was based on 'phonemes', being the perceptually distinct units of sound that differentiate words. His research showed that the farther one travelled from Africa, the fewer distinct phonemes a language enjoys, and as this decline cannot be explained by demographic shifts or other local factors, it is strong evidence of an original source, which he says comes from Africa[100].

It seems then, from an analysis of language derivation, there was indeed one language at some point in the past. The Tower of Babel story thus has a ring of truth about it.

In the book "Cuneiform Royal Inscriptions and Related Texts in the Schøyen Collection"[101], the 'Tower of Babel Stele' is represented as being built by Nebuchadnezzar. The text says:

> "The House, the foundation of heaven and earth, Ziggurat in Babylon. [there is a picture identifying the great ziggurat of babylon, the tower of babel. The Royal Inscription of King Nebuchanezzar continues: "Nebuchadnezzar, King of Babylon am I – In order to complete E-Temen-Anki and E-Ur-Me-Imin-Anki I mobilised all countries everywhere, each and every ruler who had been raised to prominence over all the people of the world – the base I filled to make a high terrace. I built their structures with bitumen and baked brick throughout. I completed it raising its top to the heaven, making it gleam bright as the sun."

The picture shows a seven-staged ziggurat topped off with a temple, pictured on a black stoned stele dated around C604-562 BC (reign of Nebuchadnezzar II). The outer walls an inner arrangement of rooms is also shown and according to Herodotus, had a room with a large richly covered couch in it, and a gold table. The ziggurat, according to these sources, was built around 1792-1750 BC, fell into some significant disrepair because it was later restored and enlarged under Nabopoassar and finished under Nebuchadnezzar II in 604-562 BC. The manner by which Nebuchadnezzar takes credit for the completion is that it was significant, as it took all countries everywhere to do. This was no minor repair. To build such a monument, it has been estimated that some 17 million bricks had to be fired, so it was indeed large.

Alexander the Great took down the tower in 331 BC.

This stele is direct evidence of the existence of the actual tower, though it is clear that it no longer stands.

Compare the description of the tower as cited in Genesis:

there was a journey of the survivors of the Flood from the East (Genesis 11:2) – compare this with the statement of mobilisation of all countries everywhere, above

they came to rest on a plain in Shinar (Genesis 11:2) – believed to be Nebuchadnezzar's country in Mesopotamia

the Bible states that they decided, together, to make a tower of thoroughly baked bricks, with 'asphalt' or bitumen for mortar. This also accords exactly with the stele's inscription

the tower is to reach the heavens – and this compares precisely with the stele's description that its top was to be raised to heaven

some event caused the tower to fall into disrepair originally, before restoration and its eventual destruction

Josh McDowell adds additional commentary. He states that Ur-Nammu built a tower around 2044 to 2007 BC under direct instruction from the gods; that it appeared to be built with mortar as there is a depiction of him setting off with a mortar basket (and hence the tower was built with brick rather than stone), and that it offended the gods. The gods threw down what the men had built and scattered them abroad, making their speech strange.

McDowell also starts his commentary stating that the Sumerians recorded that everyone once spoke the same language[102].

Indeed, the Epic of Gilgamesh talks of a golden age, when no animals threatened people and all spoke one language to praise a god, Enlil. Enki, a different god, finds some human behaviour

169

inappropriate and puts an end to a single language system, sending confusion among humans which brought about conflict, war, and different language.

Whether these are all one and the same depiction it is hard to tell; though the Nebuchadnezzar account describes him as the builder of the tower of babel. Either way, this is remarkable evidence for the building and the destruction, at the hand of divine power, of the tower.

It is also remarkable that peoples of one language are clearly described several times, and can be attested to using a study of phonemes, but that such peoples were thus scattered and thereafter had strange speech.

What is clear is that the existence of many, many ziggurats has now been noted in Iraq, and that the biblical account can no longer be simply dispelled. That the tower existed is no longer in doubt, and that something happened to language that caused its diversity and spread abroad to the rest of the world.

Ezekiel's burial place in Iraq

Ezekiel lived and died in Iraq. I chose to write about him because he lived with the Jews exiled to Babylon under King Nebuchadnezzar in 597 BC, so he sits squarely within this vital part of history. The incredibly beautiful tomb of the prophet Ezekiel can be located at Al Kifl, which is in South Eastern Iraq. Until the mid-twentieth century, up to 5,000 Jews would travel to the tomb for Passover. The so called 'Vicar of Baghdad', Canon Andrew White, travelled to it in May 2010 to inspect its condition on behalf of the Iraqi Jewry and reported that it was still "intact, glorious and beautiful"[103]. That was before so called 'Islamic State's' arrival, at least.

170

Biblical places

Apart from the obvious – Jerusalem, the following constitute newly discovered biblical towns and cities that are all mentioned in the Old and New Testaments. These attest to the truth, historically, of accounts that took place in these real places: take Jericho; Beth Shemesh; Beth Shean; Beersheba; Haran; Hazor; Dan; Lachish; Megiddo; Shechem; Samaria; Shiloh; and Gezer for example.

Ebla tablets

Archaeologists found these tablets in Northern Syria in 1975. They used writing to evidence contracts and to build archives and libraries of historical accounts. The importance of these tablets to Bible scholars is that doubt had been cast upon the assumption that Moses could have written the first five books of the Bible – the Pentateuch. The assumption had been that, as writing had not 'been invented' then, a later author must have written them with credit given to Moses, but somewhat undermining the credibility of the Torah in the process, which asserts itself to be the infallible word of God for which not a jot or tittle must be changed.

However, it is known that the kingdom of Ebla existed in 2500 BC, and clearly the find shows that they very much used writing.

The Ebla texts wipe many smiles off cynical faces. For example, the word 'tehon' or 'deep' was thought to be a later use of writing and had not existed at the time that the Pentateuch was supposedly written by Moses. However, the Ebla tablets, which pre-date the date of writing of Genesis by several hundred years, uses the word. The tablets also revealed the use of patriarchal names such as Abraham, David and Ishmael, which attest therefore to the truth of the biblical account in the supposed first use of those names. In fact, the names were more common that had originally been understood, it seems.

The Hittites are also described in these tablets. Hitherto they had been a mythical race, not thought to exist. However, these authentic tablets refer quite clearly to them.

The Pentateuch therefore sits apart from the scoffers, with barefaced truth ringing out from all of its pages, as time and again, it's simple stories are beginning to show themselves to be truthful to a discerning eye.

Herod the Great

Herod the Great is a misnomer. He was a barbaric and rotten puppet king who exerted his tyranny over all Jerusalem. He is remembered for the massacre of the innocents, being the order to kill all male infants below two years old[104] in order to eradicate the possibility that another king – one who was prophesied, might rise to overthrow him. He needn't have bothered, as Jesus, the prophesied king, was a king of peace. Herod's act proved to be, therefore, one of total, indiscriminate waste and butchery, of the highest order.

Herod is of ongoing interest owing to his character. Whilst scholars doubt whether the massacre took place (noting that they have doubted many biblical accounts of history that archaeology later proves to be true), his penchant for murdering close relatives (his wife and three sons), certainly means that the death of a few hundred children was not beyond him. He taxed his own countrymen to extinction to pay for his vanities, one of which was Herodium. Herodium is a vast conical shaped hill, in which Herod built a palace fortress which descends down into the core of the hill. However, it was covered over following Herod's death, with earth, adding to the height of the hill by some 65 feet, and creating an eerie mausoleum in which Herod was buried.

Herodium was first identified in 1838 by Edward Robinson, a US scholar. He compared his find with the works of Flavius Josephus, the Roman Jewish historian, and confirmed that he had found it.

However, no one knew where the tyrant was buried. For almost 200 years the search was on, and in 2007, the Daily Mail announced that "A New Discovery May Solve the Mystery the Bible's Bloodiest Tyrant", with the discovery by Hebrew University's Ehud Netzer. Netzer had spent 35 years looking for him[105]. We have yet to hear the outcome of this find, centred on Herodium.

Josephus wrote that he was conveyed after death to Herodium, after being covered with purple, a diadem was put on his head and a crown of gold above it and a sceptre in his right hand. It is therefore probable that he was entombed there.

Code of Hammurabi

This Code was discovered in 1901 in Iran. It dates slightly before the time of Moses at around 1754 BC and sets out 282 laws and scaled punishments, and adjusts the precept: "An eye for an eye and a tooth for a tooth" depending upon social class. One law for the rich and one for the poor, so to speak. The code is thematic, dealing with matters such as contract, relationships and sexual behaviour, and civil service.

There have been obvious comparisons with the law of Moses, and question marks over whether Moses was inspired by or even stole his ideas from Hammurabi, the Babylonian King who inspired the setting down of this law. However, there are very significant differences between the two sets of laws. The Hammurabi system is based on class and social status, to which the Mosaic law are blind. The Hammurabi laws appear to be cited as case law – based on edicts given in response to specific cases whereas the Mosaic law is not, but given as an overarching system for all purposes.

The State owns the Hammurabi laws, but God Himself owns the Mosaic law; and lastly Mosaic law is set within a covenant relationship with God – the so-called Sinai or Mosaic covenant. This requires that God's servants will obey His laws and thus be blessed if they do and punished if they don't. However, it sets them apart from other cultures in which a law or civil obedience might exist, because God's side of the bargain is a promise to make Israel a kingdom of priests and a holy (set apart) nation. They are blessed in a way with which no other nation compares, as is made evidently clear within the whole of the Old Testament. What is equally clear is that when they transgress the law, they are roundly punished, perhaps like no other nation, since the Hebrews were considered at times worse than any other nation:

> "As surely as I live, declares the Sovereign Lord, your sister Sodom and her daughters never did what you and your daughters have done." (Ezekiel 16:48)

As Christopher Wright points out in "The God I don't Understand":

> "...we might point out that over the whole history of the Old Testament Israel, far more generations of Israelites felt the judgement of God at the hands of their enemies than a single generation of Canaanites experienced the judgment of God at the hands of the Israelites."[106]

In other words, under the covenant, Israel had God and no mere mortal ruler to deal with, which led to times of vast blessing (witness Solomon's splendour, or the clearing of the evil empires of Canaan), but also times of total routing for transgression of the Mosaic covenant, by worshipping other gods and intermarriage.

So, whilst the Hammurabi Code and stele shows that laws were indeed written down by the time of Moses, the Mosaic law could therefore have quite easily been put down in written form at the time recorded in the Bible. However, what sets the Mosaic law apart is the righteousness, strength, simplicity and global nature of it which speaks to a higher influence. Indeed, it is this version upon which all civil society has based its entire legal system, particularly across the Western World, and not some other, lesser law. That has set it in good stead for hundreds of years. The fabric of society is breaking down now, as a result of a diminishing respect for God and God's law.

The Tel Dan and Meesha steles[107]

The Tel Dan stele records an inscription of 'The House of David". It is dated around 900-850 BC. Likewise, the Meesha stele (846 BC) records Omri and King David. These steles are vital evidence in support of the existence of these Jewish kings as currently there is a paucity if evidence surrounding their existence outside of the Bible. Here now is proof. We await proof outside of the Bible for the existence of Solomon.

Nabonidus Cylinder[108]

King Nabonidus left a cuneiform cylinder dated 550 BC which attested to Belshazzar as his eldest son. Nabonidus reigned in a co-regency with his son Belshazzar. The biblical text says:

> "Now, if you can read the writing and make known to me its interpretation, you shall be clothed in purple and have a chain of gold placed around your neck, and shall be the third ruler in the kingdom."

The importance of the Nabonidus cylinder, therefore, is that it attests to the truth of the book of Daniel, who became, in effect,

175

part of the ruling monarchy of Babylon, as the third ruler: not something that could have been worked out from the Bible itself without this important extra information about the father and son ruler-ship.

Caiaphas Ossuary[109]

Caiaphas, the high priest who presided over the execution process for Jesus Christ, was buried in an ossuary. It was discovered in 1990 in the Peace Section of Jerusalem in a burial cave containing twelve such ossuaries, and thus silenced critics who believed that that whole of the new testament was made up.

Caiaphas existed and we even have his burial box.

Pilate memorialised[110] in the Pilate Stone

Likewise, the existence of Pontius Pilate is given weight by a discovery in 1961 of a dedication stone found at a Roman Amphitheatre in Caesarea Maritima, upon which an inscription read:
"Tiberium, (Pon)tius (Praef)ectus Iuda(aea)"

Therefore, the existence of Pontius Pilate, which is the only extra-biblical evidence of his existence has been categorically confirmed. The approximate date is recorded somewhere between 26 and 37 AD, so it accords with the time of Pilate of the Bible. It is thought that Pilate resided in Caesareas Maritima, where this stone was discovered, and travelled, as required for official duties, to Jerusalem. The stone can be seen in the Israel Museum, in Jerusalem.

Cylinder of Cyrus the Great

Cyrus the Great was a good king towards the Jews and began to reverse the restrictions placed on them under the exile. The tolerance exhibited in 2 Chronicles and the book of Ezra is borne out by the discovery of a nine-inch clay cylinder found at Babylon which dates from the time of its conquest. It reports Cyrus' victory and his policy of permitting captives to return to homelands and to rebuild temples.

Conclusion

The inescapable conclusion from archaeology is that the Bible is the reliable word of God. Events, people, times and places discovered from sources outside of the Bible attest comprehensively to its truth.

10. Prophecy fulfilled

"The testimony of Jesus is the Spirit of prophecy"

(Revelation 9:10)

How do we know that Jesus Christ was and is the only son of God? We can only know this if we are given, in advance, tools to measure Him by. These tools should talk of His characteristics, what His purpose and His plans are; and should sketch out His life.

But, surely, that is crystal ball gazing! However, there is a very large gulf between 'magic and crystal ball gazing' on the one hand, and the plans that God Himself, reveals through men and women to whom He reveals his plans in advance, because the truth of his prophetic statements can be tested again and again. God revealed His plans for His son Jesus Christ consistently throughout the Old and New Testaments, as the future person of redemption for the entire human race. His son's purpose was so essential, so important and unrepeatable, that God the Father made sure that not just snippets, but the entire life of Jesus Christ was mapped out and known hundreds of years in advance.

The evidence must be compelling, because I have read many accounts of Jewish rabbis, no less, who now accept that Jesus was indeed the messiah, and have given their lives to Him.

Even Albert Einstein, a Jew, whom I understand did not believe in God[111], at least the God of the Bible, was however attracted to the person of Jesus. He said this:

> "I am a Jew, but I am enthralled by the luminous figure of the Nazarene...No one can read the Gospels without

178

feeling the actual presence of Jesus. His personality pulsates in every word. No myth is filled with such life."[112]

Einstein, whatever his state of faith, was prepared to believe in the truth of the personality of Jesus: *"No myth is filled with such life"*.

Mahatma Ghandi was a Hindu, but he was hugely moved by the person of Jesus and recognised the power of the Bible itself. Here's what he had to say about the good book:

> "You Christians look after a document containing enough dynamite to blow all civilisation to pieces, turn the world upside down and bring peace to a battle-torn planet. But you treat it as though it is nothing more than a piece of literature."

He had a point. We have strayed from the Bible into disbelief, and it is time to take it at its word. One way to do that is to look at what is said about this luminous person, using the Bible as the source of evidence, to spell out the truth concerning Him.

We can do this by reference things that were foretold within it, and can therefore be measured subsequently.

The life of Jesus

In order to show that Jesus Christ was the Messiah, the Holy One of Israel, around whom the whole of history revolves, we need to document the main features of His life, and death and then see what the Bible had to say hundreds of years before he came to earth, by way of comparison. When we have done this, we will need to consider if there has been any real, documented person in the whole of the history of time, that has ever fulfilled or been able to fulfil these prophecies. As will become evidently clear,

179

there is only one: Jesus Christ. As the Bible says that He is history's central figure, that He is not only the son of God but God Himself, then if these multitudinous prophecies all make statements that are truthful about Him, then He simply has to be who He is said and claims to be.

In order to be sure of its correctness, it is important – so that there can be no question of a particular prophecy being open to some generous interpretation or ambiguity, for there to be serial prophecies fulfilled. Only that way can it be said that this specimen being examined is in fact, without question, the person about whom prophecy spoke.

The following is a synopsis of Jesus Christ's life and death

Jesus was born to Mary and Joseph. However, Mary was a virgin, as far as the conception of Jesus was concerned, because the bible says He was conceived via the 'unction' of the Holy Spirit. This was explained to Mary by the angel Gabriel, who, as Gabriel clarifies, stands in the presence of the Lord[113]. Jesus takes His lineage from David and ultimately from Abraham, the Old Testament patriarch. He was born in lowly state, in Bethlehem, and three wise men (aka 'kings') from the East came and bowed down and worshipped Him, offering gifts of gold and frankincense and myrrh, by way of tribute to Him.

Shortly afterwards, Herod, who had heard that a king had been born who would be 'king of the Jews' – a title nailed eventually to Jesus' cross of crucifixion – had every male child under two years old murdered to prevent his ascendancy; but Mary and Joseph escaped to Egypt to lie low until matters settled down. About the same time, Jesus' cousin, John the Baptist, was born.

On the eighth day, Jesus is presented at the Temple, and is circumcised as a Jewish boy by Simeon, who was informed beforehand that he would not die until he saw the 'comfort of

180

Israel' – the 'Lord's Christ' or chosen one, who would be their salvation. Anna, an ancient prophetess present there at the same time, also recognises the boy and prophesies that he will be the redemption of Israel. Once all the ceremonies had been fulfilled as the law required, they returned to Galilee and their own town of Nazareth.

We don't hear a lot about Jesus' life until he is twelve, except that He grew in strength and wisdom and the grace of God was on Him. At twelve, He is presented to the temple on the Feast of the Passover, and Jesus stays there, unbeknownst to His parents, but they find Him after three days of loss[114], and are surprised by His retort that they should not be concerned because He was in His 'father's house' – the temple courts.

We hear little of the intervening years. But when Jesus reaches thirty years old, His acetic cousin initially takes centre stage, living in the wilderness on locusts and wild honey, dressed in garment made from camel's hair and a wearing a leather belt. He takes to baptising his followers with water.

But he knows that a time is coming for one greater than this final Old Testament prophet, and he booms out to his audience that they are to make 'straight paths' for the coming of the saviour Himself. People wondered if John was the Christ – the chosen one, but he reminded them that he was not, and that he was not even worthy to untie the thongs of the saviour's sandals.

Then one day, as John is baptising, Jesus arrives. We are not told how well they know each other, or whether John recognises Jesus, but at some point, John realises that he is in the presence of the saviour, and acknowledges that he should be baptised by Jesus and not the other way round. Jesus, ever mindful of the law, affirms John in his ministry by saying that for the time being (frankly, until Jesus is crucified), it is necessary for all to be fulfilled and is baptised by John.

181

The heavens open, a dove representing the Holy Spirit descends on Jesus, and an audible voice from heaven confirms that Jesus is God's son, and that He is pleased with Him. Immediately Jesus leaves for the wilderness to be tempted by Satan in a long fast for forty days; but Jesus overcomes all temptation and is ministered to by angels.

Jesus returns back home where, as a prophet in His home town, He is roundly rejected. He confirms that Isaiah's scroll is an announcement that He is the fulfilment of the prophecy of the one who would heal the blind (a miracle reserved only for the saviour as no Old Testament Prophets could achieve it), and says that unless Israel accepts Him, God's message of redemption would issue to the Gentiles instead.

This is what infuriates His own townsfolk, and they attempt to kill Him. But He walks straight through them.

Jesus leaves to begin His ministry by calling His disciples, issuing His manifesto (the beatitudes) and undertaking extraordinary healing and other miracles. Notable are turning water into wine at a Wedding in Cana in Galilee; raising Lazarus; healing the Centurion's servant at a distance, casting out a legion of demons into pigs; raising Tabitha and Lazarus from the dead; walking on water; feeding 4,000 and 5,000 respectively from a few loaves and fish; His transfiguration; and of course, His greatest miracle, but one which was not from Himself, but given through the other persons of the Trinity, His resurrection.

During this time, He teaches in parables – stories – instead of with rules, covering a wide range of themes.

John is beheaded, but only after asking Jesus by messenger if Jesus is in fact the Christ. Jesus confirms that the blind and deaf are healed – the sure sign of the saviour. John's head is presented to Herod in court as a gift for the dancing daughter of Herodias, who promptly displayed it on a platter to her mother and Herod's guests.

Jesus invokes the ire of the Pharisees and teachers of the law, calling them 'a brood of vipers' and 'hypocrites' amongst other names, as they appear like 'whitewashed tombs': perfect looking on the outside, but full of evil intent, inside. This constant theme eventually leads to Jesus' crucifixion. However, in the meantime, every trap they set for Him is confounded by His genius and wit.

He side-steps them all with His skilful rhetoric, to the point that every challenge they raise backfires, and they are left speechless.

His disciple Peter recognises Him as the Christ, the Son of the Living God. For his reward, he is handed the spiritual keys to heaven. Later, in spite of this impressive award ceremony, hubris befalls Peter, and he denies Christ publicly three times.

Jesus predicts His death. He then travels with Peter, James and John, disciples, up a high mountain and is transfigured before their eyes, glowing brilliant white, at which point Moses and Elijah (the law and the prophets) appear with Him, showing Him as the fulfilment of the whole Bible story, and confirming the manner of His return.

He enters Jerusalem in a display of triumph on a colt, and is worshipped and adored by rows of followers, who spread their cloaks and cut branches on the ground in honour.

His prophecies begin to sound eschatological (talking of the end of times), turning to themes like the signs of the end of the age; and the day and hour of the second coming of Christ (referred to as the Son of Man) being unknown to all except God in Heaven.

Those days, He reports, will be like the days of Noah – which were of course so evil that the earth had to be destroyed. He warns that all should keep their righteous wits about themselves, lest they are caught napping (un-repented sin), when the end comes.

Jesus hosts a last supper at Passover, at which it is revealed that one of His own, Judas Iscariot the scribe, will betray Him. Jesus explains that it is the one who dips his hand in the bowl at the same time as Jesus, to which Judas retorts; "Surely not I, Rabbi?" but as prophesied by Jesus, he duly dips his hand in at the same time as Christ. Presumably Judas thought he was doing Jesus a favour by ensuring his political case for a King of Israel would be raised at the highest levels in Jewish society. This later backfires, spectacularly.

During this supper, Jesus teaches them about the taking of bread and wine to represent His body and blood under a new covenant, a covenant for forgiveness of sin. They all sing a hymn together and retire to the Mount of Olives.

At the garden in Gethsemane, Jesus sweats blood with the stress of what He knows He is about to face as He is pleading with God to take the cup of death from Him, but agrees to His father's will to proceed with His certain death.

Jesus is arrested by a posse of soldiers accompanied by Judas, who betrays Jesus with a secret sign – a 'kiss of death'. Jesus, however, knowing what is to follow, simply asks him as a friend to do what he came to do. Jesus is taken away.

Peter, who had confessed undying loyalty, and who had been told by Jesus that He would deny Him three times before the cock crows duly does so when challenged whether he knows the accused. Judas then hangs himself as he realises that his political aims he swapped for 30 pieces of silver in return for Jesus did not turn out as he had expected and that he has, in effect, simply betrayed an innocent man to death. The money he threw back was used to purchase a potter's field.

Jesus is brought before Pilate, where they discuss a number of matters, including the essence of determination of truth. Pilate, conscious that he must appease the crowd, lets a convicted murderer, Barabbas go. But Pilate's wife warns Pilate that he should not interfere with Jesus for He is an innocent man, as revealed to her in a dream. Pilate tries to find Him innocent on no less than four occasions and seeks to get others to judge Him, including Herod. His plans come to nothing and, at the pressure of the baying crowds, who all now reject Him, Pilate famously 'washes his hands' and hands Jesus over to be crucified.

Crucifixion is not a punishment recognised in Jewish criminal law. It is a Roman punishment, reserved for the most damned and shameful. Only the Romans could administer crucifixion. It was so torturous that even the barbaric Romans banned it eventually, but not in time for Jesus.

He is taken, flogged, and soldiers mock Him and His 'kingly' status. They strip Him, cast lots for His clothing, and dress Him in scarlet. They make a crown of painful thorns to adorn His head and hand Him a staff, kneeling in front of Him in a cry of fake deference: "Hail, King of the Jews". They spit on Him, beat Him up, and then lead Him to His murder – the murder of an innocent man, on a cross, the bar of which He is made to carry.

Simon of Cyrene helps Jesus carry His cross-bar outside of the city. At Golgotha, the place of the skull, Jesus is offered wine with gall. They placed a plaque with 'King of the Jews' over His head on the cross and taunted Him to save Himself. Jesus' fate is discussed by two 'robbers' who are hanging on crosses either side of Jesus. Both mock Him, but one comes to his senses and suggests that whilst the two robbers are there for good reason, Jesus is innocent and asks to be remembered when Jesus comes into His kingdom.

Despite the immense pain and effort required to mouth any words (given His mouth is completely parched), Jesus confirms that this man will be with Him in Paradise that very day.

The time for Jesus' death draws near. At that point, the scenery changes. Darkness rolls in across the land from the sixth hour (noon) until the ninth hour (3pm). At His own darkest hour, Jesus cries out: "Eloi, Eloi, Lama Sabacthani?", which means "My God, my God, why have you forsaken me?" He is offered wine vinegar on a sponge, but refuses it. He cries out loudly once more, gives up His spirit, and dies. His body is then pierced to reveal that blood and water pours forth.

The earth shakes violently and rocks split. The four-inch thick temple curtain tears from top to bottom as the Lord's spirit explodes forth from the Holy of Holies and out, into the world. Tombs crack open and the dead start to rise to life, walking into cities and appearing to hordes of people. Truly this is a remarkable scene of the clash of the material world and the spiritual world. Something has changed forever in this moment, and the Romans knew it. One Roman exclaimed that "surely this was the Son of God" that they had just crucified.

Jesus is buried in a rich man's tomb after wrapping His body in funeral linen and attending to the funeral and embalming arrangements. The tomb belongs to that of Joseph of Arimathea. After Jesus' body is laid to rest, a heavy stone is rolled into place at Pilate's orders, to protect the tomb from robbers. Pilate instructs the authorities to make it as sure a seal as possible, to answer the request of the Pharisees. Both Mary, mother of Jesus and Mary Magdalene witness the internment.

The resurrection

After three days, another violent earthquake shakes Israel. An angel of the Lord comes to sit on the tomb stone seal, which is now rolled aside from the entrance. This angel shines, and the tomb guards noticed this luminosity and are afraid. Both Marys arrive at the tomb and see the state of affairs and the angel, and the angel informs them that Jesus has risen and is not there. [He has risen from the dead]. The angel invites the two to see where Jesus formerly lay and to tell others, as Jesus is at that very moment going ahead of them into Galilee. As they go, Jesus meets them. He too tells them to meet His brothers in Galilee where He will arrive shortly.

They duly do so, and no one believes them. Peter runs to the tomb, sees the strips of linen, and wonders to himself what has happened. He cannot quite make the connection that Jesus has risen and is even at that moment walking among them.

On the road to Emmaus, two followers were walking when Jesus appears. His risen form evidently changed the way He looked as they do not immediately recognise Him. He opens their eyes to the things the scriptures had said about Him, then arriving in their destination village, he breaks bread and they recognise Him, for their hearts had been burning within them as He had spoken. He instantly disappears from their sight. They spread the news to others. Jesus then appears to His disciples and doubting Thomas issues a gory challenge, that he will not believe it is Jesus unless he can put his hands into the places where Jesus' wounds are. He does so, and duly understands that Jesus has and is risen. Jesus then explains what the scriptures said about Him to the disciples and lifts up His hands to heaven to bless them. While He is blessing them, He is taken up into heaven at which point they return to Jerusalem with great joy.

The prophecies about Jesus Christ's life and death

Room does not permit me to cite in excess of 350 prophecies concerning the life, death and character of Jesus Christ, but there have been at least that number fulfilled.

There is no one else about whom so many prophecies have been fulfilled in all of history. This is what sets the Holy Bible apart from any other religious book. Jesus Christ is the rigorous and testable person of truth, the Son of God and the second person of the Trinity, being God Himself. His life was set out, in remarkable detail, from His birth, to His death and resurrection, and many fine details in between about His ministry and His personality, His deity, and His humility.

No one else in all of time could qualify for Messiah

It is simply impossible for anyone else other than Jesus ben (son of) Joseph to fulfil these prophecies, because such a would-be saviour would require extensive collusion, even from his enemies, to convince the world of his bid for Messiah-ship.

For example, to be a Messiah, a person would willingly have to 'hang on a tree' – a euphemism for crucifixion. This requires their agreement (as Jesus did) to being flogged beforehand to within an inch of their lives.

They would need to be able to perform genuine miracles by curing the blind and deaf: not something any Old Testament prophet did. They would also have to raise people from the dead; and rise from the dead themselves, which is something that God the Father did, in the power of the Holy Spirit, for Jesus, His Son. This likewise implies that even God the Father Himself would need to be complicit in the events for the bid to be successful.

These and many other factors weigh heavily against the

possibility of anyone else being Messiah, and yet 365 prophecies about Jesus can be readily identifiable as having been fulfilled. After centuries of textual analysis and exegesis, even many Rabbis have been convinced that Jesus was indeed Messiah. As the veil is being lifted now from Jews' hearts[115], who hitherto have not been so favourable to believe that Jesus was the Messiah, it is a sure sign that we are near the fulfilment of the whole biblical story. Belief by Jews that Jesus was the Christ, the Messiah, does not take away from Jewishness. Quite the reverse. The coming of the Messiah is the very fulfilment of everything they have been seeking. Many have rejected Him, which was required for a time, so that His message would spread outside Israel to the whole world[116]. That era continues, and many nations' peoples have come to believe in Jesus.

Even many Rabbis are turning to Christ as Messiah: the veil is being lifted

But now the tide is turning, and many Rabbis, some of whom are well known, have turned to belief in Yeshua (Jesus) Massiach (Messiah). Those listed in the endnote have given testimony and can be read at the link in the endnote[117].

There is also the controversial case of the highly-revered rabbi, Rabbi Yitzhak Kaduri, who died in Jerusalem in 2006. Before his death, it is said that he believed the Messiah would arrive soon, and that he had met Him a year earlier! A controversial note, to be opened only following his death, appeared to reveal that he believed that the Messiah was 'Yehoshua' (Yeshua – i.e. Jesus Christ). The name was derived by acronym, following the Hebrew use of the words. "Concerning the letter abbreviation of the Messiah's name, 'he will lift the people and confirm that His word and law are valid."[118]

The Rabbi's funeral was attended by some 200,000 Jews. Yet when the note was opened, little press coverage appeared about the 'shock' findings that a notable Rabbi believed that Jesus Christ was Messiah. You can see a list of hundreds of Jews who have shown belief in Jesus Christ at **www.israelinprophecy.org**, as well. Among those listed, is Sir William Herschel. I can confirm that he came from Jewish stock, but that he believed in Jesus Christ. The veil is being lifted, as more and more of our Jewish brothers and sisters begin to see that Christ did indeed fulfil all of the Law and that the prophets all spoke about Him.

So, let us now turn to the life, in prophecy, of the remarkable God-man, Yeshua Messiah.

His birth

He was to be born of a virgin. Isaiah 7:14, written 700 years before Christ, states:

> "Therefore, the Lord Himself will give you a sign; behold, the virgin shall conceive and bear a Son, and shall call His name Immanuel" [which means God with us]. The verse was reiterated in the New Testament in Matthew 1:23 to show its fulfilment about Jesus being born to the virgin, Mary.

He was to be born from interaction of humanity with Holy Spirit, and not humanity with itself.

For Mary's sake, the angel Gabriel appeared to explain that the Holy Spirit would cause her to have Jesus:

> "In the sixth month, the Lord sent the angel Gabriel to Nazareth, a town in Galilee, to a virgin..." (Luke 1:26-27);

> "The Holy Spirit will come upon you, and the power of the Most High will overshadow you. So, the one to be born will be called the Son of God." (Luke 1:35)

190

An angel of the Lord, almost certainly Gabriel, also appeared to Joseph, Mary's intended, in a dream, to smooth over the rough waters that were beginning to swell regarding Mary's unexplained pregnancy:

> "[Joseph] planned to send her [Mary] away secretly. But when he had considered this, behold, and angel of the Lord appeared to him in a dream, saying "Joseph, son of David, do not be afraid to take Mary as your wife; for the child who has been conceived in her is of the Holy Spirit..." (Matthew 1:19-20, NIV)

Jesus was born in Bethlehem, in Judea

Micah the prophet was prophesying between 750 and 686 BC, and said this in verse 5:2:

> "But you, Bethlehem Ephrathah, though you are small among the clans of Judah, out of you will come for me one who will be ruler over Israel."

He would be lowly in nature and not full of pomp and circumstance

Zechariah 9:9 says: "...yet He is lowly"

He was born in a lowly manger for animals, as we see fulfilled in Luke 2:16: "...they [the shepherds] hurried off and found Mary and Joseph, and the baby, who was lying in the manger." [Feeding trough for animals]

Three wise men (often translated 'Kings') would come and worship Him

These men would sometimes be referred to as kings, hence the

Christmas carol: "We three kings of Orient are":

"Nations will come to your light, and kings to the brightness of your dawn" (Isaiah 60:3) "Merchants from Sheba will come, bringing gold and incense" (Isaiah 60:6)

They would offer Him gifts, and bow down to Him

"The Kings of Tarshish and the coastlands will offer gifts; the kings of Sheba and Seba will bring tribute. All Kings will bow down to Him; all nations will serve Him....May they offer Him gold from Sheba..." (Psalms 72:10-15)

The Old Testament explains centuries beforehand that Jesus would attract kings to His light, and presents as a sign of their deep respect for His senior kingship. This was all confirmed in Matthew 2 generally.

The arrival of the saviour will be as a child, a son, who will rule over all

Isaiah's famous prophecy says in 9:6:

"For to us a child is born, to us a Son is given, and the government will be on His shoulders. And He will be called Wonderful Counselor, Mighty God, Everlasting Father, Prince of Peace...Of the increase of His government and peace there shall be no end."

The arrival of a King-saviour-child was confirmed in the New Testament:

[The angel said to the shepherds] "Today in the town of David a Saviour has been born to you; he is Christ the Lord." (Luke 2:11)

The truth of Jesus' ever-increasing government foretold in Isaiah 9:6

His government has never decreased. It may appear within the West that Christianity is temporarily ebbing away, but it is rapidly growing in Africa, South America, India and especially China. In China alone, in 2010 there were around 58 million Christians[119], and some reports suggest that the actual figure is far higher at around 130 million[120]. This may be overly generous and it is difficult to get accurate statistics given that the biggest church is the unofficial and unregistered body of churches that have no official status. An apparently conservative rate of growth is put at 10% per annum in one article[121] which, on the basis of the article, suggests that 10 million Chinese are becoming Christians annually, or just over 190,000 per week. By 2030, at the present rate of growth, there will be some 160 million Christians, overtaking the USA with a declining population of Christians presently at 159 million. God blesses nations that believe in Him. China therefore has a blessed future, however the West might seek to criticise her.

One thing is very certain from global growth. Christianity, and therefore the government of Christ, has grown consistently since He came to earth and left His legacy and is growing worldwide faster than ever before. Woe to you atheists: you are on the wrong side of this battle and are fighting against the inevitable prophesied tide.

It is a battle that the God of the Christians wins, so if you can't beat 'em, do join 'em!

Massacre of the Innocents: Herod attempts to stop a rival king taking over

Herod orchestrated the "Massacre of the Innocents" having concluded that the birth of Jesus was competition for his kingly

193

authority. In undertaking the butchery, he fulfilled the prophecy by Jeremiah, the prophet, who in about 625- 586 BC had this observation:

"A voice was heard in Ramah, Lamentation, weeping, and great mourning, Rachel weeping for her children, refusing to be comforted, because they are no more." (Jeremiah 31:15)

Herod himself was referred to this verse by his own counsel, as it confirms in Matthew 2:3-6 in the New Testament:

"When King Herod heard [that Magi had travelled from the East to enquire about the whereabouts of the one who had been born King of the Jews], he was greatly disturbed, and all Jerusalem with him. When he had called together all the people's chief priests and teachers of the law, he asked them where the Christ was to be born. "In Bethlehem in Judea", they replied, "for this is what the prophet has written:

"But you, Bethlehem, in the land of Judah are by no means least among the rulers of Judah; for out of you will come a ruler who will be the shepherd of my people Israel.""

Without doubt therefore, Herod's own advisers believed this section of Jeremiah referred to the time of Herod's massacre of his citizen children, and Matthew cites at verse 2:18 the actual verse (which is slightly different to the way it was expressed by Herod's advisers). The prophecy was therefore cited in both the Old, and New Testaments.

Holy Family in Egypt

The Holy family would flee to Egypt to seek to avoid this

massacre and, following its cessation, God called them back from there:

"...God calls Him out of Egypt" (Numbers 24:8)

"...Out of Egypt I called my Son." (Hosea 11:1) (as cited in fulfilment in Matthew 2:15)

<u>John the Baptist was born around the same time as Jesus to fulfil the prophecy of Isaiah that he would arrive to announce, some thirty years later, that the Saviour had arrived</u>

Isaiah, seeing the saviour come 700 years before His arrival, said that an oracle would arrive saying:

"A voice of one calling in the desert, "Prepare a way for the Lord, make straight paths for Him.""

This was fulfilled in the New Testament:

"When it was time for Elizabeth [who was barren] to have her baby, she gave birth to a son.....His name is John." (Luke 1:57 and 1:63)

This oracle was John the Baptist, the embodiment, we later learn, of an earlier prophet, Elijah. Now John wore camel's hair clothes, and a leather belt. This is significant because he was the last of the Old Testament prophets and is referred to by Jesus as the greatest. But Elijah also wore a leather belt, and was Israel's greatly loved prophet, and is in many ways 'the greatest' as we will see shortly. John's wearing of such clothes rounded off the period of pre-Christ prophecy. It says in Malachi that the Lord would:

"...send my messenger, and he shall prepare the way before me..." Malachi 3:1, ESV)

195

"...Send Elijah before the great and awesome day of the Lord" (Malachi 4:5, ESV)

Now Elijah wore:

"...'a garment of hair and had a leather belt around his waist'. The king said: 'That was Elijah the Tishbite." (2 Kings 1:8)

So very clearly then, John is the assumption of Elijah in all ways, as the greatest of Old Testament prophets who would foretell the coming of the Messiah. And we know also that Elijah is the greatest, as he stands as the figure of 'the prophets' with the figure of 'the law', being Moses, at Christ's transfiguration[122].

Jesus Himself confirms that John is the fulfilment of Elijah:

"...For all the prophets and the law prophesied until John. And if you will believe it, this is Elijah, which was to come." (Matthew 11:14)

There is no inconsistency in there being two 'greatest prophets', as in fact, as Jesus made clear, they were in effect one. If you find that difficult to understand, just remember that this comes from a God who is one God, but three different persons!

Jesus is baptised by the Holy Spirit

The Old Testament makes clear that the Spirit of God will rest on Jesus:

"The Spirit of the Lord shall rest on Him" (Isaiah 11:2)

It is fulfilled in the New Testament when Jesus is being baptised by John the Baptist:

196

"As soon as Jesus was baptised, He went up out of the water. At that moment heaven was opened, and He saw the Spirit of God descending like a dove alighting on Him." (Matthew 3:16)

<u>Jesus reads from the scroll from Isaiah, about Himself, and confirms this to the synagogue to whom He is reading</u>

Isaiah 61:1-2 [broadly, as recanted by Jesus in Luke 4:18] "The Spirit of the Lord is upon me, because the Lord has anointed me to preach good news to the poor; He has sent me to proclaim freedom for the prisoners and recovery of sight for the blind [Isaiah 35:5], to release the oppressed, to proclaim the years of the Lord's favour"

Then Jesus says in Luke 4:21: "Today this scripture is fulfilled in your hearing." It spoke directly of Jesus and His ministry. Jews knew from the Old Testament that healing the blind and deaf was reserved only for the Saviour. No Old Testament prophet would be able to accomplish these miracles. Therefore, Jesus confirmed this when John the Baptist enquired of Jesus whether He was the 'coming one' or whether Israel should wait for another. Jesus confirmed that He was indeed healing the blind.

<u>Jesus performs many miracles and teaches in parables (stories)</u>

"I will open my mouth in parables..." (Psalm 78:1)

Jesus indeed taught many parables. One can see these generally for example in Matthew 13 (parables of the sower, weeds, mustard seed and yeast, and hidden treasure and pearl)

The Messiah would heal and have a ministry of miracles:
- the blind, deaf, lame and dumb: (Isaiah 35:5)
- as a ministry, generally: (Isaiah 53:4)

197

These miracles were fulfilled in the New Testament, in, e.g., Mark 10:51-52 and 7:32-35; Matthew 12:10-13 and 9:32-33 and 9:27-30 and in Luke 6:17-30.

But Jesus is despised and rejected by the teachers of the law and the Pharisees

> "He is despised and rejected by men, a man of sorrows and acquainted with grief. And we hid, as it were, our faces from Him; He was despised and we did not esteem Him." (Isaiah 53:3)

And the fulfilment:

> [when Jesus explained that He was the fulfilment of Old Testament scripture] "All the people in the synagogue were furious when they heard this." (Luke 4:28)

> One might also cite Matthew 27: 21-23, in which the baying Jewish crowd requests for a murderer to be set free and for Jesus, an innocent man, to be crucified.

In spite of the Pharisees trying to set traps for Jesus, He outwits them all

> "Therefore, I will do an amazing thing by these people – an absolutely extraordinary deed. Wise men will have nothing to say, the sages will have no explanations." (Isaiah 29:14)

This is indeed fulfilled several times in the New Testament, some examples being Jesus teaching on Marriage at the resurrection, in which the crowds were 'astonished at His teaching' (Matthew 22:23- 33); and the queries of the Pharisees as to whether it was right to pay taxes to Caesar. The Pharisees were '...amazed. So, they left Him and went away.' (Matthew 22:15-22)

He is recognised by Peter as the Son of the living God

In 2 Samuel 7:14 it states: "I will become His father and He will become my son."

Peter says in Matthew 16:16: "You are the Christ, the Son of the living God."

But shortly thereafter, Peter, Jesus' friend, disowns Him

Psalms 5:12-14: "Indeed, it is not an enemy who insults me, or else I could bear it."

Jesus says to Peter: "I tell you the truth...you will deny me three times" (Matthew 26:34)

Peter fulfils all the prophecy, by denying Jesus three times in Matthew 26:69-75.

Enter Jerusalem triumphantly as 'Lord', on a donkey

Zechariah predicted this in chapter 9:9: "Rejoice greatly, daughter of Zion! Shout, daughter of Jerusalem! Look! Your king is coming to you; He is legitimate and victorious, humble and riding on a donkey – on a young donkey, the foal of a female donkey"

This was spectacularly fulfilled in Matthew 21:2-10:

"Go to the village ahead of you. Right away you will find a donkey tied there, and a colt with her. Untie them and bring them to me. If anyone says anything to you, you are to say: 'The Lord needs them'...This took place to fulfil what was spoken by the prophet...They brought the

199

donkey and the colt and placed their cloaks on them, and he sat on them. A very large crowd spread their cloaks on the road. Others cut branches from the trees and spread them on the road. Crowds went ahead of Him and those following kept shouting: 'Hosanna to the Son of David! Blessed is He who comes in the name of the Lord! Hosanna in the highest!'"

He is betrayed by Judas, a friend, at the last supper

Psalm 41:9: "Even my close friend who I trusted, he who shared meals with me, has turned against me."

Again, this was sadly, but convincingly fulfilled when Judas left the dining disciples and Jesus at the Last Supper, to betray Jesus to the chief priest:

"The one who eats my bread has turned against me." (John 13:18); and "...after that, Judas took the piece of bread, Satan entered into him. Jesus said: 'what you are about to do, do it quickly.'" (John 13:27)

Judas then betrays Jesus by using a secret sign, a kiss, which Jesus knows all too well is loaded with betrayal. The guards take Him away once He has been identified that way, to His eventual death.

He goes through intense stress in the Garden at Gethsemane, knowing what is to face Him

Jesus sweats blood[123] with the intense pressure He knows will face Him. It is a true medical condition brought on by extreme anguish, called Hematidrosis. Being God, He knew what He would face. He knew all that was going to happen to Him[124]. He knew His face and body would be disfigured beyond recognition to the point that it was 'beyond human likeness[125]. He knew that

200

His body would be flogged using a whip like a cat o' nine tails, which use sharp sheep bones and metal balls as weapons that sink into, and bruise the skin respectively, and score deep lines down the victim's back. The purpose was to bring the victim to a point just short of death. The first few lashes excoriate the skin after which the next series of lashes damage the muscle leading to extreme blood loss. They stopped short at 39 lashes, as 40 would have killed Him.

He knew that crucifixion was the most painful of deaths – from which we obtain the word 'excruciating' or, literally, 'from the cross'. Alexander the Great introduced it, and the Romans perfected it to a point where the victim would die, but only after intense agony. The victim was required to carry their cross bar across the shoulders, after having been flogged first – a pre-requisite. That way they were weakened. Inevitably they would fall in the long walk to their death but, as their arms were tied to the cross bar, they could not use their hands to break the fall. With a 100-pound bar on their shoulders, their fall, on to stony ground, would smash their face. The condemned is then offered a drink with myrrh in it as a mild anaesthetic: in Jesus' case, He did not drink it[126] but chose to suffer the full agony of death presumably lest anyone might suggest He did not suffer the fullness of the anguish of men. The ropes then make way for nails as the arms are nailed to the cross-bar. Then person and crossbar are raised onto the post, and the pain of the nails can be felt as the victim's bones rub on them to support body weight. In the case of the legs, they would usually be placed together, with one nail driven through both. It saves some steel, after all.

The victim lives for hours or days, depending on how severe the scourging was. If the body was thought to have passed away, a guard would send a spear into the body to ensure death, before the body was handed to those who might come to bury it. Otherwise it was left for wild animals to devour.

201

The victim dies of a combination of factors. As the nails hold the body in an upright position, the victim cannot take full breaths of air for long. To do so is an exceptionally painful exercise, requiring him to push up on nails through his feet, which grate against nerves. This action grinds the back against the rough wooden cross, exacerbating the pan in wounds received during flogging and opening them up again to let out more blood. Eventually, through weakness, lack of breath and massive loss of blood, he passes away.

Jesus is omniscient. Unlike human beings, He can foresee all that will happen to Him with this knowledge acutely in mind. It is entirely understandable that even God the Son would ask if this 'cup' can be taken from Him. What is all the more remarkable, and makes this person above any other worthy of our admiration and praise, is that in spite of knowing how it would feel, He agrees to God the Father's divine will and proceeds. It is fully understandable, therefore, that He sweated blood. If I were capable of seeing my grisly fate in such detail, I think that I would do so too.

<u>Psalm 69:19 reveals that Jesus' state of mind was full of reproach</u>

"Reproach has broken my heart, and I am full of heaviness..." It is quite clear that this is talking of the Messiah, as we shall see shortly, as a couple of verse later, the sufferer says: "As for my thirst they gave me vinegar to drink" (vs 21), which was, as we shall see, fulfilled during the crucifixion process. The Psalm continues: "But I am poor and sorrowful" (vs 29)

Jesus in the Garden of Gethsemane said:

"My soul is overwhelmed with sorrow to the point of death."

202

Overwhelmed to the point of death. The sentence is simple and understated, but powerful. It implies an 'ultimate' anguish, which is precisely why Hematidrosis took hold.

Judas betrays Him for 30 pieces of silver:

> Per Zecharaiah 11:12: "If it is agreeable to you, give me my wages; and if not, refrain". So, they weighed out for my wages thirty pieces of silver."

Again, this man who was prophesied to betray Jesus, is fulfilled in Matthew 26:14-16:

> "Then one of the twelve, called Judas Iscariot, went to the chief priests and said: "What are you willing to give me if I deliver Him to you?" And they counted out to him thirty pieces of silver." So, from that time he sought opportunity to betray Him."

Money used to purchase a potter's field

And in the Old Testament, Zecharaiah 11:13 continues with a theme about a potter's field:

> "And the Lord said to me: "throw it to the potter" - that princely price they set on me. So, I took the thirty pieces of silver and threw them into the house of the Lord for the Potter."

It was also prophesied by Jeremiah, as the fulfilment New Testament section of Matthew's gospel makes clear. In Matthew 27:3-10, it confirms:

> "Then Judas, His betrayer, seeing that He had been condemned, was remorseful and brought back the thirty pieces of silver to the chief priests and elders, saying, "I

203

have sinned by betraying innocent blood." And they said, "What is that to us? You see to it!" Then he threw down the pieces of silver in the temple and departed, and went and hanged himself. But the chief priests took the silver and...consulted together and bought the potter's field, to bury strangers in." ...Then was fulfilled what was spoken by Jeremiah the prophet, saying: "And they took the thirty pieces of silver, the value of Him who was priced, whom they of the children of Israel priced, and gave them for the potter's field, as the Lord directed me"

Jesus is led away by guards after an unjust trial with Pilate, who washes his hands to appease the baying crowd

Isaiah 53:7 – "He was led away after an unjust trial"

He is flogged and His blood is revealed variously through flogging, piercing by a crown of thorns, nails of the cross and the spear that entered His side post death to ensure He was dead

Isaiah 53:5 explains that He was "wounded because of our transgressions". He was innocent after all, as Judas recognised. Judas had betrayed Him in some vain hope of encouraging His rise as king of Israel to trump Roman occupation; but he has misunderstood the Messiah and, even though he may not have agreed with Jesus continued peaceful mission, became instantly remorseful when he recognised that Jesus was not going to be pushed into an uprising. Recognising he had just condemned a friend to certain death, he takes his own life.

Jesus was initially flogged.

<u>He was then spat on:</u>

Isaiah 50:6: "I did not hide My face from shame and spitting."

...As confirmed in Matthew 27:30: "Then they spat on Him..."

Stripped:

Psalm 22:18: "They divided my garments among them."

Luke 23:34-35: "They divided His garments..."

John 19:23-24: "They took His clothes, dividing them into four shares, one for each of them, with the undergarment remaining...."Let's decide by lot who will get [the undergarment]". This happened so that the scripture might be fulfilled which said, "They divided my garments among them and cast lots for my clothing.""

<u>...And indeed, they did cast lots for His clothing:</u>

Prophesied in Psalm 22:18: "...and cast lots for my clothing..."

Fulfilled in Luke 23:34-35: "...and cast lots"

<u>He was mocked:</u>

Psalm 109:25: "I am an object of scorn to my accusers; when they see me, they shake their heads."

This was fulfilled by many parties when He was going through crucifixion:

Matthew 27:39-44: "And those who passed by

blasphemed Him, wagging their heads and saying "You who destroy the temple and build it in three days, save yourself! If you are the Son of God, come down from the cross'. Likewise, the chief priests also, mocking with the scribes and elders said, "He saved others; Himself He cannot save. If He is the King of Israel, let Him now come down from the cross, and we will believe Him....Even the robbers...reviled Him with the same thing."

Luke 23:36: "The soldiers also mocked Him, saying, 'If you are the King of the Jews, save yourself'"

...and nailed to a cross

Psalm 22:16: "The congregation of the wicked has enclosed me.

They pierced my hands and feet."

This action forms a necessary part of crucifixion. It says in John 19:23:
  "The soldiers crucified Jesus."

Amazingly, Psalm 22:16 begins to predict this, although Psalm 22 was written many years before the invention of crucifixion. Crucifixion was invented some four hundred years later in BC 70, and 'perfected' as a cruel torture under the Romans, in time for Christ's sentence. Psalm 22 talks of His hands and feet being pierced – which is representative of crucifixion.

Jesus bones are not broken

However, not a bone in His body was broken, yet the soldiers, seeking a way to bring a more rapid end to the process, broke the legs of the robbers either side of Jesus.

In the Old Testament, it said:

"Not a bone of Him broken." (Numbers 9:12); and "I can count all my bones" (Psalm 22:17); and "He guards all His bones. Not one of them is broken." (Psalm 34:20)

And in John 19:32, it says:

"The soldiers therefore came and broke the legs of the first man who had been crucified with Jesus, and then those of the other. But when they came to Jesus and found that He was already dead, they did not break His legs. Instead, one of the soldiers pierced His side with a spear, bringing a sudden flow of blood and water."

This is interesting medically as, upon death by crucifixion, blood separates into water and blood, and so Romans used this test to assure them and their masters that death had been truly administered. This account gives an eye witness testimony of the process. It is a detail likely to be omitted were it to have been made up.

He was crucified outside the city:

In Leviticus 16:27 it was predicted that He would suffer "outside the camp". This was fulfilled Matthew 27:33:

"They came to a place called Golgotha, that is to say, Place of the Skull." (Outside the camp)

The Sun would be darkened at the point of His crucifixion

Amos 8:9:

"I shall make the sun go down at noon, and I will darken the earth in broad daylight."

Luke 23:44:

"Now it was the sixth hour [noon], and there was darkness over all the earth until the ninth hour" [three pm]

Before He died, He exclaimed: "It is finished"

Spoken of in the Old Testament in Psalms 22:31;

...and confirmed in the New Testament in John 19:30

And at the point where His strength fades, he quotes: "Into thy hands I commend my Spirit"

Prophesied in Psalms 31:5;

...and confirmed in Luke 23:46

It was intended that His corpse should be buried with criminals but burial was prophesied to be with the wealthy (Joseph of Arimathea's own tomb)

Prophesied in Isaiah 53:10;

...and fulfilled Matthew 27:57-60 and Luke 23:33

Jesus rises from the dead

There are many Old Testament prophecies about this. Here are a few:
In Psalms 16:10: "...you will not abandon me to the grave, nor you will let your Holy One see decay."

And in Isaiah 53:10, it states: "After the suffering of His soul, He will see the light of life."

The book of Job saw Job three days in a whale in the Abyss of the sea, in a prophetic allegory of the three days Jesus would spend in the darkness of the grave, before rising again.

These were fulfilled in John 20:17, in which Jesus meets Mary and the disciples, and allows 'doubting Thomas' to put his fingers in Jesus' hands and side (where the spear entered).

They are also attested to in Matthew 28:6: "He is not here; He has risen, just as He said." Finally, in Acts 2:31, Peter spoke of the resurrection of 'the Christ' and that He was not abandoned to the grave, nor did His body see decay.

Conclusion

The Biblical record set out, hundreds of years before Christ came to earth, exactly how the life of the true Saviour could be tested. Jesus is the only one capable of fulfilling that prophecy. It is not feasible for anyone else to do so, as we have argued, for they would have had to ensure natural disasters and other phenomena could occur when required, such as rocks splitting and the sun eclipsing. Further, this person would have to do something outside of his control: He would have to be raised up exactly three days after He died by a third party – God.

The mathematical likelihood of some person fulfilling just 8 of these prophecies is, according to one report[127], 1 chance in 10 with 16 noughts after it. That's a very small number, and from some commentaries I have read, may be grossly understated (and so is conservative). However, we saw from the 'Evolution's evolution' chapter that for something to be scientifically impossible, the chance has to be 1 in 10 with 50 noughts after it. When someone fulfils forty more (i.e. 48) prophecies, this chance reduces to 1 chance in 10 with 157 noughts after it[128].

209

These figures are far, far smaller (more unlikely) than, for example the statistical impossibility of cells coming together from amino acids organised in the correct order to form the correct proteins, or species developing by natural selection and mutation[129]. So, the fulfilment by such a person of all of these prophecies is even less likely to be achieved than the emergence of life by random chance!

Yet Jesus fulfilled somewhere between 300- 360 prophecies! The clear message is that Jesus Christ is the only person who could, can, or ever will be capable, mathematically, of being the prophesied person about whom the entire bible focusses.

There is no point looking for anyone else! Either it was indeed Jesus, or it can be no one. It is as simple as that. There will never be another, different Saviour, and there never was one before Him or after Him. When this mathematical truth is realised by, for example, Jews, Jew and Gentile will indeed come together in peace as 'one new man' in the same Lord, Jesus, as Jesus purposed[130].

Jesus Christ is therefore the unequivocal Saviour as attested to in the intimate detail laid down in the four gospels and attested to by the prophets of old.

The notable thing about prophecy in the context of this book, is that it also attests to intelligent design. In the case of Jesus Christ, His life was mapped out before He came to earth. He always had a choice whether to step into that 'calling', that 'prophecy' over His life, and at times we know that He would rather have had 'that cup' taken from Him. But His life, which has been attested to in secular sources external to the Bible[131], attests strongly to a provable pattern of events that took place and were witnessed by many people after which they were written down.

210

It points to a carefully planned process, an intelligent designer, as Herschel would have it. Therefore, from statistics, intelligent design can also be inferred, as in the case of the strong evidence of prophecy of the life of Jesus Christ.

"For God is not a God of disorder…" 1 Corinthians 14:33

11. Truth within a godless post truth society

"If God does not exist, then everything is permitted."

(Ivan Karamazov in Dostoevsky's The Brothers Karamazov)

Whatever your particular view of one or other parts of this book, it is becoming increasingly evident to believers that there is enough scientific and other evidence from all things made, visible and invisible, to attest to the handiwork of an intelligent, supreme being, who Christians call 'God'.

I cannot show you God directly, as it will be your decision to take a step of faith as to whether the door to that relationship is opened. But I hope that I have referred you to a sufficient body of evidence and reason, to demonstrate that you can take an informed risk to believe in God.

Our choices without God have got us where we are: it's a total mess

But if that is still too difficult, even after several chapters of this book, then I ask readers this: "Would you rather have a world in which He does not exist, where man is left to his own devices?"

Look at the state of the world. The West is not better off for rejecting God, but is instead now descending into moral chaos, the likes of which we have never seen before. Can an argument for atheism possibly be right, given that moral chaos has accelerated since the West rejected a loving God?

Take for example pornography; the abuse of children; grand economic failure; terrorism and wars of all kinds; nuclear brinkmanship; and the massive displacement of people from their traditional homelands. Do you really think that God is responsible for those things, or do you think we brought them about ourselves?

I suggest we were responsible for it all – after all, God put us in charge of the planet, so we must be responsible[132]. These are our choices. Choices made without God.

These are our destructive, society-imploding, choices.

<u>If God does not exist, then where do we turn for a consistent standard of truth?</u>

If one is content to live in a world where we suggest God does not exist, then may I ask where one obtains the yardstick for 'the Truth'? What principles of ultimate wisdom can one point to, by which our lives must be safeguarded, so that we can avoid all of this evil?

A. The failure of leadership is a failure to believe in God

<u>For who owns and upholds The Truth?</u>

We must all have and understand "truth". We crave the right answers to these global problems.

Does this truth, for example, belong to the West? How about the global bastion of democracy - America, which has proudly projected its values of freedom and democracy around the world, like a moral policeman? After all, US citizens all wipe moistened eyes when their boys go off to defend her shores with a resounding: "God bless America". And even the good old Greenback keeps reminding everyone that "In God we Trust".

213

But we all know very well now that those days, if they ever existed, were the good old days. They have long since gone, particularly given the latest *political* theme that has affected US and UK politics: "Post Truth" – a tacit recognition that it is somehow acceptable not to tell truth when pursuing some political goal or other. This must surely find its way into society, as we all know leaders affect those they lead, given we all know the phrase: 'a fish rots from the head down'. In support of that view, let me turn to a latter-day prophet and someone who caused great controversy in the US, Alexandr Solzhenitsyn. This prophet said that we talk of 'truth' in the West, and we espouse it as a name over our porticoes, but it eludes us:

> "Harvard's motto is 'Veritas'. Many of you have already found out, and others will find out in the course of their lives, that truth eludes us if we do not concentrate our attention totally on its pursuit. But even while it eludes us, the illusion of knowing it still lingers - and leads to many misunderstandings." (From his 1978 address to Harvard "A World Split apart")

Now, some of the collective statements he made in his speech may seem a little unfair, avant-garde or perhaps extreme for their time, but I think that had he given them now, more people would have accepted what he said as fair criticism. He was prophetic, after all. We look at his speech in more detail below.

A compromised Church

Does 'The Truth' belong within the church? Well, it should do, but sadly the handling of scandals that have occurred within the ranks of some Western churches have caused the wider church to lose much moral authority. This undermines the ability of the church to speak with conviction on moral issues, but I do believe that this terrible wrong is being routed and look forward to the church regaining its moral authority again (and in my opinion the public need and want it to, actually).

Thankfully, the failures of humans within the church do not diminish God, who is not human and so not subject to human failures.

Due deference to God in humility assures complete strength and reliability: it's what heroes do

Turning back to politicians - I often wonder when I last heard a world leader say to his or her nation, in times of need:

"...Let us, as a nation, confess our wrongdoings and seek God's guidance in such and such a situation...."

Perhaps fearing that it might give vent to allegations of zealous and unbalanced religiosity, or that it might offend this or that group of voters, the subject is avoided even if believed.

Some of you may think me naïve to suggest such a thing! Really? Yet, in one of the greatest examples of modern statesmanship that set apart a leader and his nation, and upheld him as a shining example to the world of how to resolve the seemingly impossible, this is exactly what one government did.

South Africa, facing the possibility of civil war, *did apply Christian principles of peace and reconciliation* during the post-Apartheid regime led by Nelson Mandela (Methodist) and Desmond Tutu (Anglican). No one seemed 'offended' that the very public Truth and Reconciliation Commission was overtly Christian, and it worked during their leadership. The results stunned the world. So, *it can be done*. We have seen it's like in our own times, so there is no excuse.

It of course takes enormous courage and dignity to speak with humility, and to defer the strength and position of temporal premiership to an unseen God. But as Solzhenitsyn made clear in his speech to Harvard, we lost courage to speak of the things of God, a long, long time ago. Express refusal to 'do God' was notable in a previous UK Labour government in spite of its leader expressing Christian belief; though the Conservative leader David Cameron did make reference to the Christian Faith in his 2015 Easter address. One of the only major leaders who remains courageously steadfast in regularly proclaiming the Lordship of Jesus Christ is Queen Elizabeth II, God bless her.

However, the Jews of the Old Testament overtly deferred to and openly praised their God, Yahweh. Gideon did so before he faced an overwhelming army[133]. These are the heroes we should look to for our examples and who are to be admired. They understand where their strength comes from, particularly at times of their own great weakness. In Gideon's case, the Lord asked him to send back most of his troops, to make his position weaker! The Lord was then to demonstrate dramatically how powerful He is when we are most vulnerable. He set traps for Gideon's enemies, so that they fought amongst themselves to a man, leaving nothing for Gideon's army to do other than to walk through the ensuing carnage. For it says: "My Strength is made perfect in weakness."[134]

Powerless to take a biblical, principled stance

Collectively, the message of the gospel provided by the Western Church has also been compromised partly from an atheistic pursuit of science, which has reduced God's heroic stories, to myth. Even if we don't go so far as to overtly state that we distrust God, we find aspects of the biblical account embarrassing – the miracles, creation of individual species, the supposed age of the earth and so on.

Those who lead us in secular life also tend to avoid speaking with

216

conviction about many aspects of the Bible without hedging their position, for fear of losing votes. Our leaders, even those who believe, stay ineffectually silent.

Submitting to God sounds politically weak: but it isn't. It is exactly the opposite: it's a position of almighty strength, because whilst the nation's Premier is not omnipotent, the Lord is.

But if God is not asked to intervene, no one would think to glorify Him if He subsequently took action – indeed we may probably think it was our own efforts that resolved the issue. And some may think that He should simply intervene when disaster appears imminent on the basis that if He says He loves us so much, He should just clear up the world's messes. Yet equally, the same people are unlikely to spare Him a thought at any other stage. In other words, God should do our bidding, which perhaps touches on the heretical theology of extreme grace[135]. Such a notion attempts to reverse the roles of God and mankind, and attempts to make us God instead.

B. The failure to address problem causes

The limits of rules and a legalistic approach to society

Politicians have shown themselves increasingly incapable of sorting out the world's issues. Society is not improving; it is getting worse. The best the politicians can do to address this is **to make rules and regulations to tell us what is wrong**, and what fate will befall us if we transgress new fault lines they create. They heap us up with sins that they have invented in the form of new crimes and laws that we must not transgress. But society cannot meet all the present rules and regulations, let alone meet new ones. The result appears to show a society incapable of moral rectitude.

If rules become your highest truth, then the burden of being

217

'good' becomes relative to the number of rules in existence, and so it becomes harder and harder all the time to do the right thing or find a solution that is not unfair in the context of the introduction of yet more rules. And yet it seems, for all these new rules, society *is not* getting better. One might cite the failing of the global financial services framework for which governments are ultimately responsible. These rules have failed you, in spite of years of financial regulation. And rather than address the causes and reason for failure: governments and regulators create a "tsunami"[136] of more regulation!

This is a true statement – and we explore this in the chapter about Freedom:

'If everyone did the right thing, you would need no rules. The fact that more and more rules are needed is a reflection of the poor state of society itself.'

Rules cannot do the right thing, without the right cause, and are not in or of themselves 'creative'

Stephen Hawking believes that "because there is a law such as gravity, the universe can and will create itself from nothing"[137]. It sort of 'needed itself to happen.'

I hugely respect Stephen Hawking, and his many accomplishments, but in my personal experience, I believe that he is wrong about that. Rules like gravity cannot of themselves do anything or create anything, so they are not the solution to a cause, either philosophically or in fact. They can just limit or adjust a process started or caused elsewhere, because all they are is prescriptive.

My own job sits within the financial services industry. I know its repeated failings. To make our industry work, it takes integrity to wish to apply a rule in the first place. This ultimately comes from

God. It then takes integrity not to exploit that rule, so that it is applied with the right spirit, for in our industry we are required to apply the letter and the *spirit* of the rule.

<u>An example: the losing battle of too many rules for financial services firms</u>

Financial services firms have so many rules that they cannot precisely or completely apply them, despite hours and hours of interminable training! This is for two reasons. It is both because of the vast volume of them, and also because whilst once we were taught right from wrong on our mother's knee and from school, this has all but diminished in more recent times.

Our knowledge of right and wrong has diminished as, increasingly, mother no longer believes in God and neither do school teachers or, if they do, they are not permitted to teach about their biblical source for *fear* of causing offence. What we have learned about integrity which has been passed down consciously and unconsciously for generations, is ebbing away and we lose this at our greatest peril. It needs to be re-taught and re-claimed, but it has to be recognised that these principles are the Lord's and not ours.

Financial services firms now have to apply a risk based compliance regime, because there are too many rules. Regulators have historically recognised this, because they recognise that zero tolerance of failure to meet rules is not achievable. It is expected, as such firms *can never hope to be compliant with everything*, the resources must be deployed on a risk based approach, so that the greatest risks of failure are met, but not necessarily all of them. And yet, the current fashion is now towards greater and greater regulatory punishment for failure. It is somewhat ironic, then, that these same regulators that admit that absolute compliance is not achievable, are the same regulators that apply increasingly punitive fines for failure!

A general recognition that absolute compliance is not achievable acknowledges that all firms are to a greater or lesser extent failing to meet the standard required by rules because they cannot hope to meet all of them all of the time. Yet failures on a massive scale there will continue to be, because the system is just creaking with rules.

What a damning indictment of our world! Yet this is not a new phenomenon. It is, in fact, an ancient problem, because Jesus recognised that the Pharisees levied a similar system on their citizens:

> "And you experts in the law, woe to you, because you load people down with burdens they can hardly carry, and you yourselves will not lift one finger to help them." (Luke 11:46, NIV)

We must recognise that there will never be a 'Nirvana' when the creation of more rules will cease, because they do not of themselves resolve the cause of any issues that require them, and those issues of integrity have increased exponentially. There is not one area of financial services regulation where Mother Teresa might have rested comfortably. All of it has been corrupted – even our LIBOR setting system. And we keep finding more and more corrosion the deeper we look.

Attempts by banks[138] to invest in educational programmes to teach staff moral integrity are laudable and should be encouraged. But when we understand the real source of The Truth, and its dynamic nature, even this is bound to fail unless continual engagement with The Truth is maintained. Such a programme is after all, just another set of rules to understand how to apply integrity!

And returning to the creation of the universe analogy, this is why

I don't accept Stephen Hawking's position that creation all somehow sort of happened because it needed to and that we have the rule of gravity so that is cause enough. We only need turn to real life experiences to see the flaw in that thinking.

C. Seeking 'The Truth' and an answer to everything

<u>My own personal experience in finding The Truth</u>

When I was a young Christian, I struggled with all sorts of theological themes and was looking for the right rules to judge things by. I found the answer among two biblical stories which I will highlight next, that just showed so clearly to me that rules can never themselves be the truth, but they may point towards it. Unwittingly, through those two stories, and another biblical reference, I was then pointed directly to The Truth.

<u>A tale of two men</u>

When I read the bible, I found that there were two significant men in two separate stories, who helped conclude my search. In the first story, we meet a man called Levi. Now, Levi was a tax collector, and in Matthew 9:9, Levi is called by Jesus whilst he was sitting at a tax booth collecting taxes. Jewish tax collectors were despised by the Jews, who saw them in the pay of the Romans, and who lived lavish and often sinful lifestyles at the Jews' expense, as they often siphoned off a portion of the tax bounty for themselves.

But Jesus asked Levi to give up being a tax collector and to follow Him, and Levi took the name Matthew, the famous disciple.

Rule 1: From this I could have learned that tax collecting is sinful, so the rule must be that no one should be a tax collector.

But this statement, this rule, didn't work when we look at the next story.

There was another man. Apart from being short, he was similar to Levi in many ways. He was a money grabbing tax collector and was equally despised by the Jews. He was the chief tax collector of Jericho and his name was Zacchaeus. Now the story of Zacchaeus is rich with symbolism, for it involves a sycamore fig tree.

This is his story. In Luke 19, Zacchaeus, being short, decides to try to get a better view of Jesus Christ, and so he climbs a sycamore tree. When his and Jesus' eyes meet, Jesus *calls him by name*, and beckons him to come down quickly, *because He "must stay at your house today"*. Zacchaeus then welcomes Jesus joyfully and is quickly denounced by the crowd as a sinner. But Zacchaeus explains that he will give half his possessions to the poor and if he has wronged any man, he will pay him back four times as much.

This was the effect that Jesus had on Zacchaeus in a meeting lasting a minute or two. Now we learn a great deal from this passage. The sycamore tree, or more precisely, the sycamore fig tree is an ancient symbol for righteousness or 'good fruit'. The name 'Zacchaeus' means 'righteous'[139]. This was not a statement of his life as lived, but of what God had called him to be. He stepped into his calling the moment he recognised Jesus. The fig is also a statement of good fruit from a good tree[140].

In Isaiah 9, good 'sycamore' fruit is cut down and replaced by something else as a symbol of judgement, so here a man climbs a tree of good sycamore fruit, raises his eyes to see the person of Jesus Christ, and is made righteous, because he has fixed his eyes on Jesus Christ. Zacchaeus has therefore been made clean. He changes his life and gives 'here and now' half his possessions to the poor and the remainder will be used to right wrongs of

222

injustice by paying back four times what he extorted in taxes from the Jews in Jericho. So then, what rule do we learn from the example of Zacchaeus, another tax collector?

Rule 2: From this I could have learned that tax collectors should give up sinful ways and become better tax collectors.

Well, Rule 2 conflicts with Rule 1. So, rules, even based on very similar facts, do not provide The Truth. Truth seems to have a more dynamic and tailored nature, as otherwise the outcome of the second story would have been easy to conclude, as it would have been the same as the first story. At best rules can evidence a truth or are underpinned by a foundation of truth, but they do not create or cause The Truth in or of themselves. There is something else; something *better*, something *before* the rule which the story of Zacchaeus directly points to, in its symbolism.

The Truth has to be *alive*

As stated, there is a *lively dynamic force* behind what are otherwise dead rules. In conversing with Darwin, Herschel would call this, a *'guiding force'*. Man (a *lively force*) applied law when given by God to Moses and the Hebrews. The law didn't dispense justice by itself. Man was the Mosaic law's *guiding force*. And returning to our Evolution chapter, gravity is a law, but Newton, who held the chair at Cambridge before Hawking, said:

> "Gravity explains the motions of the planets, *but it cannot explain who set the planets in motion*"

There is a limit to what gravity can do and explain, says the discoverer of gravity, himself. Newton also suggests that the cause is a being of some sort – a 'who'.

In our stories of two similar tax collectors, two entirely different

223

outcomes have been determined from ostensibly the same source, or judge, Jesus Christ Himself. We need to ask ourselves, then, if rules don't create truth in and of themselves, where do we go to find The Truth?

What is truth? The discussion between Pontius Pilate and Jesus Christ

Pilate to Christ:

"So you are a King!"

Christ replied:

"You say I am a king. For this reason, I was born, and for this reason I came into the world – to testify to the truth. Everyone who belongs to the truth listens to my voice."

Pilate answered:

"What is truth?" (Taken from John 18:38).

John, who describes himself as the disciple that Jesus loved, is the only gospel writer to record this conversation between Pilate and Christ and it is not the only word John says on the subject of truth. Here, Pilate is suggesting, in parenthesis that the truth is *what one makes of it*. But he asks the wrong question. For the right question, and the question that is foundational to all understanding, for all people, for all ages and even beyond ages to eternity should have been:

"Who is truth?"

For you see, the truth is a **who, not a what.**

The 'who' of The Truth

This truth is evidently spiritual in nature. And John, this mystical gospel writer, gives us the 'who' of the 'Truth', for he records, writing down what Jesus says about Himself:

"I (Jesus) am the Way, <u>the Truth</u>, and the Life."[141]

So then, we finally have it. The 'who' of The Truth is Jesus Christ. The truth is not a statement, or a rule, but a person. Yes, 'truth' is a person. And now at last it makes perfect sense. Truth has to be a person to cope with the nuanced differences between our two tax collectors. It has to be a person to cope with the application of heart as well as mind, as otherwise we get sterile justice and automatic law. Such a sterile legal system does not take into account the circumstances of a case, but applies it rigidly. Jesus spent much of His three-year ministry railing against the approach of sterile justice, which was why He battled so much with those who meted it out: the Pharisees.

This body of people were the ruling political elite and thinkers of their age. Pharisees claimed they had Mosaic authority over interpretation of the Torah – the books of the old Testament (or the full Bible as they knew it in their day), in contrast to their more aristocratic brethren, the Sadducees. And because they claimed the right over, and exercised interpretation, they weighed people down with laws of all sorts: laws that people could never hope to honour. To the ten commandments had been added hundreds of laws, amounting to some 613 'mitzvot', or rules. Jesus Himself said:

> "And to you experts in the law, woe to you, because you load people down with burdens too they can hardly carry, and you yourselves will not lift one finger to help them!"

225

"...Because of this, God in His wisdom said: 'I will send them prophets *(my emphasis - to lovingly warn them and give them every chance to change, but...)...*some of whom they will kill and others they will persecute..."

The highest personality in philosophy

Real truth can cope with our example of two different human-being tax collectors and apply the right outcome to what our eyes imperfectly and incorrectly see as a solution, because real truth is not a rule. Real truth makes room for subtle differences. Perhaps Matthew liked games and Zacchaeus liked music? Who knows? Well, the truth does, and knows more about each of us, besides. The Truth is not legalistic, but intimate.

This is why Dr SM Lockridge said of Jesus in his famous sermon that:

> "He's the highest personality in philosophy. He's the fundamental doctrine of true theology. He's the only one qualified to be an all sufficient Saviour."

True philosophy recognises that there is a God, as Anthony Flew, the 'world's most notorious atheist' recognised in his book: "There is a God"[142] and this has to mean that the highest pinnacle of philosophy is not a 'how' or 'what' or 'when', but a 'who'. So philosophically, if we humans are indeed created by a loving God and we were made in His image and seek meaning and identity, then it is right that the treatment of such beings comes from a 'who' and not a system of rules. Humans are predisposed towards worship, as the chapter "Hard Wired" made clear. This is because we are indeed meant to find a philosophical stone, for the true Philosopher's Stone *even calls Himself a rock:*

> "...the Mighty One of Jacob...the **rock** of Israel" (Genesis 49:24, NIV); and, speaking of the followers of Moses:

226

"They all ate...the same spiritual drink; for they drank **from the spiritual rock** that accompanied them, and **that rock was Christ**." (1 Corinthians 10:4, NIV)

Thus, the rock of Israel from time immemorial, and the one to which Christians turn also, is Christ the Rock, the perfect person of philosophy.

The core issue was recognised by Solzhenitsyn in 1978 – and was rejected; yet we have got worse

This is what Solzhenitsyn said of the culture in the West in 1978[143]:

> "People in the West have acquired considerable skill in interpreting and manipulating law. Any conflict is solved according to the letter of the law and is considered to be the supreme solution. If one is right from a legal point of view, nothing more is required. Nobody will mention that one could still not be entirely right, and urge self-restraint, a willingness to renounce such legal rights, sacrifice and selfless risk. It would sound simply absurd. One almost never sees voluntary self-restraint. Everybody operates at the extreme limit of those legal frames..."

According to Solzhenitsyn, who spoke before his time, the law has become a justification and an end in itself. The West has lost much of the fabric of integrity that underpinned the law, and gave it its life. It's as if the law is used to excuse behaviour, to the limits of what it will permit, now. The law in and of itself has become the vanguard of moral integrity, but actually it should be reflective of society. It should not be the *creator of its morals, but assisting the creator, yet we are using it for the former.*

One could point, for example, to the political use of UN Resolutions in times of international conflict, and ask whether these have been used entirely properly, or along the lines Solzhenitsyn described.

Solzhenitsyn also had these things to say in that same speech:

> "...Destructive and **irresponsible freedom** has been granted boundless space. Society appears to have little defence against the abyss of human decadence, such as, for example, misuse of liberty for moral violence against young people, such as motion pictures full of pornography, crime and horror. It is considered to be part of freedom and theoretically counterbalanced by the young people's right not to look or not to accept. Life organized legalistically has thus shown its inability to defend itself against the corrosion of evil..."

> "...Such a tilt in the direction of evil has come about gradually, but it was evidently born out of a humanistic and benevolent concept according to which there is no evil inherent to human nature. The world belongs to mankind and all the defects of life are caused by wrong social systems, which must be corrected..."

This is hugely perceptive. We in the West have been granted vast freedoms to exercise responsibly; yet we have turned our lives, exercising a freedom of choice, into lives of bondage – to debt, pornography, and lusts of all kinds. Libertines might argue that this exercise of free will is the height of freedom, but actually this is false freedom. True freedom is found in one place. I deal with this later.

And finally:

> "...There is a disaster, however, which has already been

228

under way for quite some time. I am referring to the calamity of a despiritualised and irreligious humanistic consciousness. To such consciousness, man is the touchstone in judging everything on earth – imperfect man, who is never free of pride, self interest, envy, vanity, and dozens of other defects. We are now experiencing the consequences of mistakes which had not been noticed at the beginning of the journey."

Here Solzhenitsyn points to how we imperfectly exercise this freedom to judge matters. One cannot rely on man as the final arbiter of what is right and wrong, because this leads to a calamity. In fact, it leads to a sinful moral relativism which will invariably pander to humanity's lowest common denominator. By placing freedom in the hands of ungodly men, who exercise freedom without consulting God or His word, society has fragmented.

The lawgiver was not man: laws were not man's idea, but God's and should be exercised correctly

Solzhenitsyn pointed to an over legalistic institutional framework in which we are now being run, and that framework was defenceless against evil. **But in fact, it was the Lord who gave us law** – His law, set out in the 10 commandments Moses received from God Himself was written on tablets the Lord provided. His intention was that we would apply those in love, to be written on our hearts, and varied according to the circumstances of each situation, so that justice and mercy could be applied accordingly.

Now Elijah was the Old Testament prophet who roundly defeated Baal. But Elijah was highly judgemental in his dispensation of the commandments; and the Lord had a 'part two' to His redemptive plan. He removed Elijah in a whirlwind to make way for Elijah's protégé, the more merciful Elisha, who received a double portion of Elijah's spirit to dispense doing the Lord's work. For mercy triumphs over judgement[144]. It does not take away from Elijah's message, but Elijah's message is incomplete.

The example points to the passing of the Old Testament to the New, and the coming of Jesus to complete or fulfil the richness of the law set out in the Old Testament. This was the Lord's expectation, that the law, with which it is so easy to condemn people, would in fact be used together with mercy and love. In this way, we hope He will dispense the sort of justice we seek for ourselves in our own time of judgement. It works along the following lines:

> "You, (let's call this person Charlie), have transgressed the law, because you killed someone, so you're guilty. But I (the Lord) see your heart for what my Son did for you, and you have acknowledged that you were wrong, and want to change and agree that He paid the price of death (life for a life) that you should have paid. *Because you recognise and have accepted* that my Son stood in your place and paid the price you should have paid with His own life – for you - I am prepared to exercise mercy. Charlie – you may go, but please continue to respect, and remind yourself frequently of this huge price that has been paid for you to give you another chance."

For, to return to an earlier theme, if we expect the law to be used to get our way, or to condemn those we despise politically or to obtain some revenge, why shouldn't the law equally be applied to us when it comes to a facing a better judge than ourselves? Why should we not then expect bad things to happen to us if we seek for judgement, and the punishment that follow it, to be reaped on those we disagree with? Revenge reaps revenge, for it says: "all who take the sword will perish by the sword" (Matthew 26:51-52).

In fact, this cycle of harm seems to be exactly what we reap. Look at the Israelis and Palestinians – no one really knows whose fault it all is, though I am sure plenty of people can offer views. They are both locked in a mortal cycle of revenge and retribution, constantly. Fuel is removed from the fire if retaliation is refused. There is real power in that. God doesn't talk of permitting us to retaliate: He wrote the law and He says that this mode of thinking gets us into trouble.

The 'who' of The Truth says:

> "Don't pay people back with the evil for the evil they do to you. Focus your thoughts on the things that are considered noble....don't take revenge, dear friends. Instead, let God's anger take care of it. After all the scripture says: "I alone have the right to take revenge. I will pay back, says the Lord. " (Romans 12: 17-19, God's Word Translation)

This quality of justice and mercy brings in connotations of forgiveness, and there is no other book I can recommend more highly than John Arnott's book, eponymously entitled: "What Christians should know about The Importance of Forgiveness"[145]. It is the finest book on the subject I have read.

But the law was not and is not being dispensed like that.

Look how Alexandr Solzhenitsyn was persecuted for telling the truth of our society as he saw it. Perhaps it wasn't so rotten then, but he was prophetic as it has most definitely become so since. Solzhenitsyn was persecuted firstly by the Russians and then later by us, following his Harvard address. But a prophet is rarely welcome in his home town[146] when he speaks the truth.

231

Isn't moral relativism similar to this person of The Truth, in that it also gives us different outcomes to similar circumstances?

If we descend into moral relativism, I must respect your truth even if I do not think it is correct, and you should respect mine, because my truth is what I make of it. Some believe that this is an advance in cultural development. It's called the 'culture of authenticity', in that to be true to oneself, one must concede to one's emotions. If it feels right, it must be authentic and true. This gives vent to all sorts of problems, such as the early termination of marriages, because they no longer 'feel' as good as they once did. If moral relativism is given sufficient importance, it can take precedence in such situations over oaths given at the time of marriage, or notions of lifelong commitment.

There is something about moral relativism that is attractive, as it *sounds or feels right*, but is wrong. As we saw from our two tax collectors, ostensibly the same facts led to two different truthful outcomes. But by its nature moral relativism requires more than one standpoint in order to be 'relative' to another.

For example, facts about similar people are not and never will be exactly the same, but may appear so even to the deepest scrutiny. In the present case, there are no facts that appear to be relevant distinguishing factors for a proper judgement. Zacchaeus was noted for his short height and appeared to be generous hearted, whatever the crowd may have thought of him. We do not know much about Matthew prior to his conversion, but he will have been different to Zacchaeus. Unless we truly have 'The Truth' undertaking the discernment, how do we assess which of the two we ask to become a better tax collector and which should give up tax collecting and follow Jesus? Moral relativists are highly unlikely to find the right solution and will differ amongst themselves anyway. Amongst a clan of moral relativists, we may find a variety of different, competing solutions.

232

But for Christians, there is an answer, given by Christ, to every situation. It will always be right, consistently applied and perfect for that person or situation. *So, the same truth is applied to all situations* (namely Jesus Christ as the person of truth), to what at first may look like two similar sets of facts but are, when the scrutiny of The Truth is applied, actually subtly nuanced and different. The solution will be tailored differently, therefore.

Moral relativists apply their own, or man's view as regards what is correct or truthful, and not that of *an omniscient, omnipotent and omnipresent being*. Moral relativists cannot hope to compete with someone who knows all the facts, is present everywhere to see everything, and has power over, and can change, everything. There is just no competition between the two positions and moral relativism is the corrosive acid breaking down our society now. It simply doesn't work. One of the best examples of that must be the serial killer Ian Brady. Brady considered himself to be a moral relativist[147] and the fruit of that was too ghastly to spend any more time on here. The lesson is simple, however. Moral relativism is wrong.

Why Jesus Christ is the only person qualified to be the truth

It makes sense then, that a standard of absolute truth would remove moral relativism, and if an absolute standard is real, it must vest in someone better than relativistic selves – this person must be perfect, in fact.

The qualities of that person would have to be extraordinarily profound. For them to act 100% truthfully 100% of the time, they would have to know everything, be everywhere at once, and have all power to exert justice correctly in every case, forever, without tiring. They could never do wrong (as otherwise this would diminish what we are asking them to do, which is to exercise judgement perfectly and infallibly, 100% of the time) and they would have to ensure that the best interests of every person were upheld in doing so. They would have to be able to relate to our most intimate difficulties as if they were in fact us so could see things from our own perspectives, so that they could act to ensure a perfect outcome and perfect justice.

It's a tall order.

Now, of all of the Gods of all cultures globally in all ages, there has only been one person who has laid claim to all of those features and has indeed carried most of these out already, with a promise to ensure that the remainder are carried out soon. The only God that claims this is Jesus Christ. That is a vast claim! We need to examine whether this is fair. Jesus was:

> **perfectly sinless** – tempted, but never sinned (Hebrews 4:5, Luke 2:40)

> **omniscient**. E.g. before Philip Called Nathaniel, Jesus knew his name (John 1:48); and he knew the thoughts of others (Matthew 12:25, Luke 6:8, Revelation 2:23)

> **omnipotent**. E.g. shown by His countless miracles and the power to lay down His life and take it up again (John 2:19); or the statement in Revelation 19:6 - "The Lord God Omnipotent reigns"

> **omnipresent** (in His risen form).E.g David's inability to flee from His presence. (Psalm 139:7-10)

> **100% truthful**. E.g. "the word of God is **right and true**; He is faithful in **all** He does" (Psalm 33:4). Note that Jesus was the Word of God (John 1). Also Psalm 119:160: "all your words are true"

> **Jesus Christ lived the human life we lived, then assumed all of our sin, even the very worst** (read the

234

whole New Testament)

Justice to all treated unfairly: E.g. "The Lord gives righteousness and justice to all who are treated unfairly" (Psalm 103:6, New Living Translation)

Many of His prophecies have come true, and the rest are waiting to be fulfilled. (Too many to quote[148])

He knows the outcome and it is good and fair: Revelation generally, but especially chapter 22.

The basis of a fair judge: all His terms are known now

A mistake that many people make and has been repeated to me often is that if they live morally upright lives and obey the law, then God will treat them well and 'let them in' to heaven. But that totally misses the point, as such a stance does not honour God or His point of view, nor is it biblical. It is in effect saying: "If God loves me then He *should do what I want*". But that stance is wrong if we think about it for just a moment.

Morality and observance of the law will not save a single soul. It's not enough. I set out the thought process:

In Romans 2, it makes very clear that the judgement of God falls on believers and non-believers alike. There is no partiality. Additionally, it falls whether someone knows the law or not. This reflects most legal systems in that ignorance of the law is no excuse the rationale being that anyone who knows right from wrong would know what to do in the situation proscribed in any case, and the law simply reflects that.

This has to be right in order to have a completely fair judge. God published His manifesto well before time (the Holy Bible), so that everyone could read it and understand His terms, so that the basis of His judgement could be seen thousands of years in advance and debated, and to give everyone an opportunity not to perish, because that is not His will.

Some people think that it is unfair or somehow deeply unattractive to have judgement at all, or that God just ought to let everyone in to Heaven who has, according to their standard, 'led a good life'. So let's look at this.

No judgement: If there was no judgement and God let everyone in, first of all you would be spending eternity with the same mess we have now, since all the corrupt characters would all be let in too. In this scenario, there wouldn't be any justice for all those egregious acts undertaken on earth. That cannot be right. What about all the abusers and murderers?

Someone who has led a good life (good works): Let us pretend for a moment that you proposed to me that the standard for heavenly entry should be: 'someone who has led a good life'. It is a common response from people who think that God should let them into heaven on that basis, even if they don't really believe in Him.

When one dissects that proposal, it is in fact no guarantee of heavenly entry at all, but a con trick, because it is essentially moral relativism! Surely the lowest of the low would think they should qualify, or that the standard should be 'just a bit lower' to accommodate them even if you do not necessarily agree that their belief that they have led a good life matches your view of their life! Further, your standard cannot be the right standard, as there will be others who think they are better than you and that you should not be let in! So, everyone will argue for a different standard. Setting some standard on the basis of a good life is so arbitrary as to be *grossly unfair to everyone*.

Under such a standard it becomes impossible to determine who is *really, really bad and should be refused*, and who is good enough to just squeeze in over the arbitrary line. It follows that it is philosophically impossible to set a standard based on "good works from a good life", since God Himself could be criticised for setting a standard at a particular level that appeared so unfair to so many, especially those who didn't quite make it.

Yet there are plenty of religions in the world that operate on a good works basis[149], so that people live in mortal fear of their god because they cannot be sure they will pass the test after they die. They strive all their lives but still fear the moment of death, because even after they have done everything they can, a voice inside of them argues that they may still not have passed the required test of good works, for what if their view of the standard of good works is not as stringent as their god's?

In fact, we learn from the biblical story of Adam and Eve, that the option of working your way to heaven through works comes from Satan. It is not of God.

The error of Good Works: In the Garden of Eden, when Adam and Eve realised that they had done wrong, they tried to sew fig leaves together to cover over their nakedness (here, representative of their shame) and in so doing did 'works' to atone for the sin they had committed. But this was a reaction to Satan's suggestion that they should eat of the fruit of the tree of the knowledge of good and evil, and not because they had followed God's instruction. Their works fell far short of what God required. Their cost was not enough. God had a different idea. We learn that He almost certainly sacrificed an animal because the story tells us that God provided animal skins as a covering for what they had done: not mere fig leaves. It was God who provided the solution by expending a life to pay for their sin, and not anything that they had done.

God's standard is impossible to attain, because it is unbridled perfection

There is no good work you can do that is enough to pass God's standard. The alternative seems impossible to fathom, as it is too difficult for us: God's standard is *so perfect* that even Mother Theresa would not be able to pass God's test. This has to be right, as otherwise we fall back into moral relativism again! Yet there has been one person who did pass the test, and who lived a sinless life, namely Jesus. But anything short of that perfect life is sinful by definition as it won't qualify someone for heaven and so the price of sin is exclusion from God eternally – in other words, death.

None of us can ever hope to pass the test of perfection, and so none of us deserve eternal life based on a test that is impossible to pass.

But God knows this, and that is why He provides a guarantee which saves people from that exclusion; that death. The clever thing about this guarantee is, that the process ensures that sin is left behind, so that everyone who enters Heaven is stainless. There is no moral relativism when it comes to judgement, though. Judgement measures up against the full weight of an absolute, perfect standard. And under this standard, there are no arguments of fairness or unfairness.

But we have to get everybody into that shape first. To remove the stain of sin requires acceptance of Jesus as saviour, as He guarantees that by placing faith in Him, a person is saved from exclusion from God because that person is made clean from absolutely all sin. And ongoing repentance ensures sin remains removed from that person. When they die, there is nothing that can be done to prevent that person entering Heaven, because God has guaranteed their salvation. On judgement, God the Father waves through those who accepted Jesus, as the standard of perfection has been passed. It's the only way. When God the Father sees a person that has accepted His son, Jesus' death provides the assurance that the price they should have paid for their sin (death) has already been paid for them. Jesus' own blood is substituted for theirs. God the Father therefore sees perfection when He looks at a saved person.

You see, the only standard that can philosophically make any sense at all is an absolute, perfect standard. Anything less does not deal with the problem of sin. We cannot attain that standard by ourselves, but God provided a way out, and made it well known to us over two thousand years ago.

That is quite awesome and has been given to us by a genius.

<u>This judge is charismatic and magnetic: you will want Him</u>

As I have endeavoured to point out in this book, God is light and three persons. God's light holds everything together and therefore transcends all matter, living and inanimate. He knows every thought, every motive and sees every act, good and bad. There is no other person or book that can provide you with better or deeper truth than God can provide. There is no other God that claims to make the claims that this Trinitarian God of the Christians makes about Himself and can be proven in so many cases to be true. He willingly invites us to explore and test the truth about Him. He does not require belief without questioning, and submission against the fear of persecution or death for choosing otherwise. He is simply the most charismatic, magnetic, and inspired personality that has existed and does still exist, and the world cannot, and never will stop talking about Him, despite the efforts of the small but vocal band of atheists!

This is what Dr Shadrack Meshack Lockridge, the Methodist inspiration behind Martin Luther King wrote about Jesus, and I cite some of the most poignant parts that speak of the themes I

239

have highlighted in this book. I was tempted to quote all of it as it is quite simply one of the best sermons ever given, and needs to be heard in his strong Southern American drawl to appreciate it fully:

"My King

My King is a sovereign King. No means of measure can define His limitless love. He's enduringly strong...He's eternally steadfast...He's imperially powerful....

Do you know Him?

He's the greatest phenomenon that has ever crossed the horizon of this world....He's the centrepiece of civilization...He's unparalleled...He's unprecedented. He is the loftiest idea in literature. He's the highest personality in philosophy. He's the fundamental doctrine of true theology. He's the only one qualified to be an all sufficient Saviour. (my emphasis)

I wonder if you know Him today?

He supplies strength for the weak...He strengthens and sustains...He guards and He guides...He delivers the captive...

I wonder if you know Him?

He's the key to knowledge...He's the wellspring of wisdom. He's the doorway of deliverance. He's the pathway of peace. He's the roadway of righteousness. He's the highway of holiness. He's the gateway of glory.

Do you know Him? Well...

His life is matchless. His goodness is limitless. His mercy is everlasting. His love never changes. His Word is enough. His grace is sufficient. His reign is righteous. And His yoke is easy. And His burden is light.

I wish I could describe Him to you. Yes...

He's indescribable! He's incomprehensible. He's invincible. He's irresistible. You can't get Him out of your mind. You can't get Him off...your hands. You can't outlive Him, and you can't live without Him. Well, the Pharisees couldn't stand Him, but they found out they couldn't stop Him. Pilate couldn't find any fault in Him. Herod couldn't kill Him. Death couldn't handle Him, and the grave couldn't hold Him.

Yeah! That's my King, that's my King. Amen!"

It speaks to the hero we all want and all seek. That hero is the person of Truth. That hero is Jesus Christ. He was and is the only person capable of fulfilling all of the prophecy about Himself.

And the truth about "The Truth" is, that this God desires more than anything else, to have relationship. He wants His relationship back with you. If you get to know The Truth (a person), that truth will set you free.[150]

So now we must consider what true freedom looks like.

12. Freedom

"In Christ there is no East or West
In Him no South or North"

(Hymn, by John Oxenham, 1908)

<u>What is freedom?</u>

True freedom implies that there are no rules. If there is a single boundary to limit freedom, you don't have freedom.

"Wonderful", I hear the existentialists say, "let us do what we want now and forget everyone else!"

"Excellent", I hear the Libertines shout, "I shall pursue my decadent lifestyle and I have nothing to account for, as everything is permissible."

But those two responses assume that true freedom is the freedom to do what we want, when we want, without consequence. That sounds like an oxymoron, but actually those who do not understand what true freedom is, pursue a chimera of true freedom and find out that it is anything but. True freedom exists, but not where these fellows are going. So we need to understand 'freedom' a little better.

<u>A city and garden for the free</u>

Let's put on our walking boots and tramp out to a garden, in the east, in Eden[151]. Here we meet the Lord and man. It says that the Lord placed the man that He had formed into this garden which the Lord had planted with all kinds of trees.

The Lord's original plan was to dwell with the man and woman He had created. He described His creation of humankind as: "very good"[152]. After he had completed the building of the heavens and the earth in all their vast array, (Genesis 2:1, NIV), He rested from all this work, to begin a different kind of work. That kind of work was to spend time enjoying His creation, and sharing it with His prize: the human beings He had created - you and me. It was a different kind of work but not rest, for there were *things that were done* during the Lord's rest from 'all that He had been doing' (Genesis 2:2, NIV).

The Lord started to teach them how to steward it all. The Lord spoke to Adam and Eve, the first stewards of His garden, by teaching them the "rules of the house", face to face (Genesis 2:15, NIV), by direct revelation. And the Lord trusted them with everything, as His whole purpose was not to Lord it over them, but to spend time co-partnering with them, and teaching them as they grew into their maturity. He no doubt would have taught them about reproduction, when they were ready, to create other similar images of God, but as offspring of Adam and Eve, and as immortal beings.

The Lord began by letting Adam choose the names of all the animals the Lord had created. So here we have the first classification system. Classification was not invented by Aristotle, or Linnaeus, or even Erasmus and Charles Darwin's work on the so called modern system, with the development of common descent.

Out of a place of the Lord's rest, the Lord and the first man started classification! They started to work on some science, together. Here is man co-partnering in scientific endeavour, face to face with the Lord Himself.

In that place of rest, on day 7, the Lord provided man with great freedoms. For example, the Lord said to the man that He could eat from any tree in the garden, except from the tree of the knowledge of good and evil. He brought Adam a helper, his co-equal, Eve. Together they had full run of the place, and it was intended that they would do so under the guidance and oversight of the Lord.

However, this was not a picture of true freedom, for there was a rule. That darned tree! Eating of it in their naïveté could spell disaster for their innocence, and so the Lord placed a curb on their freedom until such time as the Lord might reveal how to handle such knowledge safely. It is presumed that when they ate of the fruit of this tree and their eyes were opened, they lusted after each other and had sex, and lost their innocence. They tried to do 'works', to cover up their nakedness, with fig leaves. What was reserved for the Lord to reveal at such time as He saw right, had been forced by man's own fall into temptation. Adam blamed Eve, and she blamed the snake.

The truth is that they both disobeyed the Lord's rule.

<u>The question is: why was there a rule in a garden that God created, right from the beginning?</u>

This is because the person of reason[153], the evil serpent, was already there, and they needed protection from him. And this person of sinful reason introduced sin through them into the world. And the Lord's heart broke, because someone had damaged His beloved son and daughter, and He cursed the ground they stood on, and the serpent.

Though there were some painful consequences of sin, Adam and Eve were so innocent and inexperienced, and did not have the revealed wisdom and maturity to handle the effects of knowing good and evil, that they easily fell into temptation when it came about. In that state, it is very easy to make the wrong, uninformed choice. The serpent knew this and as he could not challenge the Lord directly, their weakness presented an alternative opportunity. He could reap revenge on the Lord for being cast out of heaven[154], by destroying the innocence of the Lord's creation. Result: difficulties on Earth. By submitting to the authority of the serpent and not of the Lord, they recognised an authority (or Lordship) over them which was not the Lord and so legally relinquished their God-given authority to rule over the Earth to another 'sinful lord of their lives'. Therefore, control over the earth now rested in the serpent, because he had control over them and their new fallen natures.

Their identities had changed. They had now been corrupted, and were mortal.

<u>Immortality in sin?</u>

And whilst the Bible is not explicit in this, my research suggests that the Lord was greatly concerned, because not only had they abused this numinous knowledge before time and had done so by bowing to another master, but the Lord was also aware that another tree existed in this garden: the tree of life. Clearly at this point they had not eaten of its leaves. But had they done so, they would never die (which we know from the reference to the same tree in Revelation 2: 1-2, as the leaves of this tree can heal the nations, and therefore all ailments leading to death). So, the Lord's special creation – 'mankind' – could, if he and she ate of these leaves, fall under the sinful authority of Satan and live forever: Satan's plan would be complete to challenge the authority of God through His special creation. They would be immortal like God, but would support the adversary of God – Satan.

Imagine: mankind would henceforth exist in a world, in which sin and corruption existed and which the Lord said would normally lead to death, but with no death. Eternal clanging hell. There could be no escape from torture, or abuse, or all manner of wickedness and oppression for eternity.

God's new plan to save His children

It is not surprise then to learn that in His protective love for them, the Lord instructed that the tree of life should henceforth be guarded by a Cherub – someone of incredible power. This angel could prevent access to the tree of life, whilst the Lord worked out a better plan to remove sin, and get His beloved back where they belonged again, with Him.

Now, the prerogative of being the Lord is that He knows the end from the beginning, so He always wins. It is difficult to conceive that He did not know that mankind would fall, because He is omniscient, lives outside time, and can see the end from the beginning, and therefore must have known they would fall. The paradox is that it was still Eve's and Adam's choice to sin.

God's timeless omniscience calls the created Satan's bluff

And we only have perfect choice through understanding the difference between good and evil and, Satan not being omniscient, cannot have known the entire game plan of the Lord's anyway. It is quite possible that the Lord knew that mankind's fall would provide an opportunity to deal with Satan in a manner which called his bluff and would provide a proper choice for mankind to follow the Lord willingly. In turn, this would provide the Lord with the prize He always wanted from the beginning: co-existence in true freedom with His special creation – you and me.

The freedom model from Eden: the world as it is now

Freedom in terms of Eden, then, is not quite true freedom. It has limits, for it required obedience to the Lord in one simple 'don't' task: 'don't touch the fruit of that tree'. But we started this chapter by saying that true freedom is freedom without limits, so Eden's freedom was not perfect, and it was not perfect because sin was already present in the form of the serpent from which mankind needed protection via one simple rule.

And Eden's sense of freedom is where we are in the world right now: we need God's protection to stay safe from the bad things that threaten us. Without Him, we cannot hope to have any freedom at all. But the single rule the Lord put in place – obedience to Him – is what ultimately points to total and complete freedom for mankind. That final picture of freedom is where God intends to get us all.

<u>Reason or revelation: pointers towards a truer sense of freedom</u>

When we consider what happened, we can see what was lost. The big schism that took place in Eden that destroyed a truly divine opportunity for freedom was the presence of evil which already existed there. But this served to change a dynamic and very special relationship of direct face to face revelation between God and mankind, to one of greater use by mankind of reason without God, by submitting initially to the reasoning of the serpent.

We listened and reasoned out *exclusively for ourselves* that we would be better off if we pursued a particular path, which led to our downfall. Whilst we acted without God, we did so as though *we were God*.

Turning to other parts of the Bible – the book about and of life, we see continually that when reason is used to force God's hand, it invariably ends with total disaster, and sometimes for millennia. The exile of the Jews in the Old Testament is a case in point. Where they resort to following their own way, sin enters in and they are defeated. It took Cyrus, king of Persia, to start to bring them back to Jerusalem from exile again. But humanity murdered the Lord's revealed Christ at Jerusalem and we were told by the Lord what would happen if we did kill Him, but kill Him we did nonetheless: and in AD 70 the entirety of Jerusalem was destroyed:

> "Do you see all these buildings? I tell you the truth, they will be completely demolished. Not one stone will be left on top of another!" (Matthew 24:2)

Thereafter we learned that freedom is *not about our ability to reason for ourselves in isolation from God.*

In fact, by doing things in isolation, the evidence is very clear: it often leads to great problems. The current state of the world and the way we have pursued international relationships between countries is proof enough of that. Why should it be necessary to spend so much on warships, guns and tanks, when half of the world is starving: the answer is clear. It is because of the insatiable appetite of man to have more, become personally greater, richer and more dominant than others. Naturally those attitudes must come with force and adequate defence.

In contrast, if *everyone* followed a different model, and cared for each other to the point of selflessness, this world would provide rich abundance for generations. But we fear that we cannot do that, since many in the world do not allow the revelation of God to take precedence over their reason, and they put their desires, their logic and will, first.

God made clear how we should behave with regard to reason. Reason is guided by our wills, and these wills are fallen. But our spirit seeks to align itself to the will of God. That is why God needs to ensure our will comes into alignment with His own good purposes for us, and why He says (as we quoted before):

> "Let us reason together..." (Is 1:18)

248

In fact, God never once mentions anywhere in the good book that man should reason out life for Himself, because it was never intended to work that way. But man has decided not to trust God, and to pursue his own agenda. Yet if man *did* trust God, he would find that the Lord would bless him and all mankind in abundance, for God says:

> "I have plans to prosper you and not to harm you, plans to give you hope and a future."[155]

But using our reason only, by taking matters into our own hands and working out our futures without God, things go wrong. Take the apostle Paul. He was a brilliant theologian, but when he relied on his reason only, before his eyes were opened on the road to Damascus, Christians were slaughtered at his command. He gave approval to the stoning of the man who became the first Christian martyr, Stephen. But when Paul had his revelatory, Damascene moment, something incredible happened. The scales[156] were removed from his eyes. His perspective was changed forever, and Paul the brilliant, but flawed murderer became Paul who would die for others to show them the person of The Truth. There was nothing in it personally for him in conventional terms. He was not made materially wealthier, given adulation during his lifetime, nor great political power. Yet untold millions have been saved through the doctrine of salvation through faith that Paul espoused at great personal cost to himself. He was beaten up, imprisoned, flogged, shipwrecked and yet driven to tell the world about Jesus. He knew from what happened to Jesus, that death might surely follow. He knew the cost, but his saviour revealed himself to Paul and when that happens, nothing else can satisfy a person. Even the threat of death will not outweigh the experience of the saviour, as those who have seen Him have seen what is waiting for them, post death will testify. The experience is so real that death holds no further fear.

Paul was in that privileged position.

We are therefore not to trust our own reasoning, but to "trust in The Lord with all [our] HEART, and lean not on [our] own understanding"[157]. We are to lean on the Lord's reasoning, putting our thoughts to Him for consideration, together. This is because the Lord says: "My ways are not your ways and My thoughts are not your thoughts", because they are higher than our thoughts and ways[158]. You can trust those thoughts of His, because unlike us, He can see the end from the beginning, because He is omniscient. He already knows whether your intended course is going to be fruitful and positive for you, or not, so it is always worth involving the Lord in your plans, to 'reason together' with Him.

The divine paradox of freedom

In the secular sense, the more we think we're free to do what we want; the more history has shown us that we simply shackle ourselves to things that can harm us or even lead to death. Without God, we die – physically – never to be raised again. Yet with Him we are raised to life.

But the principle of divine freedom is a divine paradox. The more we align ourselves to God's will, the more we are free.

But wait! That sounds odd, as it sounds like I don't have perfect freedom, as I have to shackle myself to something, or someone, so I cannot be free, can I....?

Yet it makes sense if we compare the nature of God to the nature of what a person's choice to do what they want outside of God looks like.

Who can offer you eternal life? Who can remove your failures and shortcomings as far as the East is from the West? Who is omniscient, omnipotent, and omnipresent? Who lives outside of time in an ever present now? Who is infinite in nature, so that there is no end?

In contrast, can your choices taken by yourself do these things? Does the world operate well, now, having this type of freedom? I suggest (strongly) not.

There is one book that makes all of these benefits available, because it describes one person only, who can offer these things. But He offers it in a spectacular way, as He asks that 'in' Him we find these things. There are 92 references to *'in Christ'* in the New Testament. This is an odd phrase, so as it is used so many times, we should understand its meaning. Here are a few of the references to 'in Christ':

> "For the law of the spirit of life has <u>set you free *in* Christ Jesus</u> from the law of sin and death" (Romans 8:1-4)

> "...the gift of God is eternal life *in* Christ Jesus our Lord" (Romans 6:23)

> "neither height nor depth, nor anything else in creation, will...separate us from the love of God that is <u>*in* Christ Jesus our Lord</u>." (Romans 8:39). This attests to the eternal size of God. It is not possible to get to the end of Him in any direction, and throughout it all, His love reigns throughout all of that space.

> "*In* Christ, all will be made alive" (1 Corinthians 15:22)

> "if anyone is *in* Christ, he is a new creation" (2 Corinthians 5:17)

> "the dead *in* Christ will rise..." (1 Thessalonians 4:16)

"salvation...*in* Christ, with eternal glory" (2 Timothy 2:10)

"...called you to eternal glory *in* Christ" (1 Peter 5:10)

From these collective references, we learn that there is love and freedom *'in*' Christ'. Not just following Christ, or reading about Him, but being *'in'* Him.

So, we are to imbue and be fused with Christ in some way, in order to take advantage of that immortality and that eternal freedom. Freedom then, without boundaries, exists only 'in Christ' and nowhere outside of Him. This is because He is eternal and there are no boundaries to Him. Being in Him is the only place where there are no limits because there is eternity. There is nowhere else that this promise can be made with conviction.

<u>Fusion with Christ to be 'in Christ'</u>

Paul makes clear that salvation for us comes by placing our faith in Christ and that this simple act, which includes turning away from the choices we have made to follow our own desires and back to Him, saying sorry to Him for those wrong choices is enough.

That act of itself guarantees eternity and fusion with Christ, and He states categorically that there is nothing thereafter that will ever be able to take you away from that fusion (other than your own choice). Nothing created can remove you from that promise of eternity again.

This freedom came when Christ died on the cross, to show how sin could be demolished, and to show how you can be raised with Him again. When we place our faith in Christ, the finished work that He did on the cross over 2,000 years ago buries the past we endured and raises us to life fused in Him. That act gives us direct access to heaven and to all persons of the Trinity.

Hang on! Your argument appears inconsistent! You're saying that freedom requires me (your reader) to obey a rule – obedience to Christ. Yet you started this chapter by saying that the definition of freedom requires that there is nothing that can reduce that freedom, such as a rule.

My answer to you is that on one level you'd be right, so let me develop this slightly further and all will be revealed. (after all, revelation comes before reason – right?!)

Obedience points to true freedom, which comes, but is not enough

There is a story of a rich ruler, set out in Luke 18:18, who asks what he must do to inherit eternal life. And a painful paradox emerges. (The Bible is full of paradoxes, which makes it so fascinating).

In response to Jesus reply which is to obey the commandments, he replies that he has obeyed all of the commandments of the Old Testament. You would have thought then, that Jesus' reply would be unequivocal: "you're in", because unlike Adam and Eve, according to his account, he had not broken any of them. But actually, what he said wasn't correct. Jesus saw right through to the problem. He was obeying outwardly – keeping the form of the rule, whilst not obeying the spirit of the rule. In His reply, Jesus avoids quoting the most important commandments[159] and quotes the lesser commandments choosing to focus in on the spirit behind them – he sees that this man's god is money and the power that brings, and says:

> "You still lack one thing. Sell everything you have and give to the poor, and you will have treasure in heaven. Then come and follow me." (Luke 18:22)

253

But he turned away. His god, Mammon, was far bigger than Jesus Christ in his mind. He wasn't in fact obeying the law at all, and particularly the senior law, which requires that we are to love the Lord our God with all our heart, soul and mind. His eyes were not focussed on Jesus, but on rules that have no empathy, or spirit to them. By themselves they are dead, because they can be acted out in form, without a true heart behind them. What Jesus required was not obedience outwardly to God's law, but obedience to keeping his mind and heart and eyes totally focussed firstly, and only, on the person of Jesus. The young ruler had his vision of Jesus obscured by money, so he could not see Jesus properly. Jesus was asking him to clear his vision by removing that obstacle.

Obedience is not a rule, as such, as we shall see: it is simply a necessity to access the unlimited freedom that is 'in' Jesus.

Obedience (to Christ) and complete unfettered freedom are essentially the same thing. We now need to turn to Revelation to see what the promised picture of freedom actually is.

Revelation: the perfected picture of freedom

In Genesis, we learn that the first city was created by a murderer – Cain, the brother of Abel. Cain of course killed Abel, so our memory of cities starts from darkness. And our memory of the Paradise of the Garden of Eden has been diminished by the fall. The serpent was there, and man lost his right to control the world and his immortality in Eden because of the choices he made.

But in Revelation, God puts right all those curses set up aeons ago. For in Revelation 21 and 22, we are given a picture of the promised New Jerusalem and the river of life, which is our ultimate dwelling place in a restored relationship with our heavenly father. Here, we are looking at a 'garden city'. There are a few special features and some missing things in this place. The serpent has already been thrown into the lake of burning sulphur, never to trouble God's saved, ever again. Judgement has already come and gone, removing those who will not turn to God. In this garden city of freedom, the missing pieces are these: there's no more temptation, evil or sin. Neither is there any mention of a particular tree: the tree of the knowledge of good and evil is missing.

There is no need for a tree of knowledge of good and evil, when the person of evil is no longer present, and there is no longer such a thing as evil present in this realm. Therefore, it is no longer possible to make another choice, other than a good one. Everywhere you turn in this incredible place, it's all the same: perfection and beauty and joy and complete satiating happiness that is almost edible in its fullness – without tears, curses, sadness, or pain.

And yet the people who occupy this place are there **by their own choice**. They were not forced; there was once an alternative (deadly though it was). Here God gets what He has patiently sought – a relationship with children who want to be there completely under their own free will. No one could say they were forced: the God of the bible does not act like this, as we know.

Now as free people, who have learned of the knowledge of good and evil and yet chose the good of God, there is something else missing in heaven: rules. There are no rules! Rules are only for people who do wrong things, but these occupiers had the right to choose that wrong path if they wanted to, and they rejected it. They chose to keep their eyes fixed on Jesus, so were saved in doing so. Having decided to follow Christ, and having had all evil removed from them through His promised sanctification, there is no need for rules in heaven. God knows that all the incumbents there will do His will anyway out of love, because when a choice did exist to disobey, they chose to follow Christ, because they knew that only in Him does true freedom exist.

Look for yourself at Revelation 22! There are no rules in heaven. You don't need rules when the Holy Spirit is your internal guide, for He leads His followers into all truth[160] and in heaven the fullness of His glory and truth is ever present, everywhere, so all actions will be automatically correct. And to address the heading above, this means that the logical concept of 'obedience' disappears. For obedience only makes sense if there is an alternative tempting our disobedience. But there is none. Therefore, whilst heaven is totally and completely about freedom, there is simply no possibility for disobedience or bondage! These concepts don't need to exist in the heaven of Revelation.

It is quite a hard and mind-bending truth to swallow, because we are not used to it, and it has taken me many years to understand it's depth. But this is God's great prize, and it is, again, pure genius. No one but God could have inspired the last few chapters of Revelation to be written that way, because it is so clever, so inspirational, so philosophically perfect, that man could not have made this up by himself. For a start, it is what has not been described in Revelation 21 and 22 that is so astounding: the lack of rules, the lack of necessity to defend anything – the lack of a tree of the knowledge of good and evil; and finally, the change in time itself as we understand it (see below). Enjoy your expensive Rolex watches now, as they may well be pointless in Heaven. The whole story rings out with credibility and absolute unfettered truth, because its signature is from God.

In this place, there is something to which man finally gains access once again. The tree of life. The cherub guard with his flaming sword stood aside and man gains access once more to the tree whose leaves are for the healing of the nations. These spiritual trees then, ensure our immortality and, since all of the

256

incumbents of heaven have been perfected through the finished work that Jesus did on the cross, there is no concern that an imperfect person could be immortalised – such a person does not exist in heaven.

And this heavenly picture of freedom – what does it look like?
1 Time

I believe that time changes in the sense or time of reference as we understand it. (See my chapter on Evolution's evolution). Whether we experience it like that, I do not know. I know Randy Alcorn's book on "Heaven"[161] continues to uphold that there is still space time in heaven. He provides many good biblical quotes to show that heaven measures time in seasons, months, etcetera, and that the new heaven and new earth are a better reflection of physicality that we already have. I am not sure that there is, in the sense we understand these things. I struggle to see that it is possible for time to make sense as we now understand it in the context of eternity. Einstein's theory of Special Relativity suggests at least that the pace of time could change if we experience time as God does. There are a number of reasons for this set out in the endnote[162].

Only time will tell!

2 Other aspects of freedom in heaven

It is also fair to say though, that God is different from us and will always be so. He is omnipresent[163]. We are not, nor ever will be. This means that He is not limited by time, which slows down as speed increases, until it stops ticking at the speed of light, because for God to be omnipresent, He has to be able to overcome the limit of travelling at the speed of light to get anywhere, since He is already everywhere. Whilst it is true that God is light, He is also so much more than that.

Because God is omnipresent, this is how He can see the end from the beginning[164], whereas we who exist in our own dimension of decaying space time, cannot. But the perpetual nature of Christ's light means that there is nowhere that anyone can go to take their eyes off that beauty. There is no darkness by way of an alternative. Those in heaven will be guided for ever by Christ's light as it is everywhere and throughout everything.

And the sea (which biblically can symbolise the Abyss) has been removed. It has been removed so that there is no physical obstacle between people, and between God and His people. This is perfect communion. This, then, is the true picture of freedom. It is a freedom given to those who accept Christ for *in* Him and in no other is absolute eternity to be found.

It's all there in Revelation: we will have to wait in the fullness of time to see it come to its eternal conclusion.

13. Your choice: Kingdom Blessings

"Unless you assume a God
the question of life's purpose is meaningless"

(Bertrand Russell, atheist)

So, to the conclusion of the book.

If you have read this far, then it has probably spoken to you. I am hoping that by now I will have been successful in presenting sufficient evidence to you to show that the atheists do not rule this debate, and at the very least, there is a significant case for the existence of God.

But that was never the point of this book. Evidence is one thing; the real deal is another. The real deal is *not about knowing* that God could exist, but is about finding out that He actually does by learning to *have a relationship with Him.*

God (Father, Son and Holy Spirit) is desperate for a relationship with you, and you hold the keys to make it happen. Your choice to believe in Him releases His gift of faith to you.

If you would like to take that step of faith, then please say the prayer in the next section. Write down the time and date that you said it. The reason that this is important, is that you will begin to see things change from that point forward, and you will need to reflect on that date and time, because you will come to realise that this specific moment in time is the most important time in the whole of your life: nothing else will compare. You will be able to look back and say to others that on such and such a date, you

259

gave your life to the Lord, and like me, you will be able to recount stories of things that you turned to Him for, which have no other earthly explanation than that this God reached down and touched your life.

So, I set out the prayer of faith, followed by the "Kingdom Blessings" which you may choose to read first.

<u>The prayer of conversion to faith</u>

If you have read this book and you recognise that your heart is urging you to respond, it is almost certainly the presence of the Holy Spirit speaking to you and drawing you to Him. Don't delay; see how your life will be changed forever. You can say the following prayer if it helps focus your mind. You can say it out loud, or under your breath, but do it in such a way that you know you have said it. It is really simple, but words are powerful things:

> "Dear Lord Jesus, I know that I have transgressed Your high standards and have not followed Your ways. I ask for your forgiveness. I believe that You died for me to remove those transgressions by rising[165] from the dead, which conquered sin which leads to death. I turn now from those transgressions and invite You into my heart and into my life. I want to trust and follow You as my risen Lord and Saviour to be my guide for the rest of my earthly life and for eternity thereafter. Thank You Jesus. Amen"

He just heard every word. As I explained in the chapter on 'God is Light' He sees and hears <u>everything</u>. What you just said changed everything, even if you do not feel anything. Some readers will, however. You may feel tingling, or a goldenness flow through you, often from the top of your head down; or possibly waves, like electricity, or sensitivity at the ends of your nose or fingers.

Warmth is another and so is cold, and some people's eyes may flicker. Some people laugh, and some cry. This is just a sign of the Holy Spirit being with you, and starting to change you. There is nothing to worry about with these experiences: as will become clear.

You remain fully in control. You can switch out of that or stay in it in complete freedom, because the Holy Spirit is a gentleman and He never forces Himself on you.

But if you did not feel anything, do not worry. Your life is still changed forever. You may find instead that you experience a change in attitude towards others, or a greater conviction to do what Jesus has asked you to do.

Often people find a compelling need to read more about Jesus, and they find this from the Bible. Sometimes people find the things of the Spirit come later, but there is no difference in the strength of what just happened between those who felt something and those who didn't. All are members of the Kingdom.

Kingdom Blessings

Being a member of the Kingdom has important eternal blessings. No membership of a gym, golf club or credit card can offer you such free blessings (or gifts). Your membership starts now and so there is both a sense that the Kingdom has come in your life, but also that there is so much to look forward to in future as well: the fullness of the Kingdom yet to come. The Bible upholds both those senses about this Kingdom: it is 'at hand' (here now) and yet is also 'to come' as well. Here are some of the many blessings of the Kingdom.

In no particular order, are the following blessings. All of us are sons and daughters of the King of Kings, as part of a family in

261

relationship with each other...

<u>1   You become adopted as a son/daughter into His worldwide family, as a household member</u>

You gain over one-and-a-half billion brothers and sisters who all believe the same thing as you. His means that you *belong to a large, loving family*. You can walk into a church anywhere in the world, and these people are in the same 'fold' as you. You will be spending eternity with these people. You need never be lonely in the Kingdom. It's a family of children, whose father is the King of Kings.

Now, not all of them will be your best friends. But we are all a work in a process of perfection and we all have rough edges which need smoothing over time as Jesus heals us. As Christians, we endeavour to encourage each other as a family and to build each other up.

<u>2   You get special access rights to the King, whenever you want</u>

You get personal access to the governor of everything. He makes time just for you, whenever you want, about whatever you want to talk to Him about. You therefore get a most privileged and reliable relationship to a person who loves you and has all things under His control.

Which President can offer you those terms? Our prayers are heard all of the time by Him. He always responds. Sometimes you may have to wait a little while for an answer, but you get to know His ways and you get to start to understand how He works.

<u>3   You become someone new</u>

When you ask Jesus into your life, you become a new creation.

This is often referred to as 'born again'. What it means is that your heart of stone is replaced with a heart of flesh[166], because the Holy Spirit now lives inside you and convicts you of what is right and wrong and what to do with your life. Your old self dies, replaced by a new self, which increasingly becomes more like Jesus. Read the New Testament: what a shining personality He had. Who wouldn't want to be more like Him?

You become inspired by the Holy Spirit and not merely your own will, and by exercising your choice to listen to the Holy Spirit, you can engage in powerful ministry, again directed by God, because you're executing the exciting plans that He set out for you.

4   He wants to lavish blessing on you

But if you agree to let Him influence your life and decisions, in faith, then you will experience what it is like working with Him as He begins to implement His great plans for you. They will move you, make you laugh, cry, and gaze in wonder at how marvellous He truly is. He makes this promise to you:

> "For I know the plans I have for you. **Plans to prosper and not to harm you, plans to give you a hope and a future.**" (Jeremiah 29:11).

Now that is a God of design who has designed a tailor-made future for you that is different to anyone else's future. He spent eternity designing it for you. It will be so blessed. It will be so right for you. Surely this is enough to make anyone inquisitive...

5   You regain heavenly immortality

This sounds quite important!

We all die physically. However, your *eternal* life with Jesus, which survives physical death starts from the moment you make

263

that prayer in faith. Now, if nothing else is worth taking a risk for, this certainly must rank highly as a reason for making that leap of faith. You regain what was lost through Adam and Eve, which is immortality with Jesus. If you want some clues about the exciting resurrected body you will receive following death, read the last chapter of Luke. You may look a little different, but many of the details will be remarkably similar. Jesus was unrecognisable among those who knew Him, possibly because they were seeing Him out of context (in their minds He had died after all), but partly because He had a new body. He kept His wounds, but in every sense, this was flesh and bones and renewed. He could eat and talk – but He could also pass through walls.

6   You will get to see God face to face one day

If you want to know how ecstatic and awesome an experience that will be, have a look at the opening chapter of Revelation starting from Revelation 1:13 or Ezekiel starting at 1:26. Here is Jesus, in His ascended body, with eyes like blazing fire, with a body that looked like brilliant burning metal, surrounded in a light so luminous that it glows more brightly than the sun. Yes, one day your relationship with Him will be fully restored and you will get to see Him in His heavenly, spiritual body. Just to see Him would be exciting enough for a thousand lifetimes.

7   You become empowered to live a life like Jesus

The Holy Spirit will come and make His home in you. As you will have gathered by now, the Holy Spirit is more powerful than the 300 million suns per square centimetre of residual energy that exists throughout the known Universe, yet He is also highly sensitive! His form is like a dove which can rest on you if you choose to live according to His ways and there is nothing that cannot be achieved for His plans and purposes when you co-partner with Him. Yet this gentle dove can be easily grieved by our actions and behaviour, so that power rests lightly on and in us and we need to learn to act responsibly according to His wishes. But that power is there, for our use in accordance with His purposes, if we co-partner with Him in His exciting work of love.

8   You increasingly become more and more like Him

The more you engage yourself in Jesus Christ, the more you will become like Him, and this changes the atmosphere and the world around you. Sometimes you will not notice it. Sometimes it may not always be immediately obvious to those around you, but you bring heaven with you wherever you tread, and things change around you.

You were made to change the world for the better, so sign up to the Kingdom, and change it!

9   What is the cost to you of membership?

In some senses, we can say that this cost you *nothing*; but paradoxically it is also true to say it cost you everything. It costs you nothing in the sense that membership is free to all who wish to believe in Christ as their personal saviour. This is called salvation through faith. St Paul talked a lot about this in Romans and you can see that we can become 'justified freely by Jesus' grace through the redemption that came by Christ Jesus' (Romans 3:24). It is a choice that costs you nothing to make *in one sense* because you do not have to expend any money or make large sacrifices in time or other resources to achieve membership.

But in another sense, it does cost you everything (after all, it cost Jesus His life to give these blessings to you). Jesus asks you to trust Him with your life. Is this unattractive? No: quite the reverse. You are saying to Jesus, that frankly life doesn't work without Him. With His guidance, which is never forced, you will be better off. When you make this commitment, He makes His home inside you. Yet you always retain control.

You can have as much or as little of Him as you desire.

Church

However, we were not designed to change the world by ourselves, but in a brotherhood with others. We call this 'fellowship'. Just as God created us in the first place to have fellowship with Him, so we are designed to have fellowship with each other. My church has my closest family outside my immediate family and I can turn to many of them for all sorts of troubles, to seek encouragement and the Lord's direction. My life is richly blessed and I live in a place of excitement and joy. There are many challenges that run alongside that joy, but the difference is that I have God watching over me, and the encouragement of other Christians at church looking out and praying for me, to overcome all sorts of battles. This becomes fun after a while, as it builds character.

Conclusion

Bertrand Russell is right. Life has no meaning without God. Without God, it is just a process, through which we pass, without any rhyme or reason as to why we should have done so in the first place. The fact that life comes into existence is irrelevant, because without purpose there is no difference between a world with life and a world without life. And ultimately, this is the root of the problem atheists face. Evolution is completely pointless if it points to a world without God. All of this complexity: for what? Yet all of science suggests that this level of complexity makes no sense, and the laws of thermodynamics assume that it should all stabilise at a point of less complexity: but it didn't! Humanity – the most complex of all animals, came into play, and that, my dear readers shows that it all had one purpose:

> God did it all for the single designed purpose that you would have an eternal relationship with Him.

May Aaron's blessing[167] be upon you:

> "May the Lord bless you and keep you. May He make His face to shine upon you and be gracious to you. May the Lord turn His face toward you and give you His peace".

Amen

Index of endnotes cross referenced to chapters

Chapter 1

1 Jeremiah 29:11
2 Though Newton's faith was not a conventional Trinitarian faith, and he dabbled in the Alchemical sciences
3 There is a God, Anthony Flew, who in chapter 7 of his book that explores DNA concludes with the words: "The only satisfactory explanation for the origin of such "end-directed, self -replicating" life as we see on earth is an infinitely intelligent mind". As a former atheist of many years, who wrote the seminal 1950s essay: "Theology and Falsification", he changed his philosophical view about the existence of God on discovery of such brilliantly designed complexity.
4 Brewster, Sir David. A Short Scheme of the True Religion, manuscript quoted in Memoirs of the Life, Writings and Discoveries of Sir Isaac Newton, Edinburgh, 1850

Chapter 2

5 Colossians 1, 16-17
6 "First hint of 'life after death' in biggest ever scientific study", Telegraph, Sarah Knapton, 7 October 2014
7 ibid
8 Psalm 139: 17-18
9 Romans 8: 27
10 Psalm 139:1
11 Romans 8:26-27
12 1 John 4:8
13 This was the second time that God made this statement, which was made at points of heightened significance. The other time was at Jesus' baptism. (See Matthew 3:16)
14 Complete Jewish Bible, JNTP, David Stern

Chapter 3

15 Luke 23:42, NIV
16 Luke 23:43
17 Genesis 1:3-4
18 Isaiah 45:7
19 Revelation 21:23-25

[20] This reminds us of Isaiah 64:8, in which it says that 'Oh Lord, you are our Father; we are the clay, and you are our potter; we are all the work of your hand.' (English Standard Version)

[21] Leviticus 17:11: "For the life of a creature is in the blood", ESV

[22] Genesis 3:17 and 18

[23] See Ezekiel 1:26 and Exodus 24:10

[24] Numbers 15: 38-41

[25] Volume 3, pages 118-119

[26] Psalm 13:2-4, NIV: "I will bow down toward your holy temple and will praise your name...for you have exalted above all things your name and your word...may the kings of the earth praise you, O Lord, when they hear the words of your mouth."

[27] Mishne Torah (Code of Jewish Law), Hil. Kelei Ha – Mikdash, 9:7

[28] Holy Temple, Rabbi Chaim Richman, 1997, page 39 50 Antiquities, Josephus Flavius, at 3.8.9

[29] Antiquities, Josephus Flavius, at 3.8.9

[30] A Dictionary of the Targumim, Talmud Bavli, Talmud Yerushalmi and Midrashic Literature, 1903.

Chapter 4

[31] See 1 Corinthians 15:45

[32] Joshua 2:12-13

[33] Numbers 4:6 NKJV

[34] Numbers 4:11 NKJV

[35] 2 Chronicles 3:14 NKJV

[36] Esther 1:6 NKJV

[37] Ibid, 8:15 NKJV

[38] Ezekiel 27:7 NKJV

[39] Www. Cymascope.com

[40] Ernst Chladni was a German physicist and musician, often called the father of acoustics. It was he who first used a vibrating membrane to create forms from flour

[41] There are many websites on this. A good one can be found at xww.cropcircleconnector.com

Chapter 5

[42] 2 Timothy 3:16
[43] See Max L Day's 'The Golden Ratio Format of the Bible' by JLS Publishing 8.9.2015. He updates this work from time to time.
[44] Genesis 1:26, NIV

Chapter 6

[45] A good example of this is given in 1 Samuel 13:13-14 and Acts 13:22, where King David replaces Saul as King, as God is seeking a man after His own heart, being David of course. Thus, God sees in David aspects that reflect his own emotions.
[46] "Five day 'fasting' diet slows down ageing and may add years to life", Telegraph, Sarah Knapton Science Editor, 18 June 2015
[47] Sonia Anand, professor of Medicine and Epidemiology, Michael J Groote School of Medicine, McMaster University and researcher, Population Health Research Institute: "The Effect of Chromosome 9p21 variants on cardiovascular disease may be modified by dietary intake: evidence from a case/control and a prospective study", October 2011.
[48] JM Baker, M De Lisio, G Parise, 2011. Endurance exercise training promotes medullary hematopoiesis. FASEB Journal. DOI 10.1096/fj.11-189043.
[49] "How the food you eat changes your genes" – article from the website Mindbodygreen.com by Dr Joel Kahn, 23 April 2014, citing scientific programs including Dr Ornish's work under the title "Changes in prostate gene expression in men undergoing an intensive nutrition and lifestyle intervention", Department of Urology, The Helen Diller Family Comprehensive Cancer Center, University of California

Chapter 7

[50] "Bible in one year" commentary on What is Faith? (Part 1) 12 November 2014, Nicky Gumbel
[51] Romans 1:16
[52] Matthew 5:17
[53] The Cambridge Companion to Darwin by Gregory Radick 2009, Cambridge University Press, page 187
[54] ibid
[55] ibid

[56] ibid
[57] Herschel, Physical Geography 1861
[58] Charles Darwin and John Herschel, South African Journal of Science 105, November/December 2009, B Warner
[59] Barlow N, (ed.) (1958) The Autobiography of Charles Darwin. Collins, London.
[60] Darwin to C Darwin (1986). Correspondence of Charles Darwin, vol 1, page 497. Cambridge University Press, Cambridge.
[61] Darwin to Henslow (1986). Correspondence of Charles Darwin, vol 1, page 500. Cambridge University Press, Cambridge.
[62] Darwin F. (ed.) (1887). The Life and Letters of Charles Darwin, including an autobiographical Chapter, page 74. John Murray, London
[63] ibid
[64] Barlow N, (ed.) (1958) The Autobiography of Charles Darwin. Collins, London, page 435.
[65] Herschel, JFW (1833). A Treatise on Astronomy. Longmans, London
[66] Also, earlier by Socrates and Plato: "Follow the argument wherever it leads"

Chapter 8

[67] At page 357
[68] It suggests that if one could accelerate past the speed of light, time would travel backwards, since we would begin to overtake light carrying events that had happened some time before. God is light but He is also omnipresent, which tends to suggest *He has attributes that are not limited by the speed of light* since He can be in all places at once. He does not need to travel there limited by the speed of light to be there. As He is omnipresent, this suggests that He is able to look back at our past from a position beyond a place where our light has reached, in a way that has the effect of moving time backward...He is, after all, the one who was and is and is to come...(Revelation 1:8). We now know that the speed of light can be exceeded. See next note.
[69] It is now believed that the speed of light *can* be exceeded, as scientists have shown during tests at CERN where neutrinos (that are particles formed by nuclear beta decay hat occurs for example in the sun) appear to have travelled faster than the speed of light. "CERN scientists 'break the speed of light", reported in the Telegraph 23 January 2016.
[70] Ibid.
[71] Malcolm W Browne, New York Times, 22 July 1997, Science section.
[72] Genesis 1:14 "...let them serve as signs to mark seasons and days and years..."
[73] In Revelation 21:23, we see that the Holy City of God has no need of the sun and moon to shine on it, because the glory of the Lord gives the city its light.

Therefore, there is an unending day and no night (Revelation 21:25). So. it seems that the Lord's experience of a day by reference to a night does not exist. Its permanent day.

74 Ibid. (...and CERN scientists have now proven that the speed of light is no the fastest velocity in the universe).

75 "From the beginning of creation, God made them [man and woman] male and female" (Mark 10:6)

76 Romans 1:20

77 God's Undertaker, page 98

78 John C Lennox, God's Undertaker, ibid, at pages 113-114.

79 John C Lennox, God's Undertaker, ibid, at page 114

80 Niles Eldridge quoted by John C Lennox, God's Undertaker, ibid, page 114

81 Dr David Menton, Answers Magazine, 'Soft Tissue in Fossils' 11 September 2012

82 Institute for Creation Research, Squid Fossils, Ancient DNA and a Young Earth – Evidence for creation.

83 Polystrate fossils: evidence for a young earth by Tas Walker

84 Letter Charles Darwin to Sir JFW Herschel, 23 May 1861

85 One such definition might be found in Conservapedia

86 Henry Morris, Ph.D. 2003.The Mathematical Impossibility of Evolution. Acts & Facts. 32 (11)

87 J.Richard Middleton, "A New Heaven and a New Earth – Reclaiming Biblical Eschatology", published by Baker Academic Chapter 9, page 188

88 Mike Riddle, New Answers Book, Chapter 7: Doesn't Carbon-14 dating disprove the Bible?, 20 September 2007

89 R. Humphreys, The mystery of earth's magnetic field, ICR Impact, Feb 1, 1989 www.icr.org/article/292.

90 J. Roach, National Geographic News, September 9, 2004.

91 A brief tour of the internet can reveal some interesting accounts. TruthinGenesis.com is one such site, but there are others, and together they provide the following by way of examples:

- Dinosaur blood cells, vessels and proteins point to a younger age than the supposed evolutionary ancient age (Note that the book of Job assumes an eyewitness account of land and sea based monsters – dinosaurs, perhaps?)
- The rate of decay in human DNA – i.e. the human the genome, from progressive degenerative mutations is such that it is consistent with a much younger origin of a few thousand years.
- Some stars in dwarf galaxies in the so called Local Group are moving at intensely high speeds of 10 kilometres/second. At this rate, they should have dispersed in a few tens of millions of years, not the

claimed age of 14 billion years. They just wouldn't have remained within the galaxies.

- Helium contained in granite as a by-product of radioactive decay, is consistent with an earth of 4,000 – 8,000 years old not billions of years old.

- The current population of the world at 7 billion in 2011 has increased from 5 billion in 1985 and from around 1 billion in 1800. Before that it was an estimated population of around 250 million at the time of Christ. The growth is entirely consistent with a population that had been wiped out by the flood 4,400 years ago, leaving only 8 survivors. The population growth is consistent with a model of only 4,400 years.

- Supernovas are stars that have exploded. Astronomers have observed that supernovas happen about once every 30 years. However, there are only about 300 supernovas, not hundreds of millions, leading to a time frame of 9,000 years – whatever the actual number of supernovas, there is a vast difference between 15.3 billion years and 9,000 years.

- Short period comets have a life expectancy of less than 10,000 years calculated at the rate of attrition of materials. We should not see comets at all in a universe billions of years old.

- Magnets lose their magnetism over time. Earth has lost 10% of its magnetic strength in the last 150 years and 40% in the last 1,000 years. The earth's magnetic field limits the earth to being less than 25,000 years old. This has an effect on carbon dating, which cannot be reliable for more than a few thousand years. Dating of millions of years is simply untrue.

- As the earth is spinning 1,000th of a second slower every day, so scientists make up for this with a leap second every year or so. A 6,000-year-old earth does not create problems for mankind, but if the earth was billions of years old, the earth would have once been carpeted with violent winds that would have made life unsustainable, as plant life could not have survived it.

- Some oil wells have a pressure within them of 20,000 pounds per square inch, which should have cracked the surrounding rocks if held more than 10,000 years.

- Oceans comprise less than 4% salt, but they get saltier each year, from rain water run-off from the land, so they were far less salty years ago. Estimates state that oceans got to the current degree of saltiness in less than 5,000 years. If the earth were billions of years old, why are they not saltier?

- [92] Men of Science, Men of God: Henry Morris, Master Books, August 2012. They include: Leonardo da Vinci, polymath scientist and artist,

273

1452 – 1519; Johann Kepler, founder of physical astronomy, 1571-1630; Francis Bacon, Lord Chancellor of England, who established the scientific method in science through induction and experimentation rather than philosophy 1561 – 1626; Blaise Pascal, mathematician and a founder of hydrodynamics 1623-1662 ; John Wilkins, clergyman and scientist, defended a review of science as supported by the Bible, and support of the Bible from science 1614-1672; Sir William Petty, statistician 1623-1687; Nehemiah Grew, medical doctor and botanist, noting the unique creative design of plants and animals 1641-1712; William Whiston, successor to Newton at Cambridge, combining the biblical record and the Flood with physics and geology 1667-1752; Gottfried Leibnitz, mathematician and philosopher, co discover with Newton of calculus and introducer of binary notation 1646-1716; John Flamsteed, founder of Greenwich Observatory and Astronomer Royal 1646-1719; Michael Faraday, contemporary of Herschel, one of the greatest physicists, particularly in the fields of electricity and magnetism 1791 – 1867; Humphry Davy, contemporary of Herschel, chemist 1778-1829; Georges Cuvier, anatomist and palaeontologist 1769-1832; Charles Babbage, friend of John Herschel, inventor of the computer 1792-1871; David Brewster, founder of optical mineralogy 1781-1868; James Joule, discoverer of mechanical equivalent of heat leading to law of conservation of energy 1818-1889; Adam Sedgwick, friend of Herschel, leading geologist (and like John Herschel, a friend of Charles Darwin) 1785-1873; William Whewell, friend of Herschel, scientific polymath and clergyman 1794-1866; Louis Pasteur established germ theory and vaccination, and probably the greatest biologist of all time having contributed to the greatest number of lives saved from disease 1822-1895; Lord Kelvin, physical scientist and child prodigy of the same stature as Newton and Faraday, **calculated a much shorter age for the maximum age of the earth (being too short for evolution). He utterly rejected evolution and held 21 doctorates**. 1824-1907 Joseph Lister, surgeon 1827-1912; James Clerk Maxwell, one of the greatest scientists of all time, developing electromagnetic theory, **and refuter of evolutionary philosophy** 1831-1879; Sir William Higgins, astronomer 1824-1910; Lord Rayleigh, successor to Maxwell, electromagnetism, similitude and dimensional analysis 1842-1919; Dr Francis Collins, leader of human genome project (current); John Polkinghorne, theoretical physicist, and Anglican priest (current); John C Lennox, mathematician and philosopher (current). Notable Nobel Laureates who believe in the biblical God: Max Planck – physics; Erwin Schrodinger – physics; Guglielmo Marconi – physics

274

[93] (Biblical Archaeological Society, 'The Siloam Pool: where Jesus healed the blind man, a sacred Christian site identified by archaeologists', Biblical Archaeology Society Staff, 6.2.2014)

[94] See **answersingenesis.org**, "the story that won't be told, the planned Lake Missoula Flood Interpretive Pathway", M Oard, 9 December 2003

[95] (Oard, Evidence for only one gigantic Lake Missoula flood, pp. 228–229)

[96] "The New Evidence that Demands and Verdict", Josh McDowell, page 101, Nelson 1999

[97] Ibid, page 105

[98] Genesis 6:7

[99] Genesis 11:1

[100] Africa the birthplace of human language, analysis suggests. 15 April 2011, Dr Quentin Atkinson, University of Auckland, featured research in Science Daily, reported also in The Daily Telegraph, Richard Alleyne, Science Correspondent, 14 April 2011: "Language like people came out of Africa"

[101] Ed Andrew George, Cornell University Studies in Assyriology and Sumerology, Vol 17, Manuscripts in the Schøyen Collection, Cuneiform texts VI. CDL Bethesda, MD, 2011, text 76, pp.153-169, pls. LVIII-LXVII.

[102] "The New Evidence that Demands a Verdict", Josh McDowell, page 105, Nelson 1999

[103] Jerusalem Post, Jonah Mandel, 14 May 2010

[104] Matthew 2:16

[105] "Finding King Herod's Tomb", Smythsonian Magazine, Barbara Kreiger, August 2009

[106] Page 96

[107] Answersingenesis.org "6. Archaeological Finds, Seven Compelling Evidences" Scott Lanser, 20 March 2011

[108] Ibid

[109] Ibid

[110] Ibid

Chapter 10

[111] "Albert Einstein's 'God Letter' expected to sell for £2m at auction", Telegraph, 3 October 2012. The article quoted Einstein as writing in his letter to a philosopher, Erik Gutkind who had written a book called: "Choose Life: The Biblical call to Revolt" that: "The word God is for me nothing more than the expression and product of human weaknesses, the Bible a collection of honourable, but still primitive legends which are nevertheless pretty childish. No interpretation, no matter how subtle, can (for me) change this"

[112] What life means to Einstein: An interview with George Sylvester Viereck

[113] Luke 1:19
[114] A significant but often overseen detail. Here Jesus is 'lost' for three days going about his father's work. Three days later, he is found again, in his father's house. This has significant parallels with the resurrection timetable, when Jesus is killed, disappears for three days about his father's work, and rises again at the third day to be with his father in his father's 'house'.
[115] Paul says in 2 Corinthians 3:13-18 that a veil is placed over hearts of those who contemplate only the Old Testament – probably referring to the Jews, so that they cannot see that Christ is saviour (as per the doctrine of soteriology).
[116] Romans 11:25 – a "partial hardening has happened to Israel until the fullness of the Gentiles has come in, and so all of Israel will be saved, as it is written: 'The deliverer will come from Zion; He will remove ungodliness from Jacob'.
[117] From Messianicgoodnews.org: Rabbis Daniel Zion; Leopold Cohn; Isaac Lichtenstein; Max Wertheimer; Harold Vallins; Philipp Philips; Sam Stern; Joseph Teischman; Kaufmann Kohler; P Daniel Weiss; Dr. Müller; Henry Bregman; Ephraim Ben Joseph Eliakim; Jacobs; George Benedict; Chil Slostowski; Charles Freshman; Berg; Asher Levy; Rudolf Hermann Gurland; Dr. T. Tirschtiegel; Azriel Ben Isaac; and Marcus Hoch – later known as the Rev. John Neander
[118] Israel Today 30 May 2013 "The Rabbi, the Note and the Messiah"
[119] Telegraph "China on course to become 'world's most Christian nation' within 15 years' Tom Phillips, Liuishi, Zhejiang province, 19 April 2014
[120] According to China Aid, spit between house and state-run churches, as reported in the Guardian, "Chinese Christianity will not be crushed" Nicola Davidson, 24 May 2011
[121] Ft.com "The rise of Christianity in China", Jamil Anderlini in Beijing, 7 November 2014
[122] Matthew 17:2
[123] Luke 22:44
[124] John 18:4
[125] Isaiah 52:14
[126] Mark 15:23
[127] Christian Broadcasting Network, "Biblical Prophecies Fulfilled by Jesus", www1.cab.com
[128] Christian Broadcasting Network, ibid
[129] See chapter entitled Evolution's evolution.
[130] Ephesians 2:15
[131] For example: Antiquities of the Jews by Flavius Josephus, in which Josephus refers to James, brother of Jesus, John the Baptist, and the life and crucifixion of Jesus.

Chapter 11

[132] See, for example, Genesis 1:28, or by analogy Matthew 24:47

[133] See Judges 6 and 7. Gideon faced an overwhelming army with 300 men, whittled down from 32,000 at the Lord's instruction. With 300 men, he defeated the Midianites and Amalekites who covered a valley like a 'swarm of locusts.' (Judges 7:12)

[134] Corinthians 12:9, King James 2000 Bible

[135] ...which says, in summary, it doesn't matter how much we sin, God is bound to forgive us...

[136] 'Regulatory Tsunami Floods Business' – David Ricketts of ft.com 12 May 2013. A typical article using the now common vernacular of a flood of regulation hitting Western financial markets.

[137] Hawking and Mlodinow, The Grand Design.

[138] "Anthony Jenkins to staff: adopt new values or leave Barclays" Telegraph 17 January 2013. He was appointed CEO and determined to alter the culture in response to a string of scandals

[139] Who Cares that it was a Sycamore? Climbing Trees and Playing on Words in Luke 19.1-10, by J. Lee Magness, Pepperdine Digital Commons. J. Lee Magness is Britton Professor of Bible, Milligan College, Tennessee.

[140] Ibid, and also Luke 6:43-45

[141] John 14:6, NIV

[142] "How the World's Most Notorious Atheist Changed His Mind", Anthony Flew, Harper One, 2007

[143] All quotations taken from his speech to Harvard, 1978, from "A World Split Apart"

[144] James 2:13, and demonstrated in the story of Elijah and Elisha

[145] Published by Sovereign World Limited, 1997

[146] Luke 4:24

[147] "Ian Brady: Myra Hindley was as ruthless as I was - and it was she who drew first blood", The Daily Telegraph, by Danny Boyle, 17 may 2017. In the article, Brady is said to have quoted, in relation to his accomplice, Myra Hindley: "I was never conscious of having to exert myself to coerce her into accepting my belief in relativist morality."

[148] See "310 Old Testament Prophecies Fulfilled by Yeshua the Mashiyach", Randy Lane, Amazon.co.uk, Ltd, Marston Gate, and my earlier chapter on the subject

[149] The Christian faith is based on salvation through faith; but the eternal reward once saved is based on good works in line with God's will through revelation and knowledge of the Word (bible).

[150] John 8:32

Chapter 12

[151] Genesis 2:8, NIV
[152] Genesis 1:31, NIV
[153] Most occult practices involve reason and working out a pathway to enlightenment. By definition this cannot include all of society, since there are many people who are mentally impaired. Consequently, occultism is a form of elitism for 'adepts' only; it does not have room for those who cannot aspire to its intellectual depths. In contrast, belief in the loving revelatory God of Abraham Isaac and Jacob includes all genres of humans, as revelation comes before reason, but includes reason within it.
[154] "I saw Satan fall like lightning from Heaven" (Luke 10:18, NIV; and "How you are fallen from Heaven, O Lucifer" Isaiah 14:12-19, NKJV)
[155] Jeremiah 29:11
[156] The Bible implies that the Jewish race has been said to have a veil placed over its eyes in order that the message of Christ would reach the Gentiles, until the time of the Gentiles has been fulfilled. The exception is when a Jew turns to Christ, whereupon the veil lifts. The account of Paul on the road to Damascus explains that he saw something like 'scales' fall from his eyes. Thus Paul, a Jew, meets his saviour, Christ, and the veil is taken away.
[157] Proverbs 3:5-6 NIV
[158] Isaiah 55:8-9
[159] To love God above everything with all that we are; and love our neighbour likewise
[160] John 16:13
[161] Heaven by Randy Alcorn, Tyndale House Publishers, Inc. 2004. Chapter 26 suggests that space time as we understand it will continue to exist.
[162] 1) How can it be possible to measure movement forward or backward for that matter, in the context of *eternity*? How is 'tomorrow' any closer to some sort of goal (such as death) than 'today' is, since we will never reach an end point called 'forever'? Time makes no sense in this context. If faithful man is immortal/eternal (as promised), there is no point measuring anything, since there is no more physical death or decay: man will forever remain beautiful and ageless.
2) There is no more night. No one will need to rely on the light of the sun, since God is their light. If there is no more night, and no one relies on the light of the sun (if indeed there is one) earth's revolutions around a planetary central star do not seem to have relevance to measure time by. The context of a 24-hour day is meaningless, since Jesus is the sun and there is no night. If there is no night, presumably we do not see a moon (if there is one).
3) "1,000 years is like a day unto the Lord", which suggests that the nature of

time experienced, changes as we will dwell with the Lord forever and so should experience time as He does.

4) Additionally, the Lord Himself describes Himself as the beginning and the end and one who was and is and is to come. Since God *is all of these things at the same time* and we dwell with Him gazing on His face for eternity, it makes no sense to suggest that time moves forward in heaven in a particular conventional sense.

Time may be differently understood as compared with our own space time dimension. We are physical and fallen now, so we obey physical laws (cannot walk through walls). But if our bodies are to react to the universe in the same way as the risen Christ did, then we will walk through walls. That is not what matter can do presently. That means our experience of the universe will change and the way in which we relate to a physical world will change. It may mean that, as we relate to a physical world differently, because we are immortal and *so not limited by time*, we will relate to time differently too, because time has no hold over us. The Lutine Bell will never spell out our doom. More thought is needed to reconcile these two competing views. Randy Alcorn's view that time exists in the new earth and heaven may be correct but I have to question what that looks like given what we know about time as experienced in the realm of pure light from quantum physics and other statements quoted from the bible.

[163] See my note on omnipresence under Chapter entitled: 'Evolution's evolution', paragraph three of the heading: "Creation theory attests to a similar timescale, but is less rigorous"

[164] Ibid

Chapter 13

[165] Death is the result of transgressions of Jesus' ways (sin). Jesus out paid to sin, and then having destroyed them, rose spectacularly from the dead into new life. By believing on Him who rose from the dead, He died for your sins, destroyed them, and then you are fused with Him and so rise with Him to new life.

[166] After Ezekiel 36:26

[167] Numbers 6:24-26 NIV

Hamish Ramsay is married to Louise and they have two children. He is a trained lawyer, and holds three other post graduate qualifications. He works in the finance industry. His specialisms include African cross border business and international tax information exchange obligations. He is an international public speaker and lecturer, and also preaches and teaches in his spare time, at his local church.

#0046 - 140717 - C0 - 210/148/15 - PB - DID1893350